WE
WILL
RISE

WE
WILL
RISE

A TRUE STORY OF TRAGEDY AND RESURRECTION
IN THE AMERICAN HEARTLAND

STEVE BEAVEN

Published by Little A, New York
www.apub.com

Amazon, the Amazon logo, and Little A are trademarks of Amazon.com, Inc., or its affiliates.

ISBN-13: 9781503942226 (hardcover)
ISBN-10: 1503942228 (hardcover)
ISBN-13: 9781503942202 (paperback)
ISBN-10: 1503942201 (paperback)

Cover design by Angela Moody

Printed in the United States of America

First edition

To Ruth, Paul, and Thomas, always

Contents

PROLOGUE

A Purple Flood

THE TRAIN PULLED IN at precisely 4:22 p.m., on April 27, 1943, ten minutes early, with the shades drawn at the back of the last car. The visit was meant to be top secret, a matter of national security. No *Evansville Press*. No *Evansville Courier*. Nobody in this little corner of southwestern Indiana was allowed to know of the great man's arrival until he had left town. Yet the rumors had swirled all day and now there was no doubt they were true.

A spring downpour had washed over the city, dropping nearly an inch of rain, and by the afternoon the air was warm and close, with a hailstorm on the way. Hundreds of people lined the railroad tracks downtown and crowded into Evansville's Union Station. Some had been waiting since before noon, as military troops took their places along the L&N tracks, so they could see firsthand the Secret Service agents surrounding the train when it came huffing to a stop, with a familiar black Scottish terrier named Fala resting on a platform at the back, where the president of the United States often gave speeches. The crowd whispered. Franklin Delano Roosevelt had arrived.

As the train rolled past, a little girl ran alongside, trying to get a peek and shouting at a Secret Service agent.

"Is the president on there?" she said. "I don't care if he is a military secret. I want to see him anyway."

In the midst of a nationwide inspection of US military facilities, Roosevelt stopped in Evansville to meet with assembly-line workers who made the powerful P-47 Thunderbolt fighter planes at the Republic Aviation plant on the city's north side. FDR arrived at the plant at 5:00 p.m. and toured the factory from the front of a big black convertible with the top drawn back. Indiana governor Henry F. Schricker sat directly behind FDR in a snappy white fedora, sharing the back seat with two Republic executives. Trailing Roosevelt's car were eleven others that carried Secret Service agents, presidential aides, and newspaper reporters. The journalists had agreed to not report on the trip until Roosevelt returned to the White House on April 29. As the motorcade rolled slowly across the factory floor, past the red–white-and-blue bunting, the office staff cheered the president from behind a rope barrier and a wiseacre shouted, "Where's Eleanor?" eliciting a grin from the president. Then, as he signed the factory's guest register, a select few workers who had contributed suggestions to boost production were allowed to approach the president's motorcade in pairs.

Mrs. Erma Drain, of 114 Mulberry Street, had been called to the personnel office at 2:00 p.m. and told that an unidentified honored guest would arrive soon. She was informed that she had been selected to give the guest a gift and ordered to then keep quiet and return to work in the radio department.

After a wait that seemed like an eternity, the chief tool engineer introduced Mrs. Drain to the president and she gave him a miniature replica of the P-47 as flashbulbs popped to capture the moment for the press. FDR had been briefed on the sacrifices Mrs. Drain's family had made for the war effort. Like their neighbors and coworkers, the Drain family viewed the war as a righteous conflict between good and evil. Evansville was a wartime boomtown, utterly transformed, shaking off the effects of the Great Depression thanks to lucrative military contracts

for ships, planes, and ammunition. Mr. Drain—Paul Sr.—served in
the Army Air Service during World War I and now worked in the cast-
ing and forging department at Republic, not far from his wife. Their
sons served in the Air Corps. Jack remained in training in the US, but
twenty-two-year-old Paul Jr. had been captured by the Germans.

"How do you do, Mrs. Drain?" the president exclaimed, smiling
and leaning close from the front seat. It was as if they were chatting by
themselves and not surrounded by hundreds of people. "So your boy's
in Germany. Have you had official word that he was shot down?"

Mrs. Drain had so much to tell the president about Paul Jr., how his
bomber had crashed seven months earlier near Amiens, France, how the
impact had knocked out his teeth and cut both his shoulders, how Paul
begged for letters from home, how he always asked for updates on his
hometown pals. How he had written the family from a German hospital
the previous December, explaining that he hoped to "use my legs" that
day, without providing any details. He signed his letters, "Goodbye,
Mom—See you soon" and reported he had been assigned to Stalag Luft
I, a concentration camp for airmen.

Mrs. Drain's encounter with the president happened so quickly
that later she couldn't remember all that she had said. But she did recall
that he took her hand in his and assured her that the Germans were
friendlier to American soldiers than the brutes running Japanese prison
camps.

"I think he'll be all right," the president told her.

Before he left, the big black convertible rolled through the plant
exit and outside, where FDR was treated to an impressive display of
American air power. One fighter plane fired eight .50-caliber guns.
Three Thunderbolts descending at more than four hundred miles an
hour abruptly changed direction and sped away into the darkening sky.

Roosevelt left the plant at 7:00 p.m. and headed for Kentucky,
another stop on his trek across America. In all, he visited twenty states
and traversed 7,652 miles in seventeen days, appearing before cheering

crowds at a marine base in Parris Island, South Carolina, an ammunition plant in Denver, and a bomber plant in Omaha. He made stops in Colorado Springs, Corpus Christi, and Fort Knox, rallying Americans with his booming optimism, urging them to keep up the fight, and lauding their dedication to the war effort. All the newspapers covered his trip once it was over, and the stop in Evansville conferred a special status on an otherwise-sleepy outpost along the Ohio River. Roosevelt's visit to the Republic plant confirmed the deepest convictions of everyone in Evansville, that their contributions to support the war effort were crucial to an Allied victory. The people of Evansville have always been eager to prove their worth to the rest of the country. World War II was our finest hour.

Twenty-two years later, in early 1965, an ambitious young writer from *Sports Illustrated* sat down at his typewriter to tell the story of a southern Indiana factory town and its basketball team. In a few thousand words, Frank Deford hoped to capture the madness that had enveloped the Purple Aces of Evansville College. Deford was a Princeton man, just twenty-six, a dashing figure standing nearly six feet, five inches, with jet-black hair, patrician good looks, and a grandiloquent writing style that would be his hallmark over the next half century.

The four-page spread appeared in the February 15, 1965, issue, following a profile of a young boxer who had only recently given up his "slave name" and rechristened himself Muhammad Ali. The central character in Deford's story could not have been more different than the loquacious heavyweight champ. In addition to coaching basketball, Arad McCutchan was a math professor. He came to class wearing a dark suit, a white shirt, and a tie, lecturing in front of equations scribbled like hieroglyphics on a blackboard. Nearly everyone in town called the coach Mac. He was fifty-two, with thinning hair and thick black glasses. He had already led the Purple Aces to three small-college national championships, and his program provided a perfect hook for a national magazine story: the homespun tale of a hometown team that routinely beat the big-time schools. It was classic David versus Goliath stuff. The Aces played in the College Division, a group of small schools that took long bus trips all winter to play regional rivals. Each year, Evansville crossed the Ohio River to play Kentucky Wesleyan and traveled north on Highway 41 to face Indiana State. But the Aces also took on the heavyweights from the University Division, big schools like UCLA and Iowa.

These games made for lively winter evenings in Evansville, and the entire town was crazy for its basketball team, indulging in tribal traditions foreign and confusing to fans from other cities. Officially, the team was known as the Purple Aces. But for many years Roberts Stadium, Evansville's gargantuan arena, was awash in red, all because the buttoned-down McCutchan wore red-and-black socks to a game in 1959. The Aces won that night, and suddenly thousands of fans started showing up at the stadium decked out in crimson: socks, sweaters, vests. The coach wore red ties and, now and then, a screaming red suit.

Roberts Stadium held nearly thirteen thousand fans. But good seats were coveted and scarce. Couples haggled over them in divorce proceedings. Deford recounted a well-worn story about the time a season-ticket holder died one night, prompting the man who owned the seats to his left to show up at the athletic department at 8:30 a.m. the next day, asking if he could buy the deceased fellow's season pass. But he was too late. The gentleman who owned the tickets to the right of the dead man's seat had shown up at 6:15 a.m.

"I can't think of anything that drew more people to one building than what Aces basketball did," says Robbie Kent, a longtime booster whose father helped build support for construction of the stadium. "It was almost a cult."

Because enrollment at Evansville College was less than three thousand, most Aces fans at Roberts Stadium were older and not all of them were alumni. Bleacher seats were a few bucks and popcorn was cheap. Mac's basketball program was a citywide phenomenon. Each winter, Aces games dotted the social calendar. Business leaders, politicos, and alumni bought season tickets so they could see and be seen. Restaurants, bars, and country clubs chartered buses to transport their tipsy patrons to and from Roberts Stadium. Fans threw house parties before and after games. Sometimes before Saturday night games, Jerry Purdie and his wife headed to a downtown club called Central Turners, a weekend hot spot for Catholics from Evansville's east side. An eight-ounce steak and a salad cost a buck and a quarter. Purdie graduated from Evansville College in '59. He was not Catholic but had been president of Central Turners and always knew he'd see old friends there. They'd have a Jack and Coke or a twenty-five-cent bottle of local beer—Sterling or Falls City—and board the bus for the trip to the stadium.

Deford touched down in Evansville in the midst of the Aces' greatest season, and one of the best in college basketball history. Mac's boys were the defending national champs in the College Division and were on their way to a 29–0 season and a fourth title.

Deford, however, seemed more interested in the town's devotion to the team than the team itself. The Aces, he wrote, were the biggest phenomenon to hit Evansville since the Ohio River overflowed its banks and flooded the city in 1937.

"Of late, though, memories of the past are not needed in Evansville because the present is sufficiently special—the city has the best small-college basketball team in the country, the Evansville College Purple Aces. Everyone talks about the Purple Aces. They are fun, but more than that, they bring the city distinction. The people are thrilled. The Purple Aces are like a benign flood that has come to Evansville."

It was true: Purple Aces basketball brought my hometown the national renown that had otherwise eluded us since the end of the war.

Evansville didn't boast mountains, tourist attractions, or Fortune 500 companies. The B-list entertainers born in Evansville—silent-film stars and one-hit wonders—had long since moved away or died. Evansville didn't even have a memorable nickname. It was the River City, the Pocket City, the Crescent City, or Stop Light City. Some people called it the Barbecue Capital of the World. But nothing really stuck, and by the late 1950s, when the Purple Aces ascended to the top of the small-college ranks, Evansville was struggling. The economy was in a shambles and the city's reputation as a brawny military supplier had faded. Several big employers—including Chrysler—moved out of town. The boom-and-bust cycles of the industrial economy left a cloud of uncertainty over the city.

For solace, Evansville turned to the Purple Aces.

I was born in 1967—the year the college changed its name to the University of Evansville—and grew up just two blocks from UE's leafy campus. No one in my family graduated from the University of Evansville, and yet it was central to my childhood in so many ways. In the summer, I lifted weights at the campus rec center, straining to add muscle to my hummingbird frame. On snowy winter days, all the neighborhood kids went sledding on the gently sloping hill across from campus. On Saturday nights in January and February, my father drove the two of us the mile or so from our house to the giant blacktop parking lot at Roberts Stadium. Dad always bought us tickets for the hard wooden bleachers that encircled the concourse, hovering over the seats with chair backs that were closer to the court and thus out of our price range. My father, Paul E. Beaven Jr., was a frugal man, a devout Catholic who went to seminary for two years of high school so that he could study to be a priest, but decided it wasn't for him. On his car salesman's salary, my parents paid Catholic school tuition for all five of their children and still managed to drop a check in the collection basket each Sunday. Aces games were affordable luxuries for us.

I can't remember all these years later the first time we went to Roberts Stadium together. But I remember 1977, when Bobby Watson came to Evansville after Arad McCutchan announced his retirement. College basketball was changing. Instead of the College and University Divisions, there was now Division II and Division I. Within a few years, cable television stations would carry games nearly every night. The post-season tournament was expanding. Corporate money was flooding the game. Watson swept into town with the charismatic confidence to lead the Aces from Division II to Division I and recapture the hysteria of Mac's championship years. For a few brief and exhilarating months, it seemed as if he would do just that. Watson inspired hope and optimism and renewed our love for UE basketball after several disappointing seasons at the end of McCutchan's career. When the *Evansville Courier* published a photo of the team posed in the empty parking lot at Roberts Stadium, with Watson sitting front and center, I clipped it out and taped it to my bedroom wall. I was an Indiana kid, and the Aces fit squarely within Indiana's storied basketball tradition, from Bob Knight at Indiana to Larry Bird at Indiana State, all the way back to John Wooden's all-American playing career at Purdue. Basketball defined us, perhaps nowhere more so than in Evansville.

———

Frank Deford returned to southern Indiana for another story about Evansville and its basketball team in late 1978. What he found this time was not the euphoric pride that had filled the city thirteen years prior. Instead he found grief and absence. Bobby Watson and his promising young team—Mike Duff, John Ed Washington, and their teammates—had been gone for less than a year, taken from us in an explosive plane crash that forever stained the school and the city. On this trip, Deford remembered the men lost to us on a foggy December night in a muddy field at the Evansville airport and bore witness to our first tentative steps into a new era.

By November 1978, we were still finding our way, with a team of strangers whose names and hometowns and vital statistics—height, weight, et cetera—meant little to us. Dick Walters was the boy-coach, a classic antihero with rough edges and perfect hair. We didn't know him or the kids he'd recruited. But they played for us; they were our team, and we embraced them with a hunger and desperation they were too young and callow to understand.

Deford understood. UE basketball was no longer the benign flood of 1965. It had grown even more important to Evansville, even more vital to our civic pride. In the seasons to come, we would gather again and the great loss we'd suffered would fade with each victory. My father and I watched those teams. We shared the city's passion for those new players—Brad Leaf, Theren Bullock, and all of the rest. My father tried to temper my expectations, gently elaborating on all the reasons why the Aces could never compete with Kentucky and North Carolina and Indiana, the giants of college basketball. But I was eleven years old and I believed, without reservation, that they would. As the years passed, the rest of my hometown believed it, too. We filled Roberts Stadium again, for one last championship run.

"Teams play and programs carry on," Deford wrote later, "but the tradition that Evansville possesses is the greater thing, because it has a life all its own."

PART I

ACES ARE HIGH IN EVANSVILLE

ONE

The Natural

THE HELICOPTER DESCENDS FROM the winter sky and settles on the football field's frozen turf, bare trees standing at attention like sentries guarding a head of state. With rotors whipping overhead, the chopper door opens and out he steps, unmistakable in his clunky glasses, with a helmet of thick brown hair framing his round face, not a strand out of place. College basketball royalty: Joe Beasman Hall, head coach of the Kentucky Wildcats. He looks just now like a country preacher dropping into a small southern Illinois town for a tent revival. He shakes hands with the local luminaries who've come to meet the helicopter and follows them across Saline Avenue to the gym, a subterranean fortress, low-slung and redbrick, that looks as if it's been dropped into a hole in the middle of town. Entering at court level, Hall climbs the steps and takes a seat a few rows up from the scorer's table, not far from the band, holding a rolled-up program in one hand, like a maestro's baton. Beneath the harsh lights and unceasing racket, a low hum courses through the crowd like an electrical current, from one row to the next: parents, teachers, students, cheerleaders, water boys, every sentient being, standing shoulder to shoulder, gawking. The junior varsity players hurry from the locker room after their game to get a good look at the famous coach, and a couple of the band kids run out to the football field before tip-off to eyeball the chopper up close. No one in Eldorado, an isolated farm town of 4,757, has seen an entrance so grand since Harry Truman rolled through three decades before, railing against the Republicans in a noontime campaign rally.

Eldorado High School games are public spectacles, like a circus that comes through once a week each summer and sets up on the town square: every night hot, humid, and ever on the edge of chaos. Everybody knows that getting a seat for an Eagles game means getting to the gym early, before the JV teams play. By the time the varsity takes the floor and Mike Duff wipes the dust from the bottom of his rubber soles, every seat is filled. The people of Eldorado know their days with Mike are numbered, that his astonishing gifts will soon be on display for the entire country to see. So, in the limited time before he leaves to play college ball, before he's whisked away in a private helicopter by a big-time coach promising the sun and the moon and everything in between, they savor each moment and hold him close like a precious child.

With Joe B. Hall on hand, Mike plays as if everyone on the floor is moving in slow motion—everyone but him. His game is smooth and powerful, depending on what's necessary at that particular moment. Sometimes he works methodically under the basket, shooting soft, turn-around jumpers over smaller defenders, tipping in his teammates' misses, and muscling his way to the rim. At 6'7" and 210 pounds, with chiseled shoulders, he is a dominant rebounder, bigger, stronger, and more rugged than nearly every kid on the floor. But recently he's been working on his jumper, stepping from beneath the basket out to the baseline, to add some variety to his game. When he shoots, both of his arms extend fully over his head and he releases the ball at the apex of his jump with a simple flick of the wrist. It's a shot that can't be blocked. It's a thing of beauty, punctuated by a soft whoosh each time the ball sails through the net. Tonight, Mike drops thirty-seven points on Metropolis High School, breaking Eldorado's season scoring record.

His teammates, however, can't match his intensity and the Eagles lose by eight. Afterward, Joe B. Hall tells the radio play-by-play man that he likes Mike's shooting and his explosive move to the basket.

Then he makes his way to the narrow, crowded hallway outside the coach's office, where the college scouts gather after every game, for an audience with Eldorado's favorite son.

During the brutal winter of 1977, more than one hundred schools—112, to be exact—chased after Mike Duff. Indiana. Indiana State. Duke. Illinois. A young coach from the army named Mike Krzyzewski. They drove the narrow country highways, from 13 to 45 to 142, past Equality and Muddy and Dykersburg, pulling up to Mike's house on Organ Street or staking out the high school gym. Eldorado coach Bob Brown deftly managed the flow of coaches at games and practices and advised Mike on the merits of the college programs that pursued him most aggressively. He pitted schools against each other in the newspapers to drive up Mike's value. Missouri's Norm Stewart had called, Brown told one reporter, and was due in town next week. He told another writer that Jack Hartman of Kansas State sat with him till 10:00 p.m. on a Sunday night to talk about Mike. And Cincinnati was coming on hard. The coaches, in turn, relied on flattery and other inducements to gain an edge. Wake Forest sent Mike a letter from golf icon Arnold Palmer, extolling the virtues of his alma mater. One coach promised a scholarship to another Eldorado player if Mike would commit to his school. Another told Brown that Mike was good enough to start for his team at that very moment. It didn't matter whether it was true. What mattered was how it sounded and whether it matched Mike's own visions of his future.

Coach Hall's visit was a helpful barometer of Mike's place among the nation's top recruits. The year before, Hall had snatched up a hotshot guard named Jay Shidler, the Blond Bomber, from nearby Lawrenceville, and now he was taking a long look at Mike. At that moment, the University of Kentucky was ranked second in the nation, with nine players headed to the NBA. In thirteen months, Kentucky would win its fifth national championship. Hall's mere presence made a powerful impression on Mike. The Kentucky border lay only twenty miles south of town, and Mike watched UK games on TV all winter. He hoped to make a visit to Lexington in the spring.

Still, coaches from lesser schools hustled into town to make their own impression, employing every tool at their disposal. Some of them even told the truth. Indiana State coach Bob King visited the Eldorado gym that season and made a promise none of his rivals could match.

"We're sitting in Coach Brown's office," recalls Gary Barton, an Eldorado assistant coach at the time, "and Coach King told Mike, 'If you come to Indiana State, we'll have the best two white forwards in the nation.'"

It was not the last time that Mike Duff would be compared to Larry Bird.

———

Eldorado rises up out of the flatlands of southern Illinois, a cluster of modest homes and wide green lawns amid underground coal mines and uninterrupted fields of corn and soybeans. Here, in 1977, Mike Duff achieved the near-mythic status reserved solely for high school athletes in small towns. He was the best player in Illinois on one of the state's best teams. He dated the prettiest girl at Eldorado High School, and his picture was in the paper nearly every day. He was a handsome boy, with a soft, open face and feathered brown hair parted down the middle. The people of Eldorado projected their most cherished virtues onto Mike. He was polite, humble and selfless, kind to the elderly, and a fitting role model for the children. He signed autographs for youngsters outside the locker room after games and coached them at summer basketball camps. One girl used crayons to draw a picture of the two of them in purple Eldorado uniforms, standing on a green court in front of a brown basket, under a violet sky. In speech bubbles, they both said, "Hi." At the top she scrawled, "I love you."

Greg Goodley was ten years old in 1977 and obsessed with Eldorado Eagles basketball. He went to the games with his parents, and sometimes, when every seat was filled, he sat on the floor with the other kids, near the players, coaches, and cheerleaders. At Eldorado Elementary School, Goodley and his classmates wrote Mike's name on their T-shirts, as if they were wearing their favorite player's jersey. A couple of times, when Mike passed by Greg's house, he pulled over and shot a few baskets before hopping back into his car and driving away. For Greg, those few moments remained vivid decades later, after he'd had children of his own, after he'd coached basketball at the high school, after Mike left town forever, through all the sadness to come.

———

Mike found the recruiting process especially draining. He hated the scrutiny. He hated the handshakes and backslaps. The pressure wore him down. It was as if he had been strapped to a plow in the middle of a cornfield, while a long line of coaches stood by and watched, taking measurements and jotting notes. He didn't mind whether they came to the games. But if he knew a college coach was waiting at the house, he wouldn't come home until they'd left. Midway through his senior season, Mike told the Eldorado coaches he didn't want to talk to the scouts anymore. Coach Brown advised him to meet only with a select few. Otherwise, Brown banned recruiters from Eldorado practices, told them that Mike didn't want to talk, and instructed student managers to hustle him past the college coaches and out of the gym. Duff just wanted to go fishing. He was seventeen years old, overwhelmed, and unable to decide where to play. He'd made official visits to Kansas and Duke. Kentucky was on his short list. Southern Illinois was practically home. His mom liked Missouri.

And then there was a dark horse candidate: the University of Evansville, sixty miles northeast of Eldorado, winner of five small-college national titles. UE had ambitious plans for its basketball team. The College Division and the University Division had been renamed Division II and Division I, and in the fall of 1977 UE would move up to the sport's highest level. Now the university was searching for a new coach, preferably a young guy, eager to lead a once-proud program into a bright new epoch. Honestly? Everyone in the entire city of Evansville, its burgeoning suburbs, and the farm towns of southern Indiana wanted to bring back Jerry Sloan, who was nearing the end of his NBA career with the Chicago Bulls. His return had been rumored for years, since Sloan led the Aces to national championships in 1964 and 1965. It sounded so natural: as soon as Jerry retired from the NBA, he'd come home to Evansville to take over for his mentor, the legendary Arad McCutchan.

Then he'd bring Mike Duff to town. They'd known each other for years.

Duff and Sloan met on a summer day at a Catholic seminary in the St. Louis suburbs sometime around 1973. Lean and rugged at 6'6" and 195 pounds, Sloan made his name in the NBA as a fierce defender who suffered no fools and never gave an inch, even in practice. Each summer, he worked as a guest instructor at basketball camps in southern Illinois. On the day he met Mike, Sloan had come to Ed Macauley's Camp for Boys at St. Henry's Seminary to pass along, in his deep baritone, the very foundation of his competitive philosophy: diving after loose balls. Running nonstop. Playing defense with maniacal zeal. Macauley was a former college and pro star who brought NBA players to his camps every summer to work with slack-jawed boys from small towns, many of whom would never make the high school varsity. The weeklong camps cost a hundred bucks or so, and every year at least one kid played with such skill and athleticism that he left the rest of the campers to consider quitting basketball altogether and joining the Boy Scouts.

That week, Mike dominated every kid in his age group. He didn't even have his driver's license yet. But he was already as big as a grown man, nearly as tall as Sloan. When Jerry arrived at camp, the high school coaches told him that Mike wanted to play him one-on-one.

"I'm not playing anyone one-on-one," Sloan said, deadpan as always. "I couldn't beat my mother."

But for celebrity instructors, playing against the camp kids was part of the job. Games of H-O-R-S-E or one-on-one provided each boy a brush with greatness that he could brag about back home. Sloan understood the unwritten rules of the summer camp circuit, and he didn't mind squaring off against Mike Duff. After a few minutes, though, Sloan called time-out to make a point: Mike would never achieve greatness if he didn't dive to the floor for every ball like his life depended on whether or not he got it. When their game resumed, that's what Mike did, playing with a desperation that Jerry Sloan never forgot.

Mike had already been declared a prodigy in his hometown. Shawneetown, Illinois, sat at the tip of the Shawnee National Forest, less than four miles across the Ohio River from Kentucky. Shawneetown was best known as the tiny burg that was completely engulfed by the Ohio River during the great flood of 1937, when waters as high as the windows at the grocery store rushed down Main Street and destroyed everything in sight. The city was rebuilt a few miles inland, and this is where Mike showed the first signs of his immense potential. Even in junior high, he was a rare talent in a town of seventeen hundred, where one player with extraordinary skills could alter the fortunes of the tiny high school's basketball team. But by the time he was a freshman, Mike

had already outgrown the competition in Shawneetown. After Kay and
Bill Duff split, Kay moved her son and his three younger sisters seventeen miles northwest to Eldorado, where Mike enrolled at the high
school. This did not go over well in Shawneetown. The local fans didn't
want to give him up. So they fought to keep him. The state's high school
athletic association got involved. There were hearings and meetings, and
Mike's family had to hire an attorney to untangle the whole mess. But
Shawneetown's challenge ultimately failed, and Mike began classes at
Eldorado High School in 1974.

Not long after school started in Eldorado, Mike stopped by to
watch junior varsity football practice. He'd never played organized football before. But his new classmates encouraged him to give it a try, and
the coach was happy to have such a big, athletic kid on the team. In his
first game, after minimal practice, Mike started at defensive end. It was
a Monday night in Eldorado, the Eagles versus Johnston City. Mike was
a raw rookie, but it didn't show. He knocked down a pass and sacked
the quarterback twice. He also made a spectacular interception at close
range in the Johnston City backfield that Eldorado coaches remember in amazement to this day, like old men recalling their first love.
The story spread through Eldorado quickly, embellished further with
every telling. Eventually the tale ended with Mike sprinting downfield
for a touchdown. But the exaggeration wasn't necessary. Everyone in
Eldorado knew Mike possessed rare skills. They anticipated great things
from him. But they didn't expect him to make his mark so soon, and no
one figured he'd do it on the football field. It wasn't even Christmas yet,
and Mike had already made a memorable first impression.

That game, however, was the pinnacle of Mike's football career. The
next game, a week later, was his last. He planted a foot while chasing
the quarterback and tore up his left knee. The injury required surgery
and delayed his debut for the Eldorado basketball team. But it wouldn't
diminish his skills.

Ambitious and charismatic, Eldorado basketball coach Bob Brown enjoyed an outsize reputation in the small world of high school basketball in southern Illinois. Charming and profane, just thirty years old, Brown combed his thinning hair across his otherwise bare scalp and wore flashy suits, cut just right, with lapels the size of pterodactyl wings. He cultivated relationships with the media and spoke openly of his efforts to get a college head-coaching job. His flamboyance, titanic ego, and blunt demeanor didn't endear him to everyone. But many of his assistant coaches and players—including Mike—were utterly devoted to him. Brown didn't like to be alone, so some nights he'd head to a dive bar out in the country to eat cheeseburgers, drink beers, and talk basketball with his assistant coaches. He smoked a lot, even in the gym, standing beneath the basket during practice with a cigarette cupped in one hand, hidden from view in case the principal or superintendent happened by.

Brown had been a schoolboy legend in the late '50s and early '60s at nearby West Frankfort High School. He played at the University of Illinois and then served as a scout and coach for the Illinois freshman team before entering the family furniture business. In 1972, Eldorado High School hired him as a PE teacher and head basketball coach. Brown brought a youthful energy to his new job. In an era when high school and college coaches controlled their teams like dictators and used fear to motivate their players, Brown's philosophy was different. He was young for a high school coach and took his time with the kids, listened to them, read their moods, and made them laugh. If he yelled and swore at a boy in practice, later on he'd hang an arm over the kid's shoulder and praise his hustle or his smarts. Brown won a lot of ball games in Eldorado, 121 in five years. In 1974, the season before Mike arrived, Brown's team finished undefeated and ranked number one in the Class A division before losing in the state tournament.

As a recruiter for Illinois, Brown had traveled the country looking for prospects, hanging out in gyms from Kansas City to New York. But he'd never come across a player as skilled as Mike Duff. As a sophomore with a weak knee, Mike scored thirteen points a game. He averaged twenty-five points the following season, when Eldorado won thirty-one games in a row before losing in the quarterfinals of the state tournament. As a senior in 1977, he turned in one of the greatest seasons in state history, averaging thirty-two points per game—more than any player in Illinois. In four state tournament games, Mike poured in 131 points. The Illinois High School Association later named him as one of the "100 Legends of the Boys Basketball Tournament," where he joined an all-star lineup of future NBA players, including a pint-size point guard from Chicago named Isiah Thomas.

On February 3, 1977, Jerry Sloan stepped into the upscale Executive Inn in downtown Evansville for his first press conference as the new head coach at the University of Evansville. He wore a gray three-piece suit, a white shirt, and a dark tie, his brown hair nearly covering his ears, longer and more stylish than the crew cut he wore fifteen years before. But Sloan hadn't changed. He answered reporters' questions with the lantern-jawed sincerity that was his trademark.

After eleven years in the NBA, Sloan had retired and returned, duty bound, to replace the man who'd brought him to town in the first place.

Jerry Sloan grew up in poverty in Gobbler's Knob, Illinois, a splat on the map sixteen miles from the nearest post office. He was one of ten children raised by a widow who took no sass from anyone, least of all her kids. Sloan wore bib overalls, graduated from a one-room elementary school, and made a name for himself at McLeansboro High School. McCutchan was one of many college coaches who recruited him. At first, Sloan turned him down in favor of the University of Illinois. But once classes started, he found the Illinois campus big and intimidating. He grew desperately homesick, dropped out of school before practice even began, and moved home. Back in Gobbler's Knob, he took a job in the oil fields. It was nasty work: wet, cold, and unforgiving. When Sloan came in one night after a day in the fields, his mother asked him whether this was the way he wanted to spend the rest of his life. It was not. So he called Evansville to see whether McCutchan still wanted him. McCutchan didn't hesitate and Sloan soon moved to Indiana. He enrolled in classes and took a job at the Whirlpool plant as he waited to begin his college career.

In late 1962, early in his first season at Evansville, Sloan sat out practice one day nursing a sore knee when his coach sat down for a chat. "Jerry," he said, "someday after your pro career is over, I want you to come back to Evansville to take my place." Sloan didn't understand. He hadn't even played a game yet. But McCutchan was serious. He recognized the depth of Sloan's talent and drive long before Sloan realized it for himself.

So it was no surprise that Sloan was the beating heart of McCutchan's best teams. But he was not Mac's only all-American.

Larry Humes was a slender forward who came to Evansville from Madison, Indiana, perched on the Ohio River, 165 miles east of the college. He was a quiet kid with prominent ears, arched eyebrows, and a deeply lined forehead. In 1962, he'd been Indiana's Mr. Basketball—the best high school player in the state. Three years later in Evansville, he averaged nearly thirty-three points a game, maneuvering around the basket with the balletic grace of a figure skater. Walt Frazier, a guard at archrival Southern Illinois, who later won two NBA championships with the New York Knicks, once told a sportswriter that Humes was "a maestro . . . He was phenomenal, man. I couldn't stop him. Hanging shots, off-balance, fadeaway, using the glass . . ."

Sloan's game, on the other hand, was all bone and gristle. He was the team's best rebounder and its top defender, equally adept at guarding players from 5'6" to 6'11". He was McCutchan's ideal, on the court and off, with an understated disposition and a dry sense of humor.

"The only thing I regret about us being in the College Division," McCutchan told *Sports Illustrated* in '65, "is that Jerry and Larry won't get the recognition they deserve."

It was the perpetual lament of Aces fans. The College Division versus the University Division. Evansville knew its Aces could beat the big schools in the University Division. They'd seen it, year after year. And they were certain that Sloan could shut down Bill Bradley, the cerebral forward from Princeton, and that Humes would dominate Cazzie Russell, the high-scoring guard from Michigan. But no matter how many games they won or how many high-profile teams they beat, the Aces would never earn the same attention and respect of John Wooden's UCLA Bruins or Adolph Rupp's Kentucky Wildcats. They settled for perfection instead.

In the final weeks of 1964, the Aces played transcendent basketball, a stretch so mysterious and magical that it seemed as if only the Boston Celtics could challenge them. Iowa fell first. Then Northwestern and Notre Dame. George Washington, Louisiana State, and Massachusetts left town wondering why they'd bothered to show up. As the new year began, the Aces rolled on, blistering regional rivals by twenty points or more. The only true threat they faced was Walt Frazier and his Southern Illinois Salukis. The Aces squeaked past SIU on January 20, 81–80. Five weeks later, Evansville prevailed a second time, 68–67. Their third meeting came on March 12, 1965, in the national championship game at Roberts Stadium. Tied at 74 when the buzzer sounded, the teams traded baskets in overtime until Evansville led 83–82 with four seconds left and Sloan at the line. He sunk the first free throw, but the second bounced around the rim for something like eternity before finally falling through the net as Sloan threw his hands toward the heavens and leaped with joy. Those were his final moments in an Evansville uniform.

The Baltimore Bullets selected Sloan in the 1965 NBA draft. The following season, he joined the Chicago Bulls, where he played for ten years and earned a reputation as a relentless defender, all arms, elbows, and knees. He didn't back down from anyone, ever. Sloan's best friend from childhood was David Lee, who went on to be a successful high school coach in southern Illinois. Once, while Sloan was still playing in the NBA, Lee invited him to scrimmage against his team. Sloan was a grown man, playing against high school boys. But he showed no mercy. When a kid gave him an elbow on a jump ball, Lee recalls, Sloan flattened him, dropping the boy to the floor and leaving him with a broken arm. Jerry Sloan was an NBA all-star. But growing up in rural poverty had shaped his playing style.

"He was mean," Lee says. "That was the only way he could survive."

Sloan's return as head coach was a coup for the University of Evansville, a private school eager to shed its reputation as a parochial institution that drew most of its students from surrounding towns. Since 1967, the university had changed its name from Evansville College, created a satellite campus in England, and expanded its academic offerings, all under the leadership of an enterprising president named Wallace Graves. And in 1977, the coming season, the basketball program would ascend to the top rung of the college game, leaving behind many of the small regional schools on its schedule to play the best teams in the country.

But for all of Jerry Sloan's legendary grit and fortitude, he was prone to near-crippling bouts of uncertainty at pivotal moments in his life. Doubt drove him from the University of Illinois, and it plagued him again in the weeks before he took the Evansville job. He was torn between big-city ambition and hometown loyalty, between Chicago and Evansville, the Bulls and the Aces. Evansville offered him a four-year contract at $40,000 per year. It was his alma mater, practically home, and Coach McCutchan had given him so much. In Chicago, however, he could easily slip into an assistant's role with the Bulls, putting in his time before ascending to head coach, earning far more money in the process. Sloan weighed his options in public.

"I don't want to sound hard to negotiate with," he said. "I'll try to be fair and across the board with both sides."

Ultimately, his loyalty to McCutchan and his alma mater won out. His introductory press conference at the swanky downtown hotel was packed, so crowded that one sportswriter compared it to the media scrum that had welcomed Evel Knievel to town a few years before. Sloan gave a polished performance. He was no miracle worker, he said, and if he didn't get the job done, he expected to be fired. He wanted players who were big, quick, and intense. He promised that he'd recruit "fair and square. Hopefully, there are still some kids out there who think the same way."

Then he headed to Eldorado to reacquaint himself with Mike Duff.

TWO

Spiral

HOW FITTING THAT WHEN Jerry Sloan came to Evansville in 1962, he spent his first weeks on the factory floor at a Whirlpool plant. The kid and the company were a perfect match, their brief partnership evoking the city's romantic ideals of hard work and humility. But as Evansville sports fans reveled in Sloan's return, sputtering contract negotiations between the Whirlpool Corporation and Local 808 of the International Union of Electrical Workers threatened once again to fracture the city's economy. On February 17, 1977, some four thousand members of Local 808 squeezed through the turnstiles at Roberts Stadium, not to watch basketball but to consider Whirlpool's latest contract offer. It was a high-stakes vote for both sides. Negotiations between the two had been grim business for nearly a decade, punctuated by two harrowing strikes that reinforced Evansville's reputation as a "bad labor town," steeped in union-management hostility. Charles Johnson, the powerful and blunt-talking president of Local 808, told his coworkers before the vote that he couldn't recommend the contract because the pension and vacation proposals fell short of the union's demands.

"It's up to you," Johnson said, "to make the final decision."

The tension at the stadium that day and the deteriorating relationship between the company and its workers belied Whirlpool's role in rescuing Evansville's economy two decades before, when the city needed it most.

After a massive manufacturing boom during World War II, the Evansville economy crashed in the 1950s. Local plants that had supplied the home-building boom after the war, when the city proudly proclaimed itself the "Refrigerator Capital of the World," no longer had a market for their goods. Ten major employers moved or closed between 1950 and 1957. Chrysler packed up and headed to St. Louis. The Servel Refrigeration Company shuttered its factory. The International Harvester plant out by the airport also shut down. Unemployment topped 13 percent, and the federal government added Evansville to a list of "distressed areas" eligible for loans and grants to attract new employers, a dubious distinction that sullied the city's image of itself as a muscular manufacturing hub. In a panic, local leaders hired a consulting firm to assess the potential for luring industry. The firm's glum appraisal haunted the city for years to come: "Evansville is racked by pessimism, gloom, inability to work in a unified fashion; one group stymies another simply because of personal differences between members. The city as a whole is unable to accomplish anything."

In the midst of this slump, Whirlpool swooped in to rescue the city. The home appliance maker, based in Michigan, bought the International Harvester, Servel, and Seeger-Sunbeam factories in the late 1950s. As Whirlpool broadened its product line to include air conditioners and dehumidifiers, it expanded its footprint in Evansville and added thousands of well-paying jobs. Evansville was removed from the distressed cities list in 1963, and a second report from the relocation consultant praised the city's progress. Whirlpool was especially good to Evansville College. Its executives served on the board of trustees, and each year the company hired graduates of the college's engineering and business programs. Whirlpool, like Arad McCutchan's basketball teams, was a cornerstone of the city's identity. It was also the foundation of Evansville's economy. The company's impact and influence extended well beyond its own factories. Local Whirlpool suppliers—at plastics factories, fabrication plants, even advertising firms—employed thousands. Retailers relied on Whirlpool workers and so did local charities. Jobs at Whirlpool were coveted for their generous pay and benefits. Husbands and wives worked opposite shifts so they could raise families. Fathers got jobs for their sons. One generation after another relied on the company to provide a middle-class life.

Donnie Latham grew up on Evansville's west side and got hired on as a machinist at Whirlpool in 1966, a few years out of high school. Donnie's dad had worked at Servel, and his younger brothers, Billy Ray and Larry, eventually got on at Whirlpool, too. Donnie started out at $2.50 an hour, making the doors for side-by-side refrigerators, working second or third shift because he had no seniority. But he took on overtime and got a few promotions. He bought new cars and a house and raised three kids on a Whirlpool paycheck. The work was challenging and meaningful, rooted deeply in the well-being of his extended family. He was an officer in the union and retired in 2009, after forty-three years.

"I liked it there," he says. "It was good money. When I retired I think I was making $50,000."

But every three years, contract negotiations at Whirlpool brought a collective, low-grade anxiety to Evansville. There had been brief strikes and lockouts in the 1950s and '60s. It wasn't until the early '70s that the tenor of the disagreements between the union and the company turned particularly nasty.

A strike that began in October 1970 lasted for 110 days. After the strike came to an end, Whirlpool ramped up production and in 1973 sales of room air conditioners exceeded five million. This was Whirlpool's peak in Evansville, with nearly ten thousand people working at three plants. But it wouldn't last. A four-month strike in 1974

was the start of a slow downward spiral. After members of Local 808
went on strike that February, Whirlpool shifted production and jobs
to its plants in Arkansas and Ohio. Crescent Plastics and Ball Plastics,
two major Whirlpool suppliers, laid off nearly 150 workers. As the strike
wore on, community leaders pleaded with the two sides to find common ground. Federal mediators were summoned. Bishop Francis R.
Shea of the Catholic Diocese of Evansville sent a letter to both sides,
asking them to "make some gesture of genuine goodwill." Finally, on
June 19, Local 808 approved a contract after 122 days on strike. The
new deal provided a raise, but for fifteen cents less per hour than the
company's original proposal.

Three years later, when members of Local 808 returned to Roberts
Stadium for another contract vote, bitter memories of the '74 strike
lingered. Whirlpool had warned union leaders that if the local rejected
its final contract offer, the company would lock the factory doors. The
union had already compiled picket line schedules, and the county wel-
fare board was preparing for a flood of food stamp requests.

The vote, however, wasn't even close. After the union approved the
new contract by a three-to-one margin, workers cheered and hugged as
they streamed into the parking lot. In the optimistic days after the vote,
the company suggested that it would add jobs and boost air-conditioner
production in Evansville. Instead, when the market for gas refrigerators
collapsed, the company closed one of its three plants in town. Its payroll
in Evansville had fallen by more than half since '73. Three weeks after
the union signed the new contract, Whirlpool laid off 375 workers.
More layoffs followed that summer. Bills were put off and mortgages
went unpaid.

If Whirlpool was one indicator of Evansville's well-being, the company's decline suggested 1977 would be a bleak year for the city. And yet
our mood was lightened, our hopes lifted up, by our basketball team and
its new coach. Jerry Sloan passed up the NBA for Evansville. His return
was an indisputable validation of our worth at an otherwise-uncertain

moment in the city's history. As the world economy slowly passed us by, we still had basketball; we still had the Purple Aces.

In the days after he accepted the job in Evansville, Sloan seemed committed to building the program in his own image. He talked to his old teammate Larry Humes about joining him as an assistant coach. He offered another assistant job to David Lee, his childhood friend. On February 5, a Saturday, Sloan traveled to Eldorado to see Duff score thirty-two points against McLeansboro, his alma mater.

Even with Sloan in the stands, Eldorado coach Bob Brown made clear to reporters that Evansville had plenty of competition for Mike. Sloan's pedigree guaranteed nothing.

"I'm sure Mike is interested in Evansville," Brown said. "But a lot of good people are hustling Mike very hard. He's a long way from a decision."

Still, Sloan enjoyed a history with Mike that none of the other coaches could match. Everybody in Eldorado knew Jerry. His farm in McLeansboro was only a half-hour drive away. Kay's new husband, Dr. John Barrow, was an orthopedic surgeon who had operated on one of Jerry's brothers. And Sloan, perhaps more than anyone, commanded Mike's respect. His first workout with Sloan, at the summer camp at St. Henry's Seminary, seemed in retrospect like a tryout. Sloan would be Mike's mentor, one southern Illinois boy preparing another for the NBA. Mike would be Sloan's first and most important addition to the UE basketball program, a national recruit who would set off a chain reaction that would bring more talent, more media coverage, and a long-awaited resurgence at the University of Evansville.

Two days after visiting Eldorado, Sloan brought Lee to Evansville, where they met with UE administrators and stopped by practice at Carson Center to chat with McCutchan. But Lee noticed a change in Sloan's mood that day. He seemed discouraged. After seeing all of the other college coaches recruiting Mike Duff, Sloan felt that familiar churning in his stomach. It was the same way he felt as a homesick freshman at the University of Illinois, convinced he'd made a huge mistake.

On February 9, six days after the celebratory press conference, Jerry Sloan called Thornton Patberg, the UE vice president who oversaw athletics. Sloan told Patberg that he was headed to Evansville with his wife, Bobbye, and needed to meet with UE president Wallace Graves. Patberg immediately sensed the gravity of the meeting, but Graves dismissed his concerns as if picking a stray thread from his suit. Perhaps, he told himself, Jerry and Bobbye want to talk about buying a house or some such thing. After all, it was a big move with myriad details and a short timeline.

But when Jerry and Bobbye arrived at Graves's office that afternoon, the new head coach didn't want to talk about real estate. He wanted to quit. It just didn't seem right. He told Graves about that awful feeling in the pit of his stomach. He didn't offer any details and didn't make any excuses. But he'd made up his mind. He'd come to resign. Graves was incredulous. He'd courted Jerry for years, meeting him for dinner in Chicago, building a relationship, waiting for the day that Sloan returned. And now, less than a week after giving him the job, he wanted to quit? Graves urged Sloan to think it over.

But Sloan wouldn't budge. He couldn't do it.

News of Sloan's departure struck the city like a thunderbolt. What the hell just happened?

"I think I'll just get drunk," one Aces fan told a sportswriter. Another said the news "actually made me sick." In a column headlined "Black Night in Evansville," *Courier* sports editor Bill Fluty acknowledged the suffering of UE fans who had long considered Sloan as "the messiah." Fluty wrote with great solemnity that he wouldn't blame Sloan for reneging on his deal with the University of Evansville.

"But the news kicked a world of Aces fans in the gut. That's always the way it is when a dream ends."

In the days after the news broke, Sloan gave one interview after another, offered vague excuses, and apologized to anyone who asked. But he never fully explained his departure. Was it money? Was it his family? Did Bobbye want to stay in Chicago? Did the Bulls make him an offer he couldn't refuse?

"I made a mistake," Sloan said in one interview. "Some personal problems came up—some problems I hadn't anticipated."

Graves believed Sloan got cold feet when he realized the competition he faced in his pursuit of Mike Duff. Sloan didn't relish recruiting. Smooth as gravel, it was hard to imagine him glad-handing teenage boys and their parents. So he stayed in Chicago and took the assistant's job with the Bulls instead, forever leaving Evansville wondering why.

Sloan's abrupt exit not only left his alma mater without a coach during the peak of the college recruiting season. It also left Mike Duff in limbo.

———

The University of Evansville secretly flew Bobby Watson into town on a Thursday night, keeping everyone guessing until he made his first appearance as the Aces' new coach the next morning, March 11. He'd been an assistant at Oral Roberts and beat out dozens of competitors to replace Jerry Sloan.

Watson was made for Evansville. Every line of his résumé. Every word he spoke. His family. His faith. His military career. He was a commanding presence, 6'8", handsome—with the dark hair and eyes of his Italian ancestors—and he had an affable charisma that left everyone in his wake feeling like they had a new best friend. At thirty-four, he was a decorated Vietnam veteran and a devout Methodist with a wife and three daughters. He lacked Sloan's star power, but had coached at every level of amateur basketball, in high school, junior college, and as an assistant at three Division I schools, including Wake Forest and Xavier. Watson promised Evansville fans a disciplined program, well-groomed players, and closed practices with a classroom atmosphere. The Aces would play high-intensity pressure defense and a free-flowing, fast-breaking offense. Watson was a master recruiter who made clear that UE had to upgrade its roster to compete in Division I. On his first day, he met with the UE players who would return in the fall. And then he set out to find the young men who'd soon join them at Roberts Stadium.

In those first weeks at UE, with his family still in Tulsa, Watson worked from 7:00 a.m. to 10:00 p.m., attending to every detail. He hired three assistant coaches. He met with a clergyman who would provide for the team's spiritual needs. He met with student leaders to build enthusiasm for the program. He discussed plans for joining a conference that would include Xavier, DePaul, and Valparaiso. He brainstormed new slogans for team stationery and arranged for boosters to invite players and their dates over for postgame meals. He made plans for a summer camp for boys and reviewed blueprints for the new coaches' offices.

Much of the time, he was on the road, logging thousands of miles, by car and by plane, hopscotching between Terre Haute, Indianapolis, Fort Wayne, Dayton, Louisville, and Cincinnati. The pace was relentless. For ethical reasons, he wouldn't recruit the nearly twenty kids he'd been pursuing for Oral Roberts. But the standards that governed big-time college recruiting had always been malleable.

"Of course," Watson said, "if a 6'10" guy on ORU's list called and said he wasn't going there and would rather be in Evansville, I'd say, 'Come ahead.'"

Mike Duff's final decision did not come easily. Too many options. Too many people to please. A big state school with a nationally renowned program? Or a small private school with an unknown coach? Play close to home or hours away? Start immediately or ride the bench for a year? The entire process, every moment of indecision, was excruciating.

As winter turned to spring, Mike's options narrowed. Joe B. Hall didn't invite Mike to Kentucky for a campus visit and never offered him a scholarship. Kansas State was out because Mike didn't want to move so far from home.

He wasn't interested in Missouri for the same reason. But Missouri kept coming hard. It was the only way Norm Stewart knew. Stewart grew up the son of a gas station owner in rural Missouri and played his college ball at the university. By 1977, he'd been the coach at Missouri for a decade and built a program that would soon be one of the top twenty in the country. Adding Mike to his roster would send a powerful message to other coaches: Norm Stewart would pursue—and sign—the best players, anywhere. Stewart and his assistants came to Eldorado every week, for several days at a time. Mike couldn't get away from them. And yet he couldn't tell them no. Kay Barrow, Mike's mom, liked Norm Stewart. She believed that Mike could thrive academically at Missouri and felt the competition would be better at a bigger school.

But Evansville was still in the running. Soon after he was hired at UE, Watson headed to Eldorado to charm Kay and John Barrow. He wanted to meet them before he introduced himself to Mike. So the three of them sat down one day in the waiting room at John's office while Mike was at school. They hit it off immediately. Bobby wore cowboy boots, just like John. And after the monotonous parade of faceless coaches, Kay found Watson appealing. Tall and handsome, charismatic and sincere. Mike liked him, too. Evansville was an hour's drive from Eldorado, with a small campus and a storied basketball program.

On Thursday, April 14, Watson made another trip to Eldorado. Mike told him he hadn't made a decision, but promised he would drive to Evansville the following Monday for a campus visit.

Then, at 2:00 p.m., Norm Stewart and two assistants showed up at Eldorado High School. Mike told them he wasn't ready to make a commitment, and the coaches assured him they were only visiting. They knew the competition was fierce, and they wanted Mike to understand that, after investing so much time and energy, they had come to protect their interests.

Mike had a track meet that day at another school, and when it ended, one of the Missouri coaches gave him a ride home. When they arrived, Stewart awaited them inside, prepared to make a final pitch. He wanted Mike's signature on a National Letter of Intent, securing his commitment once and for all. The discussion that followed dragged on for hours.

At first, Mike agreed to come to Missouri, then and there. But later he changed his mind and called Bob Brown, who came over to talk with him one-on-one. Brown bolstered his resolve, prompting Mike to tell Stewart again that he didn't want to sign with Missouri. He'd visited the university and knew he'd never be happy there. The campus was huge. And the drive to Columbia was four hours, too far from his family and his girlfriend.

But Stewart persisted. "You told me you would sign," he said. "So let's get it over with."

Exhausted from the pressure, Mike finally signed away his college career at 8:30 p.m. Even then, pen in hand, he knew it was a mistake. Stewart and his assistants left, victorious at last.

But Mike was devastated, wondering what he'd done. He couldn't sleep that night. At 2:00 a.m., he awakened Kay and told her he would be unhappy at Missouri. She told him it was only natural that he would have second thoughts after making such a big decision and assured him that everything would be fine. But it wasn't fine, not the next morning nor in the days that followed. Mike felt certain that Missouri was wrong for him. Finally, he mustered the courage to call Stewart to renege on their agreement. Stewart wasn't having it. He promised Mike that once he moved to Columbia, he'd realize that he had made the right choice. He called Mike back three or four times that day, frantic at the thought of losing his top recruit. But Mike finally stood his ground. Missouri was out. Now he had to decide, all over again, where he'd go to college.

The next day, he met with Bob Brown to discuss his options. Stewart insisted that the letter of intent was binding, which meant that Mike couldn't go to another Division I school unless he sat out a year. If he wanted to play immediately, he'd have to settle for junior college or a Division II school. But the competition would be so weak, Mike worried that his skills would deteriorate.

When Watson learned that Mike was wavering in his commitment to Missouri, he let it be known that he was still interested in bringing him to Evansville. Watson returned to Eldorado on May 2, but swore that it had nothing to do with Mike.

"Bob Brown and I are working together on a basketball camp and we have some other business interests," Watson told a reporter, without elaborating. "The purpose of my visit was strictly to see Bob Brown."

Because, of course, Watson would never actively recruit a player who had signed a letter of intent with another school, right? But, if Brown suggested to Mike that he should call Watson, Bobby would most certainly take the call, wouldn't he? So that's what Mike did. Then, on May 3, he drove to Evansville.

Watson, meanwhile, adopted a particularly creative interpretation of the widely held tenets of the letter of intent. He claimed the document that Mike signed wasn't binding. It was merely a "gentlemen's agreement" honored by Division I schools, but not an NCAA rule. Technically, he added, UE remained a Division II school until the fall, and thus didn't honor letters of intent. Bob Hudson, the assistant athletic director, even called the NCAA to get an unofficial ruling on the matter. Then he wrote an official-looking document in his best legalese.

> To Whom It May Concern:
> This will confirm the conversation with Mr. Warren Brown by phone Wednesday, May 4, at 9:15 a.m., concerning the National Letter of Intent. Mr. Brown stated that the NCAA is not connected in any way with the National Letter of Intent, and the signing of same by any student would not affect the eligibility of any student athlete.

Later that day, Mike officially signed a scholarship agreement with UE. Stormin' Norman Stewart was furious but uncharacteristically subdued, offering a "no comment" through gritted teeth when a reporter asked about Mike.

Rather than crowing about Duff's change of heart, Watson professed wonder at such a fortuitous turn of events, as if the hand of fate had gently guided Mike to Evansville.

"It is just one of those unbelievable things that just happen," he said. "Why it happens, I don't know."

For Watson, Mike's commitment was his first victory at UE, an emphatic endorsement of his fledgling basketball program. The best coaches in the country wanted Mike Duff, and he chose Evansville.

It seemed, at the time, like a small but encouraging sign of a hard-luck town's changing fortune.

THREE

Down South

EVEN WITH ITS TEEMING factories, its slums, whorehouses, and gambling dens, its bustling banks and shops, Evansville, Indiana, has always seemed more rural than urban, more like a town than a city, more a part of Kentucky than Indiana. Evansville had much in common with the great urban manufacturing centers of the Midwest—Detroit, Chicago, Milwaukee, and Cleveland—big cities where cars, bombs, and refrigerators rolled off assembly lines by the millions. But its pace, its geography, and its approach to race relations often left Evansville out of step with its northern neighbors.

The novelist Theodore Dreiser spent four years in Evansville as a youth and wrote about the city in *A Hoosier Holiday* after returning to town as an adult in 1915.

> Evansville is a Southern city, in spite of the fact that it
> is [in] Indiana, and has all the characteristic marks of a
> Southern city—a hot, drowsy, almost enervating summer,
> an early spring, a mild winter, a long, agreeable autumn.
> Snow falls but rarely and does not endure long. Darkies
> abound, whole sections of them, and work on the levee,

the railroad, and at scores of tasks given over to whites
in the North. . . . It is as though the extreme South had
reached up and just touched this projecting section of
Indiana.

The Ohio River was central to life in Evansville, to jobs and politics,
to war and peace and race relations, gambling and prostitution, and the
economy. Early in the nineteenth century, white settlers built Evansville
on the shores of the river in the southwest corner of Indiana. Native
Americans had thrived on the deeply forested land for hundreds of
years. But in 1805, the US government pulled off an old-fashioned land
grab, taking vast swaths with sweetheart treaties and then selling its new
property on the open market for two bucks an acre. Hugh McGary Jr.,
the enterprising son of an Indian fighter, took a liking to the lush green
hills as he traveled back and forth across the river to pass the time with
a lady friend in Kentucky. But more important than natural beauty was
his hunch that he could make, literally, boatloads of money. Hugh Jr.
envisioned a port along a rising little spit of land that looked unlikely to
flood. So, in 1812, he bought 441 acres. Two years later, he donated one
hundred acres for a county seat and named the new community after
Colonel Robert M. Evans, a well-known local pol and friend of Hugh
Sr.'s. McGary's bet on the Evansville riverfront paid off. At midcentury,
locals built a wharf along the river, and soon steamboats loaded with
raw materials added Evansville to their routes. The mills and factories
built on the riverfront would dominate the city's economy for more
than a century. Furniture shops, lumber mills, foundries, and all manner of factories paid decent wages, about ten dollars a week for sixty
hours of work. The Scotch Irish and Brits who'd first settled Evansville
were soon outnumbered by Germans escaping political strife at home.
   Indiana troops fought for the Union during the Civil War. But
Evansville couldn't escape its Southern roots or the slave trade. Racial
unrest would define the city and its politics for decades.

Evansville served as a link in the Underground Railroad, as black men, women, and their children were smuggled across the Ohio River at night and given shelter in the homes of black families willing to risk their lives. Escaped slaves continued north up to Terre Haute or Lafayette, often on their way to Canada. These were dangerous missions—for the escaping families and for the people ferrying them north. Even freed slaves who had the documents to prove their status weren't safe. Slave catchers traveled from the South and patrolled the riverfront, looking for a lucrative payday, their work sometimes aided by the sheriff. Still, in the years to come, thousands of former slaves settled in Evansville. From before the war to 1890, the black population exploded from about 130 to more than 5,500.

But even as the black community grew—opening businesses, churches, and schools—its tenuous relationship with its white neighbors was defined by intimidation and mob violence. Historian Darrel E. Bigham has pieced together the escalation of slow-simmering racial tension in 1903, when blacks and whites fought over property rights, and black men were accused of assaulting a white woman and trying to kill a police officer. Then, on the afternoon of July 3, a tavern dispute ended in a shoot-out between a white police officer and an African American man named Robert Lee. The officer died the following day—the Fourth of July—and that evening hundreds of angry whites crowded outside the jail, eager to get their hands on Lee. The prisoner remained locked away. But the next night, the city erupted in violence. About a thousand people returned to the jail, and white men descended on black neighborhoods. With his city in chaos, Evansville's mayor closed all the taverns and ordered his constituents to remain inside. On July 6, the governor sent one hundred troops to restore the peace. But when the soldiers faced off against another angry mob at the courthouse, someone among the protesters fired a shot. The troops responded by firing into the crowd. By the time the shooting stopped, twelve were dead and thirty wounded. Fearing ongoing attacks on their neighborhood, Evansville's black community was consumed by panic. Many fled the city on foot along the railroad tracks leading out of town. Order was restored only after the governor sent in another three hundred troops. But the damage had been done. Black families left town for good. Plans for an African American newspaper were scrapped. Evansville grew to nearly seventy thousand people by 1910, but the black community only got smaller. In the 1920s, white supremacy had rooted so deep in the workings of the city that the men who ran for office often sought and received endorsements from the recently revived Ku Klux Klan. Or they simply joined, aligning themselves with a cresting wave of fervent white nationalism, anti-Semitism, and opposition to the Catholic Church.

The Klan was a powerful player in city politics in the 1920s, thanks to D. C. Stephenson, an ambitious, baby-faced political operative of mysterious origins who arrived in Evansville after World War I, working for a coal company and glad-handing the local power brokers. His formal education was limited. But Stephenson possessed a certain charisma that attracted returning veterans and aspiring statesmen. Stephenson lost a bid for Congress in 1920 as an anti-Prohibition Democrat. So he joined the Republican party, opened an office downtown, and adopted the title of Grand Dragon of the Ku Klux Klan of Indiana. With Evansville as his base, Stephenson built one of the most powerful Klan operations in the country. At its peak, Klan membership included more than 30 percent of the white men in Indiana. About four thousand men claimed membership in Evansville, marching in parades and burning crosses. Stephenson soon grew wealthy from his cut of membership fees and the sales of white robes and hoods. He forged alliances with politicians of both parties, in Evansville and throughout the state. In 1924, the Klan helped governor-elect Ed Jackson, a host of state legislators, and most of the Indiana congressional delegation. The following year, the Klan sent Evansville Republican Herbert Males to the mayor's office. The Klan's support was no surprise. Males was one of its own.

Far from the back rooms and saloons where Evansville's politics were hashed out, the city's elites boasted opulent Victorian homes in sunny riverfront neighborhoods and steered local social and cultural institutions. But even as Evansville grew in the early 1900s, it remained an insulated outpost 180 miles south of the state capital in Indianapolis and 170 miles east of St. Louis, the nearest big city. Evansville lacked many of the cultural amenities enjoyed by its neighbors in Terre Haute and Carbondale, where big state universities played a leading role. In Evansville, the closest four-year colleges were more than one hundred miles away. Wealthy families were happy to send their sons and daughters out of town for a university education. But the absence of a college contributed to Evansville's reputation as an unsophisticated industrial town. For the wealthy and the civic-minded, this simply would not do. Evansville wanted a college, an institution of higher learning that might smooth the city's raw edges. So, in 1917, it bought one.

Civic leaders proposed relocating Moores Hill College, a financially struggling little Methodist school two hundred miles east of Evansville. But they needed money. So, on April 15, 1917, the city launched a fundraising campaign with a goal of $500,000 and asked the Methodist Church to match it. The chamber of commerce took out a newspaper ad outlining all the benefits a college would bring to Evansville, including higher property values, trained leadership for local industry, and "an elevation of intellectual and moral standards."

It didn't take much to convince the people of Evansville that the college would be a community asset. Support came from all corners. Mayor Benjamin Bosse and businessmen from his furniture company contributed $28,500. The *Evansville Courier* featured the college on the front page for eleven days in a row. The owner of the Hercules Buggy Company contributed $25,000. School kids donated dimes and quarters, and teachers from Fulton School handed over fifty bucks apiece.

The Fulton janitor gave $25. A railroad brakeman walked seven miles to drop off $5 at the *Courier*. A giant thermometer constructed on the side of the Citizens Bank Building downtown provided a running tally of donations. The leaders of the campaign pulled up to the bank every day in a fire truck to update the steady progress toward the city's goal.

But on May 3, the last day of the campaign, Evansville came up $50,000 short. If the city didn't meet its goal that day, the terms of the campaign called for all of the money to be returned to donors. Mayor Bosse, who coined the motto "When everybody boosts, everybody wins," took the campaign into his own hands. He brought a rabbi, a Methodist bishop, the president of Moores Hill, and a minister to lobby a wealthy bank president named Francis Joseph Reitz, who promised to match last-minute donations up to $25,000. Fund-raisers pushed forward. Trinity Methodist Church chipped in another $10,000. Smaller donations trickled in. That night, more than one thousand people piled into the Soldiers and Sailors Memorial Coliseum downtown, hoping for good news. Special telephones had been installed so fund-raisers could call in with progress reports. Anticipation swelled as the clock ticked toward midnight. Then, at 11:57 p.m., Bosse delivered the news: the city had raised $514,000.

With matching funds from the Methodist Church, Evansville College opened in temporary quarters in September 1919 with 104 students. Three years later, the college moved to a permanent home on Lincoln Avenue, less than three miles east of the river. A large city block was cleared for the construction of the new administration building. The college's fledgling athletic teams were known at first as the Pioneers and dressed in purple. But the school changed its nickname in the mid-1920s when a rival congratulated Evansville basketball coach John Harmon after a Pioneers victory: "You didn't have four aces up your sleeve. You had five!" A local sports columnist convinced the college that *Aces* would be easier to fit in headlines than *Pioneers*, and the change was made.

Compared to the wider world of higher education, the college operated in a vacuum in its first decades. It provided a basic post-secondary-school education for young men and women from Evansville and surrounding farm towns. The college, a private school that relied mostly on tuition and community support, struggled financially. As its fortunes faded, so too did the city's grand visions for a center of intellectual and cultural uplift.

But then the United States entered World War II and everything in Evansville changed.

───────

It happened so quickly, the transformation from drowsy industrial town to muscular military supplier. On January 4, 1942, less than a month after the Japanese bombed Pearl Harbor, Evansville awakened to news that the local Chrysler plant had been awarded a lucrative war contract. Soon after, the US Army Corps of Engineers took over the Chrysler facility as well as a Sunbeam Electric factory to create the Evansville Ordnance Plant, which churned out millions of tons of ammunition for machine guns, pistols, and rifles. But that was only the beginning of Evansville's surging wartime economy. With well-equipped factories and a skilled labor pool, the city was ready-made to support the war effort. In a matter of months, new manufacturing plants were built, old ones were retrofitted, and workers were retrained.

Then, on Valentine's Day, 1942, a screaming two-deck headline in the *Evansville Press* announced the construction of a massive new moneymaker on the riverfront:

NAVY TO BUILD SHIPS
AT 45-ACRE YARD HERE
300-Foot, Diesel-Powered Craft to Come from
New Industry, City's Contribution
to All-Out War

Amid huge cranes and row after row of scaffolding, the first ship was launched eight months later. The yard eventually grew into the largest employer in Evansville history, with nineteen thousand workers. In April of that year, construction began on the Republic Aviation plant along US Highway 41, next to the airport. Republic was based in Farmingdale, New York, but chose Evansville as the site for a $16 million fighter plane factory because the president of the company had a business connection in Evansville and figured a plant in Indiana would be safer than one on the East Coast if there was another attack. The first fighter planes rolled off the line at the Republic plant on September 20, 1942. At its peak, more than five thousand people worked at Republic, producing two dozen planes a day. The Servel factory, which had made gas-absorption refrigerators before the war, was redesigned to manufacture parts for the fighter jets. Other plants made portable bridges, earth-moving equipment, airplane parts, and military uniforms. As the draft depleted the ranks of skilled workers, the unemployed came from hundreds of miles away to take their places on assembly lines. Because the Klan's influence had waned, prewar employment restrictions were eased and classified ads sought "white or colored" job applicants. Black workers and women got jobs that had previously been off-limits. The workforce doubled after the war began, and doubled again before it ended.

The patriotic fervor that swept across the United States in the early 1940s lifted Evansville up and carried it along. No longer was Evansville a free-floating factory town, disconnected from the rest of the world. Evansville took its place among midwestern manufacturing cities, where the automobile industry had been largely set aside in favor of lucrative military production.

The growth of jobs and wages, and the need for workers with new skills, brought new life to Evansville College. The war helped launch the school's expansion, boosted revenue during lean times, and strengthened its relationship with the most important institutions in the city. The college offered pilot training as part of a contract with the Civil Aviation Authority. A separate program for US Navy pilots included two months of preparation on the ground and forty hours in a plane. The college also trained local factory workers for plants with government contracts, including Republic Aviation and Servel. Radio communication and first aid classes were added, as were new classes in physics and math. When the war ended, hundreds of returning veterans registered for classes on the GI Bill. By 1947, enrollment had grown from four hundred to more than seventeen hundred. That year, local bankers launched a fund-raising campaign that netted $1.2 million. By the early 1950s, an engineering building and a new union building were completed. Classroom space was added and a new library was constructed. In only a few years, the college had finally achieved financial stability. The growth and good fortune extended beyond the classrooms, the library, and the circular drive that marked the campus entrance.

From a cramped concrete building on the back side of campus, a modest mathematician named Arad McCutchan built the greatest small-college basketball program in history.

FOUR

Wild Ass

ARAD MCCUTCHAN'S INTRODUCTION TO basketball sounds, a century later, like a rural fable. Born on the Fourth of July in 1912, McCutchan grew up in a family of subsistence farmers about ten miles north of Evansville. He was the youngest of six children, spoiled rotten and bossed around by his siblings, two brothers and three sisters. He milked the cows, worked in the fields, and went to a one-room country school, where he was the only student in his graduating class and liked to say he had been chosen class president and most likely to succeed. He also liked to joke that his first name was a biblical term that meant "wild ass."

He learned the game on the farm, where his brothers attached a homemade metal ring to the side of the barn. No one had a proper ball, so they stitched one together out of scrap leather with an inflated pig's bladder inside. Crude, yes. But functional. McCutchan went to Bosse High School, not far from the college, where he played well enough to draw interest from schools as far away as Montana State. But he chose his hometown team, where he studied math and physical education, played football, and served as president of his freshman class. He also played basketball for four years, led the Aces in scoring, and was named team captain as a junior. The *LinC*, the 1933 yearbook, said McCutchan was "one of the best basketball men in the state and was high point man on the team. He could place the ball through the hoops from any angle of the floor and his style of play was the joy of his teammates. He leads his team through his own example of fine sportsmanship on the floor, rather than evident discipline."

Once McCutchan graduated in 1934, the seasonal certainties of his rural youth were replaced by a peripatetic work life. He coached high school ball in Alabama, traveled to New York in the summers to earn a master's degree in math at Columbia University, and returned to Evansville to coach at Bosse High School. He also taught a full load of classes. His annual salary was $500. McCutchan married Virginia Robinson in 1940 and took stock of his life. It wouldn't be easy to raise a family on a coach's salary. Maybe it was time to consider a new career. Before he had a chance to decide his long-term future, McCutchan entered the navy a few months after the attack on Pearl Harbor and moved his family to Pensacola, Florida, where he served as a flight instructor. In early 1946, with McCutchan's discharge from the navy looming, Evansville College president Lincoln Hale sent him a letter offering the head-coaching job at his alma mater. By this time, McCutchan was thirty-four years old, the father of two toddlers, and unsure whether he wanted to commit his life to basketball. He wrote back, rejecting the offer. But he regretted his decision immediately and called Hale to accept the job before his letter crossed the president's desk.

McCutchan moved his family back to Indiana and never left again. This was Arad McCutchan's great gift to his hometown: every time he left, he came back. The athletic director from Michigan State called in 1965, after the Aces won their fourth national championship. "But by that point," McCutchan said, "it didn't seem practical to leave for a bigger school." So he stayed in Evansville, refereed high school football games, officiated at track meets, and ran a youth baseball league on the city's east side. He coached golf, served as the athletic director, and spent sixteen years as an assistant football coach. Everyone called him Mac. He earned the devotion of local basketball fans with a gentlemanly demeanor and a self-deprecating wit. He opened the Aces locker room to fans after games and adopted a no-cut policy: any boy who tried out for the team, worked hard, and maintained good grades could dress for home games. Although he was known to stomp the floor in moments of frustration, he didn't berate referees or yell at his players. He kept emotional displays to a minimum.

"In his own way, he showed his love and affection," says Bob Clayton, who played for Evansville in the early 1970s. "He wouldn't come up and hug you. He'd tell a story to whoever was standing around to build you up in some way, something you wouldn't even think he'd remember."

When McCutchan promised parents he'd look after their sons, he wasn't talking about keeping an eye on them at games and practices. He tutored his players in math at his kitchen table while Virginia helped them with English papers. A local barber offered players haircuts in McCutchan's basement every few weeks. They played badminton in his backyard when the weather was good. These visits helped players maintain their grades and the clean-cut look their coach preferred. It also provided them with a sense of community in those first, uncertain years of adulthood.

Mac stood for all the values his neighbors in Evansville hoped to see in themselves, and all of the values they hoped the rest of the world saw in them: modesty, faith in God, belief in family, stoic bravery in times of war. He was also a hometown boy in a town deeply suspicious of outsiders.

For nearly twenty years, starting in the late 1930s, Evansville College played its home games at the National Guard Armory, which was adjacent to campus. The armory, an imposing brick-and-concrete field house constructed on a gently sloping hill, included seating for roughly two thousand. Here, businessmen in starched shirts and neckties squeezed in next to each other beneath the dim lights, their cigarette smoke hanging over the playing floor like a poisonous smog.

In the mid-1940s, when Ron Brand was eleven, he convinced a sympathetic adult at the armory that he'd be an excellent soda salesman during Aces games. He'd bum a ride to the armory from his elementary school basketball coach, watch the first half from the balcony, and then hustle down to the floor to peddle popcorn and Cokes. He made decent money at those games, as much as twenty bucks on a good night. But the cash was a bonus, the cherry on top. Ron loved basketball and he loved the Purple Aces most of all. Back in those days, when Ron was selling soft drinks, the Aces were truly something to see, with standing-room-only crowds pressing forward for a better view of the court. Some nights, when one of Evansville's rivals came to town and the armory was loud and full, it felt like the Aces were playing real big-time basketball.

But for years, local politicians and civic leaders had debated the merits of building a bigger venue for concerts, games, and other gatherings. Concert promoters were especially eager for a bigger hall. When big-name bandleaders like Tommy Dorsey toured the Midwest, they bypassed Evansville for cities with bigger venues. Promoters could make a tidy profit at a sold-out show at Louisville's National Guard Armory, which seated ten thousand. There was nothing in Evansville even half that size. But it was basketball—along with a bit of community envy—that sparked the development of the new arena on Evansville's east side. Friday night high school games already drew thousands of fans at local gyms, and stray tickets to Aces games at the armory were scarce. Evansville also wanted to keep up with its neighbor across the river. Owensboro, Kentucky, was just forty miles southeast of Evansville and the home to Kentucky Wesleyan College, perhaps the Aces' greatest rival in the 1950s. Owensboro was also about a quarter of the size of Evansville, and when the town opened an arena that seated six thousand in 1949, Evansville would not be outdone. Enter Henry O. Roberts.

In 1951, Hank Roberts campaigned for the mayor's office in Evansville, promising the city he'd build an arena big enough to meet the growing demand for Aces tickets. The stadium project faced opposition from some who felt it would turn out to be a white elephant. One sports columnist referred to it as "Hank's Tank." But businessmen, civic leaders, and the city council favored Roberts's proposal, and in 1956, Roberts Municipal Stadium was completed on fifty-five acres of farmland about a mile east of the college. The price tag was $2 million.

The stadium was palatial and cavernous, with seventy-four hundred permanent seats and temporary bleachers that seated another four thousand, making it one of the largest college arenas in the country, even bigger than the field house where Indiana played its home games in Bloomington. The big bands now had a suitable venue: a year after the stadium opened, Lawrence Welk performed there for 13,780 fans. But from the very beginning, everyone knew the stadium belonged to the Purple Aces. Evansville College played its first game at Roberts Stadium on December 1, 1956, drawing nearly nine thousand to see McCutchan's team lose to Purdue on a layup with four seconds left.

In the coming years, Louisville, UCLA, Iowa, and a parade of other major schools agreed to play Evansville at the stadium. Envious coaches from big schools arrived in Evansville several times each year with their empty hands outstretched; a road game at Roberts Stadium was always a generous payday. At the armory, visiting schools might take home $300. But with the new arena, top-tier teams were willing to risk losing to a small College Division program in the middle of nowhere because ticket revenue enabled Evansville to pay visitors as much as $5,000 for their trouble. This, as much as McCutchan's genius for the fast break, is what built the Aces basketball program. The best teams came to Roberts

Stadium, drawing sold-out crowds, which in turn attracted good local players who might otherwise have chosen Indiana, Purdue, or Illinois.

It's no coincidence that Evansville College won its first national championship in 1959, less than three years after moving into Roberts Stadium. Something fundamental had changed in Evansville. Roberts Stadium became a national landmark for college coaches and their teams, an enormous arena for a small school, deafening and packed for nearly every game.

_____

John Wooden brought his weary UCLA squad to Roberts Stadium four days before Christmas in 1957. The Bruins had sprinted out to a promising start that season, winning four straight at one point to climb to number thirteen in the Associated Press poll. But UCLA's annual swing through the Midwest teetered on disaster when the Bruins limped into Evansville, following consecutive losses to Wichita and Bradley. If UCLA fans hoped that playing a tiny College Division team in the snowy wilds of the Great Midwest would provide some measure of relief, they were disappointed. On December 21, the Bruins lost to the Aces, 83–76. John Wooden had been at UCLA for a decade, but he was not yet the "Wizard of Westwood."

Still, the game was a chance for Wooden and McCutchan to reconnect and renew their friendly rivalry. They'd known each other for at least a decade, and their lives had unfolded as mirror images nearly every step of the way. Their Indiana boyhoods, their collegiate playing careers, and their coaching achievements seemed to overlap almost from the day they were born. They shared the same dry sense of humor, moral rectitude, and understated coaching style. In the mid-1960s, they were the two greatest college basketball coaches on the planet, and they had the hardware to prove it. They weren't close friends, but rather kindred spirits whose paths crossed often through the years, even after they both retired.

But their differences were stark, too. One left Indiana and lived life on the national stage, on the covers of magazines, on network television, feted always as the humble small-town genius from the Midwest, prim and proper, demanding the game be played "the right way." He disdained dunking, referred to his most famous player as Lewis even after the young man changed his name to Kareem, ordered his big redheaded center to get a haircut, and made his faith and his marriage appealing characters in the drama of his own life.

The other was Arad McCutchan, and he never left Evansville.

Johnny Wooden was born October 14, 1910—twenty-one months before McCutchan—in Hall, Indiana, a rural community about 150 miles northeast of Evansville. The Wooden family inherited a nearby farm when Johnny was six, but lost it when all thirty of their hogs died, forcing the Woodens to move back to Hall. Johnny was a basketball star at Martinsville High School, leading the Artesians to the Indiana state championship in 1927. As McCutchan's playing career got off the ground at Evansville College, Wooden had already made a name for himself as a cat-quick guard at Purdue. He graduated in 1932, after earning all-American honors three years in a row.

Wooden and McCutchan both apprenticed at high schools and served in the military before beginning their college coaching careers in the fall of 1946. While McCutchan took over at his alma mater, Wooden took the top job at Indiana State Teachers College in Terre Haute. Over the next two seasons, the Sycamores won three of the four games they played against Evansville. In 1948, after two years and forty-four victories in Terre Haute, Wooden accepted the job at UCLA and moved his family to Los Angeles. It took years for the two coaches to truly master the game and separate themselves from their contemporaries. But in 1964 and 1965, they each guided dominant teams to national titles. In '64, when the Aces finished 26–3 and won the school's third championship in the College Division, UCLA went 30–0 and won Wooden's first title in the University Division. The following year, as the Aces completed their undefeated season with a fourth title, the Bruins won twenty-eight and gave Wooden his second championship.

Beyond their quaint life stories and parallel coaching careers, the two men also shared an intellectual curiosity that shaped the way they approached the game. Wooden recited poetry from memory and inspired his players with folksy aphorisms: "be quick, but don't hurry"; "failure to prepare is preparing to fail"; "never mistake activity for achievement"; and "drink deeply from good books, especially the Bible."

McCutchan, on the other hand, saw the game through the prism of mathematics. His philosophy paired an affinity for statistics and precision with a creative flair that influenced how he dressed his players, how they practiced, and how they played. He took every advantage he could find. His teams wore long robes on the bench instead of traditional warm-up suits because it was faster to shed a robe and enter the game. His players wore white shoes because he thought black shoes were easier for a referee to see and thus resulted in more traveling calls. They also wore short-sleeved jerseys instead of tank tops because that's how they practiced and he wanted them to be equally comfortable in games. Plus, he said, short sleeves are "more flattering to the thin ballplayer." McCutchan preferred orange uniforms because orange was the most visible color, making it easier for his players to keep track of each other on the floor.

Despite all of their success, neither Wooden nor McCutchan earned handsome salaries. McCutchan's local celebrity exceeded his income. The college didn't pay him more than $20,000 until the mid-1960s. So he took on extra work to supplement his pay. He coached track and taught a basketball class in addition to math. He was the athletic director for many years and took on extra teaching assignments in the summer. The McCutchans didn't live extravagantly. But they enjoyed certain perks that came with Arad's status. Their kids went to college for free. Boosters paid for a family country club membership and gave the coach a red Chrysler 300 with gold hubcaps after he won his three hundredth game.

UCLA won eight more national titles before Wooden retired with his tenth championship in 1975, a feat that seems unfathomable today. Four of his teams finished 30–0.

The final years of McCutchan's career were far less satisfying. Evansville won its fifth and final championship in 1971. But the Aces never recaptured the glory of their best years. Evansville suffered through losing seasons in 1967, 1969, and 1970. McCutchan had never been keen on hitting the road to plead for the services of top high school players. His recruiting budget for many years was $1,500. He also believed college coaches were educators who should spend more time in the classroom than on the road, which limited off-campus recruiting but reinforced the idea that academics were more important than athletics. As he got older, he left most of the recruiting to his assistants, and several of the players they brought to Evansville couldn't meet UE's academic requirements. One kid practiced for two years but never played because he couldn't cut it in the classroom. Another was suspended from practice so he could improve his GPA, but dropped out amid accusations that his high school grades had been falsified. McCutchan didn't compromise his standards. But it didn't look good. He celebrated his sixty-fourth birthday in 1976. Boosters had grown restless.

On Arad McCutchan Recognition Night in January 1977, the old coach received $15,000 in gifts, including a television set and a new Chevrolet parked courtside. McCutchan, dapper in a red tie and red pocket square, accepted the gifts with characteristic humility after a win over Valparaiso, standing on the court near Virginia and their three grown children. Then, shortly after 8:00 p.m., he stepped to the microphone.

"Because you are my very dear friends," he said, "I have chosen this moment to give you a bit of information I think you'd like to know now. I will work for the University of Evansville next year. But I will not work as basketball coach."

McCutchan's simple retirement speech landed with a thud, stunning the crowd. He had won 514 games in thirty-one years. But the transformation of college sports had begun, and the University of Evansville wouldn't be left behind. Mac was no longer the young, maverick coach who worked miracles with local farm boys. It was time to step aside.

As one era ended, another would soon begin.

FIVE

Mr. Watson

A WEEK AFTER BOBBY Watson arrived on campus, Chris Weaver, the vice president of the University of Evansville Student Association, got a call in his office from the athletic department: the new coach wanted a meeting. Weaver was a straight-arrow kid with big glasses and shaggy blond hair who grew up in a small farming community in northern Indiana. He spent most of his waking hours at the student government offices in the back of the union building, just down the hall from the campus newspaper, the *Crescent*. Weaver enjoyed a particularly spacious and well-appointed office, with a large desk, a meeting table, a credenza, and a sitting area with two chairs for visitors. Two windows behind his desk overlooked the rose garden at the president's residence. Weaver was on the phone when Watson walked in, but ended the call while hurriedly ushering the new coach over to the sitting area. Instead of a firm handshake, Watson unexpectedly enveloped Weaver in a hug, as if they'd met a thousand times before. Weaver was a big kid, six feet tall and 185 pounds. But Watson was *massive*, with a personality as big as the Ohio River, leaving the impression everywhere he went that he stood seven feet and not 6'8".

Soon, Watson and Weaver settled into the visitors' chairs and the coach made his pitch.

It was a variation of the sermon he had delivered over and over, every day, to anyone who would have him. He spoke to the Jaycees and the Boys Club. He met with a Sunday school class to talk about "Christian Attitudes in Athletics." He called everybody "big guy"— "How ya doin', big guy?"—and worked every room he entered with a disarming magnetism. His plans for the program were every bit as big as his personality. He wanted to change hearts and minds, to create the aura of a true Division I program, with all of the amenities that other schools enjoyed. Travel, for one thing, would be upgraded. With the exception of games in Colorado and California, Arad McCutchan's team rarely flew. Most of its opponents were regional schools, and buses were fine for such short trips. But under Watson, the Aces would travel in style, on private, chartered jets.

It wasn't that Watson was going soft. Quite the contrary. At a Lions Club luncheon, he towered over a waist-high lectern and sold, in a deep baritone, his vision of UE basketball: He would run a tight program, he said, consistent with his strict, all-for-one military background. No bushy mustaches. No beards. No long hair.

"Now, people say hair length has no bearing on a guy's ability to play. To play for me, you will sacrifice. To dive on the floor or grab that last-second rebound," he said, "you must sacrifice. Hair length is that first step towards sacrificing to my rules."

Watson considered academics equal in importance to basketball and a pathway to lifetime success. He had written a letter to the faculty outlining academic expectations for his players. They would not be allowed unauthorized absences from class and were required to eat breakfast with the coaching staff every morning. "If they get out of bed," Watson wrote, "they will go to class."

Watson's disciplined approach would extend beyond the players, the coaches, and the student managers, all the way to the office staff.

"The most important person in those offices will be the reception-ist," he told a reporter. "Hers is the first University of Evansville voice a caller will hear. She has to be sharp. If I'm in conference and a prospect calls, she must know that it's far more important to interrupt me than put him on hold for five minutes."

Watson took a big-picture perspective on his role at the univer-sity. He knew he had to sell the program to the students as well as the boosters. That's why his meeting with Chris Weaver at the student government offices was so important. Watson needed Weaver's help. Even on a good day, student support for UE basketball was lukewarm. It was a matter of simple mathematics: UE's full-time enrollment was about three thousand, and capacity at Roberts Stadium was nearly four times that. The stadium was a mile and a half from campus, mak-ing it an inconvenient walk on bitter-cold winter nights for students without cars. The team's descent into mediocrity in the final years of McCutchan's watch hadn't helped.

Watson wanted to build a deeper bond between students and their basketball team, no matter whether they lived in fraternities, in the dorms, or at home with their mom and dad. He told Weaver the Aces would play on TV and in the NCAA tournament. He told him the offense would be aggressive and fast-paced. And he promised that if Weaver could get three people in a room, he'd be there to sell them on Evansville basketball. The timbre of Watson's voice changed as he got excited. He was an evangelist for Aces basketball, bringing every crowd to its feet and making everyone he met a true believer. Left in Watson's wake, Weaver felt like he'd been lifted up and swept away by the new coach's passion. In less than a half hour, Watson convinced Weaver that he was *essential* to the program, *crucial* to its success, that if he did not fully commit himself to Watson and his players, he would disappoint the entire university.

"He had this ability to personalize the basketball program so you felt like you had ownership in its success," Weaver says. "He was masterful in getting people vested in the program from very early on."

———

Mike Duff was just seventeen years old when he moved to Evansville in the summer of 1977, a mama's boy who'd never been away from home for more than a week or two. Now he had to make the transition to college, leaving the cocoon of Eldorado for a big city full of strangers with soaring expectations. The pickup games at Carson Center hadn't even started yet, and already Mike felt the pressure to restore the glory of UE basketball.

"Don't expect too much just yet," he cautioned reporters. "I'll have to adjust to being away from home. I'll have to spend more time with the books than before. I'll have to get used to better competition and work on certain things—strength, dribbling, my defense."

That summer, Mike worked a construction job during the day and played ball at night. That left little time for Cherie Bougas, his girlfriend, who'd stayed behind in Eldorado to finish high school. Mike and Cherie had lived a few blocks from one another in Eldorado and started dating when he was a junior and she was a sophomore. They went to homecoming dances and the prom and spent long lazy days at the indoor pool at Mike's house. They cruised around in Mike's purple van, maybe meeting up with friends in the Dairy Queen parking lot or stopping for a burger at Hardee's. They broke up for who knows what and then got back together. Mike was quite a catch. But so was Cherie. She was beautiful and petite, with long silky brown hair and fine cheekbones, and the top of her head barely reached Mike's shoulders. They had plans to get married someday and had already talked about moving into married student housing at UE once Cherie graduated from high school and joined Mike in Evansville.

But once Mike moved away, they spent the summer trying to bridge the fifty-mile gap between them. Mike drove home when he could, and they talked for hours on the phone. He also sent Cherie love letters nearly every week in big, loopy handwriting, each one earnest and filled with promises and yearning.

"How's no. 1 doing? That's *you* dummy," he wrote one morning that summer. "I had a good dream about us last night. But I have them all the time. It's hard to keep my mind off of you. Don't forget to ask your mom if you can go to Kentucky Lake with me for the weekend. I'll teach you how to ski if you'll get in the water. I won't go without you so you better be able to go. OK, sugar? Well, honey I'm going back to bed. See ya Friday. Love always, Mike. PS: I hope you can make something out of this letter. It's still early. PSS: I LOVE YOU."

Mike roomed that summer with Kevin Kingston, another Eldorado boy on a basketball scholarship at UE. Kevin was three years older than Mike and had graduated from Eldorado High School in 1974, three months before Mike enrolled as a sophomore. But they'd become friends during the summers, working together at Bob Brown's youth basketball camps in the mornings and hauling hay in the afternoons, heaving huge bales into the back of a truck as it rolled slowly through a farm field and then unloading the bales into a barn loft. When they played on summer nights at Carson Center, it was obvious that Mike was a natural. But Kevin's game wasn't so pretty. At 6'2", he lacked Mike's size and finesse. He made up for his deficiencies with a fearless, blunt-force playing style. Kevin was an agile defender with quick feet who wasn't afraid to step in front of bigger rivals as they barreled to the basket. That fall, during pickup games, he suffered a busted lip, a ruptured blister, and a gash in his face that required seven stitches.

Kevin came to UE as a walk-on in 1976, Mac's final season, and played in only a half dozen games. But Watson noticed him in game films, harassing ball handlers and skidding headlong across the floor. The new coach wanted a tough kid who could show his team the commitment required to defend Division I players. He decided that Kevin would be that kid and offered him a scholarship for his senior year. He also told Kevin that once he graduated from UE, he could join the Aces coaching staff as a graduate assistant. It was almost as if Watson had descended from the heavens to fulfill Kevin's greatest ambitions: he had always wanted, his entire life, to play basketball at the University of Evansville and follow his dad into coaching.

Evansville was like a second home to Kevin Kingston. Don, his father, earned a degree at Evansville College in 1957 while working full-time at the Chrysler plant to support his family. Don had planned to go to law school after graduation. But when his old football coach at Eldorado High School offered him an assistant's job, he moved back for a long career at his alma mater. He taught history, government, and driver's education and coached basketball and track, in addition to football. He also served as athletic director. In 1962, his wife, Wanda, gave birth to a girl they named Valery, and the Kingston family settled in Eldorado for good. But through the years, the Kingstons visited Evansville often because that's where Don's siblings lived. By the time Kevin was in high school, he would come to UE with his friends during the summer. One year, they played pickup ball at Carson Center and hung out with Jerry Sloan and Don Buse, another of Arad McCutchan's greatest players and a point guard for the Indiana Pacers. Kingston tacked autographed photos of Sloan and Buse on his bedroom wall. They were his heroes.

In high school, Kevin earned honorable mentions on the all-state football and basketball teams. But because he didn't draw much interest from college recruiters, he and Don plotted his path to the University of Evansville. Kevin honed his skills for two seasons at a junior college and then spent the entire summer of 1976 training with his dad to impress Arad McCutchan. The Kingstons lived on ten acres on the edge of town, and Don worked with Kevin on the concrete court he'd poured outside the old barn on their property. They played one-on-one. Don put Kevin through ball-handling, shooting, and defensive drills. And they rode bicycles for ten miles on the hot blacktop roads out in the country. Don taught Kevin to focus on the game, maintain his poise, and tune everything else out. He reminded him often of everything he could accomplish through grit and hard work. Watson shared Don's philosophy, and Kevin embodied the tenacity his new coach sought from all of the Aces.

"Kingston will show them how I want it done," Watson said. "When he gets finished with them in practice, they'll be ready to play the game."

———

Bobby Watson's path to Evansville zigzagged through military school, army bases in Texas and Missouri, the rice paddies of Vietnam, and a series of low-profile coaching gigs in high school and college. His military pedigree was especially impressive to Aces fans. Evansville was a conservative town, patriotic even during the worst of Vietnam. ROTC was a popular program at the university and the anti-war movement made barely a ripple on its small campus. Evansville sportswriters made much of Watson's service in Vietnam, consistently reporting erroneously that he'd won five Purple Hearts. The city wanted a God's-honest G.I. Joe hero and made one out of Watson, no matter the details. But Watson never flaunted his war experience, and the reality of his time in Vietnam was more complicated than anyone knew. The war marked Watson in ways that he was reluctant to share, even with his family. His experience in Vietnam informed his coaching philosophy, especially in his final days in Evansville, when grit and fortitude were at a premium.

———

In suburban Pittsburgh in the late 1950s, Bobby Watson and his team-mates wore their hair in flattops, said "yes sir" and "no sir," and arrived for every game at the Bethel High School gym dressed in dark suits and white shirts, with narrow ties knotted neatly at the neck.

"It's a policy at our school," said Preston Ditty, the athletic director. "We feel that our athletes should look like the boys they are: gentleman."

Carl Watson, Bobby's dad, loved the suit-and-tie rule. It fit nicely with the rock-ribbed conservatism that defined his life. The Watsons joined thousands of families moving to Bethel Park, ten miles south-west of Pittsburgh. In the '50s, when the borough's population more than doubled to nearly twenty-four thousand, Carl bought his family a brand-new three-bedroom brick home with a big yard and a basketball hoop attached to the house. He was a burly, outgoing guy known as Big C who'd played football at Saint Vincent College, a small Catholic school in Latrobe, Pennsylvania. He was an insurance adjuster, a Mason, a staunch Republican, and a member of the Bethel Park city council. Carl had been raised in a strict Methodist family and raised Bobby and his younger sister, Lois, in the same manner. Olga Watson, Bobby's mom, grew up Catholic but converted when she married Carl.

At Bethel High, Bobby grew about five inches between his sopho-more and junior years and cut an imposing figure in the hallways. He was an engaging kid, popular among students and teachers, and captain of the basketball team as a senior. More than fifty colleges offered him scholarships. Coaches from Pittsburgh, Duke, and Oklahoma came to Bethel Park. So did Louis "Weenie" Miller, the coach at the Virginia Military Institute. Miller showed up nearly every week, it seemed, and sat down at the dinner table for a plate of Olga's pasta. Bobby had never shown any interest in the military. But when Miller invited him to an elite summer camp he co-owned in Virginia, Bobby struck up a friend-ship with Bill Blair, a hotshot guard from Hazard, Kentucky. They were the same age, made their recruiting visits to VMI on the same weekend, and decided together they would play for the Keydets. In September 1960, they moved into the VMI barracks in Lexington, Virginia.

The Virginia Military Institute built its reputation as a training ground for generations of great American military leaders. World War II general George S. Patton Jr. followed his father and grandfather to VMI, and Stonewall Jackson taught philosophy there before becoming commander of the Confederate Army during the Civil War. VMI molded cadets through strict discipline, rigorous academics, and a regimented campus life. A bugle awakened Watson and his classmates at 6:00 a.m., and together they marched to breakfast, to class, and to meals. Classes were Monday through Friday, with a half day on Saturday and inspection on Sunday. The honor code was simple: "A cadet will not lie, cheat, steal, nor tolerate those who do." A single violation of the code resulted in expulsion. Watson was a good soldier, a three-year starter on the basketball team, and cocaptain his senior year. He took his leadership responsibilities seriously. He'd pull aside a teammate caught sneaking cigarettes to remind him that smoking was against team rules. But even the nonsmokers couldn't keep up with teams like Davidson, Furman, and William & Mary. The basketball program at VMI was historically awful. After Miller became head coach in 1958, he led the Keydets to a total of fourteen wins in his first three seasons. But in 1964, when Watson was a senior, the basketball program enjoyed the greatest moment in its long and sorry history, making an unlikely postseason run and earning a bid to the NCAA tournament. The Keydets met Bill Bradley and his Princeton teammates in the first round, however, and Bobby's college basketball career ended with an 86–60 rout.

Watson majored in biology and planned on medical school. But VMI cadets were required to complete two years of military service after graduation. He taught and coached at a Virginia high school for a year, and then joined the army. First, he was assigned to Fort Bliss, in Texas, where he played basketball and made the all-army team. But then he was ordered to Vietnam.

Watson's reserve unit was called up the first time in May 1966. He was a medic, helping treat and evacuate injured soldiers from the battlefield. Twice, Vietcong machine gunners blasted his helicopters out of the air just after takeoff, knocking both to the ground. Watson also suffered a back injury when his jeep hit a mine, contracted malaria twice, and waded through rice paddies for hours at a time, leaving his feet white, raw, and bleeding. When he came home a year later, the confidence and certainty that had served him so well at VMI had been replaced by a weary gratitude. He told a sportswriter after he returned that he felt "fortunate just to be alive."

Watson didn't share war stories. But his sister, Lois, saw the toll that Vietnam had taken. Once, at their parents' house, Bobby was napping on the couch when Lois tapped him on the shoulder to awaken him. Watson leaped off the couch, confused, uncertain where he was.

"When you wake me up," he told her, "don't ever touch me like that."

In Vietnam, he explained, they woke up soldiers by touching their shoulder rather than saying their names. For a brief, terrifying moment, he felt as if he had returned to the battlefield.

After his first tour, Watson took a job as an assistant coach for George Krajack at Xavier University in Cincinnati. He lasted for a single season before his unit was called up again in 1968. Watson returned to Vietnam with a great sense of foreboding, as if fate had dealt him a bad hand. On the eve of his second tour, he hitched a ride to the Cincinnati airport with Jack Cherry, a buddy from the Xavier athletic department. When they parted, they shook hands, and Cherry wished him luck.

"We'll see you when you get home," Cherry said.

"I won't be back," Watson replied. "Medics don't make it through two tours."

Watson survived. But when he was discharged in August 1969, he returned to Xavier with an edge, fidgety and uptight, like a rubber band stretched to its breaking point. There were moments when, at the slightest provocation, he snapped. Paul Ritter, who covered Xavier basketball for the *Cincinnati Enquirer*, recalled a night in Detroit when he shared a hotel room with Watson. Ritter entered the room first and stepped into the bathroom. When he came out, he startled Watson, who grabbed him and threw him against a wall, leaving Ritter terrified and confused. Then, just as suddenly, when Watson realized what he had done, he let Ritter go.

"I'm sorry," he told Ritter. "When I hear someone coming up behind me, I just react."

Another night, they went out for beers and Watson asked Ritter to ease up on his criticism of Krajack, whose job was in jeopardy. Watson feared his boss would be fired and worried about Krajack's wife and kids. But Ritter told him that he had nothing to do with Krajack's job security.

"The hell you don't," Watson replied, and emptied a can of beer on Ritter's head.

It was Labor Day weekend, 1977, and Ed Siegel wanted to send his son Mark off to Evansville with a celebratory cookout, maybe slap a few steaks on the grill and invite friends over to wish the boy a fond farewell. Mark was a gifted point guard and a natural leader eager to make the move from Indianapolis, eager to bond with his new teammates, eager to prove that he was a legitimate Division I recruit.

But Mark hadn't been feeling well the last few weeks and suddenly the stomach cramps were unbearable. Appendicitis? Maybe. Ed called a family friend who was an abdominal surgeon at Methodist Hospital. Their friend told Ed and Carmen, Mark's mom, to bring

Mark in immediately so he could take a look at the boy's stomach. After X-rays and tests, the doctor delivered the bad news. Mark suffered from diverticulitis, a digestive disease in which pouches that form in the wall of the colon become infected and inflamed. The doctor urged surgery to remove the diseased portion of the colon.

This wasn't how father and son had envisioned the start of Mark's college basketball career.

Ed and Mark were especially close. Mark had played point guard at Pike High School on the west side of Indianapolis, where Ed was the head coach. They rode to school together each morning, spent hours at practice each afternoon, and then rode home together in the evening. Ed was a perfectionist, a screamer, and a profane father figure to many of his players. During his summer camps, he'd drive a bus full of sixth graders across the city to play kids from other camps. The next day, he'd punish those same sixth graders for blowing a drill by making them chase basketballs he'd kicked into the bleachers. Mark was Ed's alter ego in a bowl cut, exuding a poise and confidence that earned him the respect of his teammates and opponents. When he brought the ball toward half-court, he was thinking ahead, calmly directing his teammates like a conductor in front of an orchestra. He knew where everyone should be, and he tried to get them the ball at that tiny and invisible spot on the floor where they were better than anyone else. As a senior at Pike, Mark averaged nineteen points a game and set career records for assists and steals. He was a member of the National Honor Society, vice president of the student council, and president of the school's chapter of the Fellowship of Christian Athletes. He also played baseball. But he wasn't a prima donna. He didn't need to be.

Lots of colleges wanted Mark. Butler, Wake Forest, Virginia, and Rice were especially interested. So was an Oral Roberts coach named Bobby Watson. But despite Mark's deep faith, he didn't feel comfortable with the charismatic brand of Christianity peddled by the university's founder, television evangelist Oral Roberts. The Siegels liked Watson, though, and soon after he took the job in Evansville, the Aces' new coach headed for Indianapolis. He pulled up in front of the Siegels' house at 7:00 p.m., walked through the front door, and gave Mark a hug. Then, for ninety minutes, he laid out his plans for UE basketball: No quick fixes . . . Build from the bottom up . . . Tough and hungry . . . Lots of freshmen recruits. Even more important for Mark, only one point guard would return from Arad McCutchan's last team. He'd have an opportunity to play immediately.

But the diverticulitis delayed his move to Evansville. As the first semester of his freshman year approached, Mark was stuck in the hospital, and alarming rumors about his illness had spread throughout Indiana coaching circles, where Ed and his son were well known and respected.

On a weekday before Mark's surgery, as Ed finished up a class at Pike High School, he looked into the hallway and saw Indiana University coach Bob Knight waiting for him. When the bell rang and the students filed out, Ed invited him into the classroom. Knight was only thirty-six, but his legend was ascendant. Indiana won the 1976 NCAA championship with a 32–0 record, earning Knight the dual reputation as a brilliant coach and unrepentant hothead. His genius was often obscured by tirades and tantrums of biblical proportions—on the court, in press conferences, and elsewhere. But Ed Siegel knew Knight as a generous man with a Jekyll and Hyde personality. Ed was a fiery coach, too, and understood Knight's style better than most. They had always gotten along. Knight hadn't recruited Mark, but he felt Ed's son had a bright college career in front of him.

The two men sat down in the empty classroom. Knight told Siegel he'd heard Mark was in the hospital and that the prognosis was dire. In fact, he'd heard that Mark had cancer. "No, no, no," Ed told him. Mark would be fine. The two coaches talked for a half hour, and before he left, Knight asked for Mark's address at the hospital. A few days later, Knight sent Mark a long letter, encouraging him to overcome the challenge of his illness and predicting he'd be ready for practice in no time.

"You are playing for an outstanding person in Coach Watson," Knight wrote, "and I believe that being part of the program at Evansville will be a very fine experience for you. Just make sure you don't let yourself become discouraged with a momentary setback."

On September 13, a surgeon removed two inches of Mark's small intestine. He was disappointed that his move to Evansville would be delayed. But the surgery was routine and his prognosis was excellent. He remained in Indianapolis to recover, and Watson sent the assistant coach, Stafford Stephenson, to deliver books and homework. Mark finally moved to Evansville, but doctors wouldn't allow him to begin full practices until October 24. Soon after he suited up at Carson Center, Mark realized how far he'd fallen behind his new teammates, many of whom—like Duff and Kingston—had been playing together since the summer. It would be nearly two months before he earned the starting job.

SIX

Moving Up

IN 1977, WALLACE GRAVES was fifty-five years old, a rangy Texan with a patrician air and a subtle nasal twang. He arrived at the University of Evansville from the University of the Pacific a decade before, and quickly earned credibility in a town that ran fakes and phonies to the city line. He was not always Wallace Billingsley Graves, PhD. Sometimes he was Wally, the guy in the coat and tie who celebrated with the players at Roberts Stadium after the 1971 national championship. He was as comfortable with the car dealers who funded the athletic department as he was with the music faculty at Wheeler Concert Hall. In a city where there was little distance between town and gown, Graves's dual roles were a necessity.

The Purple Aces' ascension to Division I basketball fit squarely within Graves's plans to transform an insular, hidebound university into a nationally recognized liberal arts institution. Graves proved a deft touch, re-creating the college as a destination for international scholarship while cultivating support from a community deeply resistant to change. Early in his tenure, the university opened a satellite campus in an old manor house in Harlaxton, England. He also upgraded the faculty, doubling the number who'd earned doctorates in his first ten years.

His ambition for the basketball program mirrored his hopes for the rest of the university. But, truth be told, Graves had little choice. College basketball was changing fast, and UE had to move quickly to keep up.

For decades, NCAA schools competed in either the University or the College Division, depending on the size of the institution and the scope of its athletic program. But in 1973, school presidents scrapped that alignment and created three divisions, forcing institutions to choose at which level they'd compete. Small schools that offered no athletic scholarships opted for Division III, and big state schools like Indiana and Kentucky played in Division I. The University of Evansville at first chose Division II. It seemed like a natural fit. UE had always competed in the College Division, even after changing its name in 1967. Most of the schools on its schedule played in the same division, and each year, Roberts Stadium hosted the College Division national championships. But some of UE's traditional rivals, including Indiana State and Southern Illinois, had moved to Division I. UE boosters and administrators feared that remaining in Division II would doom the basketball program, which supported the entire athletic department. Crowds at Roberts Stadium had already begun to dwindle. If the Division I schools stopped coming to Evansville, attendance and revenue would spiral, the best players would choose other schools, and one of the city's defining institutions—Aces basketball—would fade into mediocrity, or worse. UE also had to contend with Indiana State University–Evansville, the new branch campus on the city's west side that fielded an improving Division II basketball program. Graves wanted to differentiate the University of Evansville from ISUE in every way.

Dissenters among faculty and fans feared that the Aces wouldn't be able to keep up with bigger schools and that Division I would be too costly. But those fears were unfounded. Moving up was a declaration of the university's ambition that reflected the optimism of Aces fans who believed their team was poised for national prominence.

John Ed Washington, a slender lefty from Indianapolis, returned to
Evansville in the fall of 1977, eager to begin his own unlikely rise to
Division I basketball. He was a senior, 6'3", a good defender, and an
excellent passer who sliced and twisted through the lane like an acrobat.
An unreliable jump shot had scared off recruiters from big schools. But
Arad McCutchan took a chance and John Ed flourished in Evansville,
leading the 1976–77 team in scoring, with more than fifteen points a
game. By the time Bobby Watson came to UE, John Ed had played
more than anyone else on the roster. In a preseason marked by momen-
tous change at UE, John Ed was one of the few certainties.

John Ed grew up on Indianapolis's northeast side, the fourth of six
children. He was a gleefully mischievous kid who'd secretly tie your shoe-
laces together and then catch you when you tripped. John Washington,
his father, mined coal in West Virginia with a pick and shovel in the late
1950s. But when the coal industry moved toward mechanized mining,
John Washington moved his family to Indianapolis. He did welding
and such at a battery factory and then for an air-conditioner manufacturer, steady work in an era when manufacturing jobs were plentiful in
Indianapolis and paid enough to buy a house and raise a family. John
spoiled his kids, and the cars he bought for John Ed were Exhibit A.
But Sammie Washington, John Ed's mom, ran the house like a business. Sammie did not suffer fools. She paid the bills each month and
managed her husband's generosity. She sang in the choir at a Baptist
church, and if John Ed or his siblings complained they were too sick
to go with her, she told them they could stay inside all day and do
homework. When they were little, Sammie read to her children from
the Bible, a set of encyclopedias, *Jet* magazine, and children's stories like
"The Tortoise and the Hare."

The Washington family lived on a quiet stretch of Tallman Avenue,
where John Ed, his siblings, and their friends played kickball and four

square in the middle of the road. John Ed's best buddy, Wayne Radford, lived across the street. Wayne and John Ed were ferocious competitors who shared a hardheaded determination each time they stepped onto the court. The Indiana Pacers were their yardstick. The franchise was a charter member of the old American Basketball Association and one of the league's best teams, winner of three championships in the early 1970s. John Ed and his friends saw as many games as they could, scraping together money for a single ticket so Wayne could get inside the Indiana State Fairgrounds Coliseum and sneak his pals in through a side door. They played basketball all year, at school and in their neighborhood. Wayne's dad put a hoop on a two-and-a-half-car garage he'd built behind their house. The court was in the alley, part pavement, part gravel, and usually covered in coal ash that neighbors shoveled from their furnaces.

The Radford family moved out of the neighborhood before John Ed and Wayne reached high school. The boys didn't see each other as often but remained friends, and by the early '70s they were two of the best high school players in the city. As seniors, John Ed and Wayne were a study in contrasts. Wayne, who played at Arlington High School, admired the slithery moves John Ed used to get to the basket at Arsenal Technical High School. And while Wayne was built like a fullback, John Ed looked like a stiff breeze would knock him off his feet. Major college coaches came after Wayne when he was a junior. The big schools didn't seem interested in John Ed.

In early March 1974, at the very start of the state high school tournament known as Hoosier Hysteria, Arsenal Tech played Arlington in the semifinal of the Indianapolis sectional. The loser of this game would pack up, go home, and call it a season. The winner would play the next night for the sectional championship. Fans crowded hip to hip into Hinkle Fieldhouse, the historic gym on the Butler University campus. Tech led 67–66 in the fourth quarter. But when Wayne poured in six points in a row, Arlington pulled away. John Ed played perhaps the greatest game of his high school career, with twenty-nine points. But Wayne was better. He scored thirty-eight and Arlington won 85–82.

It was John Ed's final high school game. After the buzzer sounded and reality sunk in, Wayne saw tears in John Ed's eyes.

While Wayne went to Indiana to play for Bob Knight, John Ed didn't have the same high-profile options. But he had a fierce advocate in Larry Humes, the transcendent scorer from Arad McCutchan's undefeated '65 team. After his college career, Humes taught and coached at public schools in Indianapolis. He'd known John Ed since the youngster was in junior high and lobbied McCutchan to give his protégé a chance in Evansville. The old coach obliged. And now, three years later, John Ed embraced the opportunity to prove all those disinterested Division I coaches wrong.

———

At 7:30 a.m. on October 15, Bobby Watson set aside the handshaking, backslapping persona beloved by boosters in favor of a demanding and disciplined approach to college basketball. It was the first day of practice at Carson Center, a simple cinder-block slab with aluminum bleachers, two side-by-side courts under fluorescent lights, and a cramped weight room in one corner. The Aces practiced seven days a week, for two and a half hours a day, even on the weekends. Watson directed each session with authoritarian precision and obsessive attention to detail. Arrive early, he told his players. No small talk or horseplay will be tolerated. Run from one drill to another. Leave the court only with permission of the coaching staff. He planned for every probability and possibility.

In one drill, Watson blew the whistle, practice stopped, basketballs dropped to the floor, and players sprinted to the sidelines. They each took a seat on the aluminum bleachers, grabbed a towel from the student managers, downed a cup of water, and waited for the coaching staff beneath the harsh lights of the gym. When it worked, the time-out drill took fifteen seconds or less, leaving Watson with the undivided attention of his players for forty-five seconds, more than enough time to design a fast break off a missed free throw or a defensive scheme for the opponents' last possession. Watson learned the necessity of this drill at Oral Roberts, when a player who hadn't finished his water spilled it on an out-of-bounds play Watson had scribbled with nineteen seconds on the clock. That left him with little time to explain what he wanted, resulting in a botched play and a bad shot. He wouldn't allow it to happen again.

Watson's obsession with preparation wasn't limited to practice. In a series of neatly typed handouts, outlines scrawled on notebook paper, and letters to faculty and fans, Watson provided a lengthy blueprint for his basketball program. It included his philosophy on practices, games, academics, spirituality, and mental discipline. He quoted poetry and philosophers. He covered everything from the controlled-situation offense to proper restaurant behavior ("thank you—please"). He advised players to wear warm hats, so they wouldn't catch colds, and ordered them to treat student managers with the same respect they showed to teammates.

"There will be *no profanity* used on the floor or in the locker room," Watson advised in one three-page treatise on his practice philosophy. "This is a must on your part since at times I will do enough for all of us."

Watson's players wore purple shorts with the acronyms "PME" stitched on the right side and "SFE" stitched on the left, reminders to adopt a Perfect Mental Attitude and to Strive For Excellence. He quoted French philosopher and Jesuit priest Pierre Teilhard de Chardin and closed each practice with a prayer. "There is not a truly successful man," he wrote, "who has made it without *Faith in God*."

In another handout, he included an inspirational poem titled "Thinking," which encouraged hard work and confidence:

Life's battles don't always go
To the stronger or faster man;
But sooner or later, the man who wins
Is the fellow who THINKS HE CAN!

Almost as soon as classes started, Mike Duff came up against the most difficult opponent he'd ever faced: college math. He had been an average student in high school and found his first-semester algebra class especially difficult and frustrating. One assignment required him to complete two hundred problems in a single night, which took him three hours. It was soon decided, on his behalf, that this was not the best path to further his education.

"The coaches made me drop math," he wrote in a letter to Cherie Bougas, "because the teacher she gives too much homework and didn't think basketball players can handle it."

As he juggled classes, homework, and practice, Mike had even less time to spend with Cherie. He made it back to Eldorado for a weekend when Cherie was on the homecoming court. Otherwise, Cherie did the driving on the weekends, occasionally skipping school with her mother's permission and spending the night at her aunt's house in Evansville. One weekend, Mike took her to a Kansas concert at Roberts Stadium and she got to know his teammates. But during the week nearly every minute of Mike's day was spoken for: meals, class, practice, tutoring, homework.

"The days over here are getting very long and very hard," he wrote in another letter. "I haven't had time to do anything but study and play ball. Practice is so hard I don't feel like doing anything but sleep after I get back. Well, if you can get over here Friday, I'd sure like to see you. Remember to take care of that bod and your beautiful face and try to get over here as soon as possible. I love you and be good. Love always,

Mike. PS: Will have to start writing more because the phone bills cost a lot of money."

Basketball wasn't nearly as difficult for Mike as algebra. His play in the preseason intrasquad scrimmages confirmed all that UE fans had hoped. Wearing the same number 40 that he wore in high school, Mike was magnificent. On November 11, he led the white team over the purple team with thirty-six points and nineteen rebounds, dominating his teammates, proving that his size, strength, and soft touch were as impressive against college players as they were against high school boys. He scored thirty-one the following week. And in the third and final scrimmage, in front of 850 fans at Eldorado High School, he finished with twenty-two points and eighteen rebounds. The scrimmages were essentially glorified practices. But Mike's first appearances in a University of Evansville uniform provided a tantalizing hint of his potential. It was obvious to everyone who saw him play that he was the best player on the roster.

Everyone except for Mike. He didn't come across as cool and confident, like a blue-chip recruit. He sounded more like an angst-ridden walk-on fighting for a spot at the end of the bench.

"I've got a lot of work to do, particularly on defense," he said. "I know that it's not going to be anything like high school. I can't expect it to be or I'll be getting the ball jammed down my throat half of the time."

———

Kevin Kingston was not the only long shot who impressed Bobby Watson.

Open tryouts for non-scholarship players began at Carson Center in October, not long after the start of practice. Bobby Watson put a half dozen or so boys through drills and scrimmages: five-on-five and four-on-four. He didn't promise them anything. He was looking for a smart kid who played hard in practice and could help the Aces prepare for the next team on the schedule.

David Furr had been a high-scoring forward as a junior at Harrison High School, in Evansville. But when his mother remarried, he moved with her and his little brother Byron to Olney to live with her new husband. David was a redhead, doe-eyed, 6'2", lean and sinewy, with a good outside shot. He was fearless in the lane, driving to the basket, getting knocked to the floor, and popping back up to shoot free throws. When Olney played Eldorado in January 1977, Mike Duff scored forty points. But David had twenty-nine, and Tim Knox, his stepbrother, hit two free throws with seconds left to seal a 74–73 victory. David led the Tigers in scoring that year. But unlike Mike, he didn't have to duck recruiters each day at practice. A small college near Olney had shown some interest. But David wanted desperately to play for the Purple Aces. His family had a long history at UE. Elisabeth Knox, his mom, had once taught nursing there; her parents and her brother had been students at the college. David didn't want to go anywhere else. He didn't have a scholarship but it didn't matter. He felt confident he could make the UE team as a walk-on and worked hard on his game during the summer. One day, not long before David left for Evansville, Tim Knox watched as he lifted off toward the basket during a pickup game and slammed the ball through the net. Tim was impressed. He'd never seen David dunk before.

Once classes started, David threw himself into campus life. He pledged the Sigma Phi Epsilon fraternity and reconnected with old friends from high school. But he never let his social life interfere with schoolwork. David had been a member of the National Honor Society. He was a perfectionist, focused and organized. Each morning he made a list of things to do. And each night he checked back to tally his accomplishments. Larry Knox, his stepfather, thought David would be an excellent businessman.

At Carson Center, David impressed the coaches immediately, with his shot, his hustle, and his intelligence. He was the only player who made the cut and soon joined his new teammates at practice. David had been on campus for more than a month. But it wasn't until that first day at Carson Center with the team—*his team*—that he had truly arrived. He'd eat with the team, study with the team, and travel to every road game. In his own quiet way, David was elated, calling home to share the news.

But the celebration of his accomplishment ended abruptly in practice soon after tryouts when David stepped on a teammate's foot and wrenched his ankle. Practice stopped and David was helped off the court. The prognosis was grim: This was no simple sprain. It wasn't broken but it was almost as bad. David was fitted with a walking cast, and suddenly left to wonder about the future of his college basketball career.

Watson felt bad for the kid. David had worked so hard, and making the team meant so much to him. So he asked David to keep statistics on the bench during home games and told him he could try out again once his ankle healed. Of course, it wouldn't be the same. When his teammates pulled on their immaculate white home jerseys in the locker room, David would be wearing a tie and a jacket. He didn't appear in the team photo, taken in the empty parking lot at Roberts Stadium. And instead of traveling with the team, he'd stay home and listen to the games on the radio or watch them on TV. But he couldn't just quit. He'd proved himself against Division I players. No way could he turn his back on that. So, David swallowed his disappointment and accepted Watson's offer.

———

Bobby and Deidra Watson and their three daughters moved into a brand-new two-story brick house in Warrick County, a fast-growing suburb east of Evansville, where developers had begun building homes on large lots that until recently had been farmland.

The Watsons were the first residents on Bunker Hill Court, a street so new that when they moved in, their house didn't have an address and they couldn't take mail delivery. As Bobby zipped from one meeting to the next, Deidra tried to make a home for their family. But it wasn't easy. The neighborhood was empty, and it was difficult for Deidra to make new friends. She was quiet and soft-spoken, born in southeastern Indiana, not far from the old Moores Hill campus. She had met Bobby on a blind date after a Xavier basketball game, and they married on December 14, 1973. When they moved to Evansville four years later, the community showered them with attention. Twins Leigh and Chandra were two and Angela was twelve. Like Jackie, Caroline, and John-John, Watson's photogenic young family only heightened the city's awestruck reception for its new basketball coach. Bobby's prominence was a given. But Deidra and the girls got a taste of small-town celebrity, too. They were featured prominently in the UE basketball media guide, and their pictures appeared in the newspapers. A short profile in the *Sunday Courier & Press* was typically effusive:

"If there's a pretty family contest somewhere, the Watsons ought to enter it. Blonde Angela is a charmer, with poise and maturity beyond her years. The twins are dark-haired like their mother, adorable perpetual motion machines. To a stranger, Chandra and Leigh look identical, but Deidra says one has two extra freckles on her nose."

At home, a mini basketball hoop stood next to the fireplace in the family room. Leigh and Chandra liked to climb up on the hearth and slam the ball through the basket. The writer from the *Sunday Courier & Press* predicted a career change for Bobby.

"Watson is a young man. He may yet live to coach a coed team."

Deidra and the girls modeled in a fashion show fund-raiser for the UE Theatre Society. They joined a well-heeled group of luminaries that included mayor Russell Lloyd, UE president Wallace Graves and his wife, Arad and Virginia McCutchan, the sheriff, a bank president, and Marcia Yockey, a kooky TV news personality with a gray ponytail, who was known as the "weather gal." Bobby, of course, was the master of ceremonies.

Deidra and the girls also appeared on the first episode of the *Bobby Watson Show*. The premiere opened with a shot of Bobby pulling up to the house on Bunker Hill Court. Inside, he took off his brown suede jacket, greeted Deidra with a peck on the lips, and joined the twins on the floor playing with Legos.

The cohost of the *Bobby Watson Show* was Mike Blake, the affable young sports director for WFIE, Evansville's NBC affiliate. Blake and Watson had much in common: Both in their thirties, they had young families at home and prominent positions in their adopted hometown. More important, they had both staked their careers on the success of the University of Evansville basketball team.

Blake was a perfect fit for the Evansville market. He delivered scores and stats each night with a chipper sincerity that never wavered, on the air or on the sidelines. He didn't do cynicism, sarcasm, or bombast. His ever-present humility seemed ripe for caricature. But it was genuine. Blake was a devout Catholic prone to muttering "Oh lordy" when he got frustrated. He spoke at fifty to sixty community events every year and hosted the local portion of the annual Jerry Lewis telethon for muscular dystrophy. He called people "pal." Blake grew up in northwest Indiana, went to college in Iowa, and served in Vietnam, where he played records and read the news for the Armed Forces Radio network. He landed a job at WFIE in 1970, married an Evansville native, and started a family. At thirty-three, Blake had established himself as a trusted and popular presence in the local media landscape. But he had big-market ambitions. In early 1977, a Miami station offered him a weekend sports anchor job and hosting duties for a weekly Miami Dolphins show. The Dolphins had won two Super Bowls and their quarterback, Bob Griese, was a superstar in Evansville. Blake was ready to move his family to Florida.

That same year, however, WFIE reached a deal to broadcast Aces games and the *Bobby Watson Show*. Blake had always wanted to do play-by-play. And now that the Aces were competing in Division I, against top-ranked teams like DePaul and Indiana State, UE basketball was a more attractive beat with a higher profile. No one would ever confuse Evansville with South Beach. But Blake's annual salary in Miami would be only $1,000 more and he'd begun to put down roots in southern Indiana. Evansville had embraced him. In Florida, he'd be starting all over again. So he turned down the Miami station for the best job of his short career: Mike Blake was the television voice of the University of Evansville Purple Aces.

In the premiere of the coach's show, following the visit with Deidra and the girls, Watson and Blake stood on the court in an empty Roberts Stadium to talk about the first game, on November 30, against Western Kentucky.

"Bobby, of course, we hope that when you play here next Wednesday night, that this place is packed," Blake said. "It's important that the Aces of '77–'78, and from here on out, get the fans, right?"

"The city has to back us, Mike, if we're going to be the Division I team that they want to see," Watson said. "The great players in the country will come here and play only if these seats are full and if the people are really interested in our program. I can't sell an empty stadium to anybody."

The sincere gravity of this exchange reflected the city's commitment to the Aces. Watson had offered Evansville a stake in his basketball program, and Evansville had eagerly accepted.

The first four games of the season would be a gauntlet. After opening with Western Kentucky at home, UE flew to Chicago to play DePaul, returned to Roberts Stadium to face Pittsburgh, and headed to Terre Haute for Indiana State. The two road games were especially daunting. DePaul had been mediocre the previous season. But with the bruising center Dave Corzine (nickname: Lumber), the Blue Demons were poised for a Top 5 finish.

Indiana State, meanwhile, was still trying to win over skeptics who argued that their weak schedule (Tulsa, Drake, etc.) left them untested against the best teams. What was undeniable, however, was the emergence of Larry Bird. A taciturn kid with bad skin and a mop of untamed blond hair, Bird had grown up in poverty in French Lick, Indiana. After an exceptional high school career, he accepted a scholarship from Bob Knight, pleasing everyone in his hometown but himself. Committing to Indiana was a terrible mistake and Bird realized it immediately. The IU campus was huge and grand, and he couldn't figure out which building was which. Some of his classes had more than one hundred students. He was scared to ask questions. He didn't like Knight's authoritarian style. He didn't like his new teammates, who treated him like he didn't belong. He also felt intensely self-conscious about money: his roommate had plenty and Bird had little more than the clothes he wore. Larry begged his mom to come pick him up, but she refused. Finally, after less than a month, Bird gathered his meager belongings, left town without telling Knight, and hitchhiked home. He took a job with the French Lick street department, mowing grass and fixing roads for $150 a week. He was perfectly content, back home with a steady paycheck. But when the college coaches came calling again, Larry enrolled at Indiana State and moved to Terre Haute. He found its campus much more to his liking and carried the Sycamores to a 25–3 record in 1977, averaging thirty-three points a game. UE would face Indiana State on December 10.

But before Watson and his coaches turned their attention to Bird, they had to choose five starters for the opener against Western Kentucky. Duff—of course—would join three teammates who'd started on Arad McCutchan's final team: John Ed Washington, Steve Miller, and Bryan Taylor.

Taylor was the quintessential UE basketball player. A small-town Indiana kid, he'd been a star in the state high school basketball tournament and spurned a national powerhouse to play for Evansville. Taylor was TV-star handsome, like a genial street cop in a crime drama, 6'5", with thick dark hair and a matching mustache. He grew up in Tell City, a river town about an hour east of Evansville. He'd originally turned down an offer to play for McCutchan and accepted a scholarship to Louisville, which had played in the Final Four in 1975. But Jennifer Kuster—the prettiest cheerleader in Tell City, Bryan's high school sweetheart, the girl he planned to marry—had decided to study nursing at the University of Evansville. Almost as soon as classes started in the fall of 1975, Taylor escaped Louisville every chance he got, making the two-hour drive to meet Kuster in Evansville. He realized after a few weeks that he'd made a mistake. Like Jerry Sloan before him, Taylor called McCutchan to ask whether he still had a scholarship available. Then he cleared out of his dorm room and moved to Evansville. He'd finished the '77 season averaging thirteen points and impressed Watson with his quiet leadership.

Miller was 6'8" and slender, a junior center. He was Taylor's best friend and former roommate. Like Taylor, Miller had a steady girlfriend from high school. When he married Vicky Hendrix in August 1977, Bobby and Deidra Watson were among the guests. While the rest of the team lived together in a university-owned apartment building across from campus, Vicky and Steve lived in married student housing.

With four starters set, the only mystery that remained was who'd play point guard.

Tony Winburn was a whippet-quick senior listed at 5'8" who bragged that he played like he was 6'2". Winburn transferred to Evansville as a sophomore, but rarely played in his first season with the Aces. He didn't even travel with the team for two of UE's most important games, against Providence and Ohio State. He'd wanted to quit. But he also wanted a degree. Tony worked for a hometown bank every summer in Jeffersonville, across the Ohio River from Louisville, and planned on a career in finance. So he stayed at UE and played twenty-six games as a junior. His top competition for the starting point guard spot his senior year was Mark Siegel. But Mark had missed so much time in the first weeks of practice and still hadn't fully recovered from colon surgery. Winburn would start against Western Kentucky. But he still had to prove himself.

Greg Smith, another point guard, knew he wouldn't get much playing time. But he didn't mind. He felt grateful each day when he pulled the purple practice jersey over his head, slipped on the purple shorts, laced up his shoes, and stepped onto the court at Carson Center. Greg was a late addition to the team, a 6'1" guard from West Frankfort, Illinois. Watson hadn't scouted him. But Bob Brown, Mike Duff's old coach, knew Greg's game and his family. Brown grew up in West Frankfort and had known Art and Carolyn Smith for years. Art owned a radio station—WFRX—that had broadcast Bob's games when Brown was a high school hotshot. Now Brown's mother lived near Art and Carolyn and their three kids, and sometimes Greg's younger sister babysat for Bob's children. So when Bob Brown called to recommend Greg, Watson invited the young man to try out. Greg hit the weight room that fall, added some muscle to his 165-pound frame, and impressed the coaching staff with his work ethic and enthusiasm. He earned a roster spot and a scholarship after Mark Siegel got sick. Greg was elated, so pleased to make his parents happy.

"I've gone on a full ride lately," he wrote a friend that fall. "My parents were tremendously happy. My father seems to be really proud. It's a good feeling inside."

The older fellow with the heavy black glasses took his seat at Roberts Stadium in section E, row 5, seat 6. Legs crossed, he watched impassively in a suit and tie as the crowd around him welcomed Bobby Watson for his Evansville debut, November 30, UE against Western Kentucky. The seating arrangement—with Arad McCutchan in the southwest corner of the stadium and Watson on the bench—drew little attention from the fans that night. But it represented a tectonic shift, from one generation to the next, for Evansville and the university. In a town resistant to change and outsiders, the sixty-five-year-old homegrown coach with five national championships had stepped away to make room for an ambitious newcomer three decades younger. No longer was UE a Division II behemoth, routing small schools and big basketball factories the way it had in McCutchan's prime. The certainties of the past three decades had changed. Nothing made all of this clearer than McCutchan's presence in section E.

He still taught math and a basketball fundamentals class and coached the golf team. He was supportive of Watson and his staff and looked forward to seeing the players, the ones he'd coached as well as the freshmen the new coach had recruited. But McCutchan kept his distance. He hadn't visited practice or come to the scrimmages. He didn't make appearances with Watson or offer his thoughts on the players he'd recruited before he retired. Mac didn't want anyone laboring in his long shadow.

"It's something I thought about and planned for," McCutchan said. "I'm still very interested in the players and the school, but I want to stay in the background, out of the picture. That's the way it should be. That's where I belong."

McCutchan didn't regret his decision to retire. But he admitted that it felt odd, watching the game amid UE fans instead of from the bench. He caught himself thinking about strategy, then remembered that was no longer his job. Nor did he have to endure the road trips, practices, and questions from reporters who wanted to know why, exactly, the Purple Aces had lost. When the game ended, after Western Kentucky had spoiled Watson's big moment with an 82–72 victory, McCutchan was happy to leave Roberts Stadium with no regrets.

"It hurts to lose," he said. "But not nearly as much as it would have hurt last year."

———

The first few weeks of the season seesawed back and forth, from a promising stretch of play one night to a ghastly whipping the next. After losing to Western Kentucky, UE traveled to Chicago, where the Aces were dismantled by Dave Corzine and the Blue Demons. No surprise there. But three days later, Bryan Taylor and Steve Miller carried Evansville to a 90–83 win over Pittsburgh at Roberts Stadium. It was UE's first victory in Division I, and it was particularly meaningful for Watson. Pitt was his hometown team, and he'd known Panthers coach Tim Grgurich since they'd played against each other as high school kids.

"I've been involved in a lot of wins," Watson said afterward, uncharacteristically gleeful in the locker room, "but few sweeter than that one."

The victory was a hopeful sign. Maybe Division I wouldn't be so difficult after all. Maybe this brutal stretch to open the season wouldn't leave the Aces broken and defeated. A few days later, when the UE bus pulled onto Highway 41 for the two-hour trip north to Terre Haute to face Bird and the Sycamores, Watson's players felt quite pleased with themselves.

Before heading to Indiana State, Watson wrote his players an impassioned letter, typed, double-spaced, and barely more than a single page. He wrote about Einstein, Edison, and Booker T. Washington, great men who were underestimated before taking their rightful places in history. He wrote about 150 Australian and American soldiers who attacked a thousand North Vietnamese troops and prevailed. He wrote about prisoners of war who survived unspeakable torture and deprivation for years but ultimately walked away. All of these men were underdogs, Watson wrote, and they all overcame great odds. The Purple Aces could make their own history against Indiana State.

> With all of us doing our job, we can commit ourselves to *beating the odds*. If you feel what I feel, we too can *UPSET* Indiana State University. This will be no easy task, but there again, nothing good comes easily. However, you have worked *HARDER* to prepare and your desire to succeed is above and beyond any team I have ever been associated with.

The letter was a rousing call to arms, and typical of Watson's motivational repertoire. He was realistic about UE's chances in Terre Haute. But he meant every word he wrote.

On the day of the game, Mark Siegel's dad made the eighty-mile drive to Terre Haute. Ed Siegel took a seat along the baseline at the Hulman Center, about six rows from the floor, because he watched every game like a coach, scouting each team as if it was next on the Pike High School schedule. Ed felt good about Mark's progress in the first three games.

UE's point guard play had been awful. Watson wanted his point guards to put teammates in the best position to score, limit turnovers, and play solid defense. Scoring was not their top priority. Still, Tony Winburn was clearly overmatched. He lost the starting job after going scoreless on a total of two shots against Western Kentucky and DePaul. Freshman Kraig Heckendorn started and played well against Pitt, hitting two crucial free throws down the stretch. But to Ed, Mark looked more comfortable and confident with each game. He had fully recovered from his intestinal illness, regained the weight he'd lost, and scored four points against Pitt. It appeared that he and Heckendorn would split time at point guard for the foreseeable future. Ed had also had an intriguing conversation with a coach from Miami University in Ohio, which had recruited Mark in high school. The Miami coach was scouting a kid at a Pike game and told Ed that if Mark wasn't starting in Evansville, he could always transfer. Ed didn't think that was necessary. But it was a nice reminder of Mark's potential.

Kay and John Barrow, Mike Duff's parents, sat so high up at the Hulman Center that Kay felt like she could barely see the court. The rows were so narrow and her legs were so long that squeezing into her seat was a tight fit. But Kay wouldn't miss a chance to watch Mike go head-to-head with Larry Bird. They could have been teammates, two of the best players in the country. Imagine that. The UE scouting report on Indiana State provided a harsh reminder of what exactly Mike could expect of Bird: "Fine passer as well as shooter with 25-foot range; can put ball on the floor to get shot; will penetrate and hit open man; good rebounder. Can and will throw three-quarter-court pass to hit open man off rebound." But Mike wouldn't be alone in defending Bird. Watson planned to play Bryan Taylor and John Ed Washington on him as well, to keep him from getting too comfortable. UE's strategy was simple: if Bird scores thirty, shut down his teammates and hope for the best.

For Aces fans, the Indiana State arena felt like the white-hot center of college basketball. The Sycamores were 5–0 and ranked eighth in the country. The largest crowd of Indiana State's season to that point—9,653—had squeezed into the gym. The hostile energy, a top-ranked rival, the best player in the country—this is why the University of Evansville moved up to play in Division I. The players felt it and so did Watson.

The Aces were clearly rattled, from the moment the two teams walked onto the floor to the sound of the final buzzer. No matter how much they had practiced. No matter how good they felt about that victory over Pitt. None of it mattered.

Indiana State center DeCarsta Webster was three inches taller than Steve Miller and easily controlled the opening tip. The Aces barely had time to set their defense before Indiana State threw two quick passes, getting the ball into Bird's hands for an easy drive to the basket. Just like that, after nine seconds, the Sycamores led 2–0. It was Indiana State's smallest lead of the night. The Sycamores played like the Harlem Globetrotters. The Aces, meanwhile, played like the Washington Generals. In the first few minutes, John Ed Washington dribbled the ball out of bounds. Mike Duff was whistled for a foul. Steve Miller traveled and Bryan Taylor threw the ball away. Indiana State moved effortlessly on offense, whipping the ball around the perimeter and then to the baseline: Jimmy Smith to Harry Morgan and back to Smith, and then to Bird for another easy layup.

Indiana State led 4–0 and then 6–0 and then 8–0.

Bird seemed to be in the middle of every play. When Duff drove on Bird, Mike was called for charging. When Leroy Staley took a pass from Bird, he knocked down a jumper from fifteen feet. When Bird grabbed a Heckendorn miss, he passed the ball but got it back on the other end for a sweet baby hook. Now it was 10–0 and Bobby Watson quickly called time-out.

The respite didn't stop the free fall. It did, however, give Mike and his teammates a moment to consider the facts: Yes, the first few minutes were humiliating. Yes, Bird was wily and brilliant. But all was not lost. More than thirty-seven minutes remained, plenty of time to save face. And it certainly couldn't get any uglier. So the Aces returned to the court with a new resolve, led by an emboldened Mike Duff.

His first basket came on a fifteen-foot jumper with 16:36 to play. That's when he started feeling comfortable, the muscle memory kicking in. A few minutes later, he dropped one from the baseline. He'd found a rhythm. Back on the baseline, he sank his third basket from eighteen feet. Only Bird could interrupt this reverie, and that's what he did, over and over and over, all night. A layup. An eighteen-foot jumper. Another layin. A dunk. Two free throws. Bird had twenty at halftime, and Evansville trailed by twenty-one.

The opening minutes of the second half were just as brutal as the opening minutes of the first. Bird started with a twenty-foot jumper, a dunk, a layup, and another dunk. Eight points in a row, a scoring binge to finish off the Aces and another middle finger to anyone who ever doubted him. Final score: Indiana State 102, Evansville 76.

In a somber locker room afterward, Watson searched for a silver lining.

Mike scored twenty-three, with eight rebounds, and Watson offered an unusually generous assessment of his potential. "By the time he's a junior," Watson told reporters, "Duff will be as good as Bird."

It sounded like wishful thinking. Bird finished with thirty-five that night, and demonstrated what the rest of the country would soon see for itself: a mean streak born of humiliating poverty, the same seething anger that drove Jerry Sloan, the same grit and resilience that drove Lieutenant Robert Watson in Vietnam. This was the attitude Watson wanted to see in the Aces.

"All I can say," he told reporters, "is that two years from now, we'll have the courage to knock people around."

The players gathered for practice at Carson Center on a pale gray Monday afternoon, less than forty-eight hours after the debacle in Terre Haute. Watson was in a sour mood. The bus trip home after the Indiana State game had been solemn and quiet, a promising sign after a twenty-six-point loss. Now he hoped to see a renewed sense of passion and purpose. The following afternoon—December 13—UE would fly to Nashville for a game against Middle Tennessee State, and Watson wanted his boys in the right frame of mind.

But once practice started, it was obvious they weren't and Watson did little to hide his irritation. Early on, he tested his team's commitment to transition defense. He split the Aces into two squads and ran them—hard—from one end of the gym to the other. One squad pushed the ball up the court while the other, backpedaling, tried to stop them. Then Watson blew his whistle. The squad with the ball dropped it beneath the basket, and the other team picked it up. It was a simple drill, but it required fresh legs and maniacal commitment to defense. It was like a pop quiz with only one question: How bad do you want to play Division I basketball?

Watson stood off to the side, evaluating each kid. He didn't like what he saw: sloppy fast breaks, no hustle, one mistake after another.

Finally, after ten minutes, he blew the whistle one last time and called an early end to a dismal practice.

"Go take a shower," he said. "I don't even want to see you. We're wasting time here. Yours and mine."

Thus ended Bobby Watson's final practice.

SEVEN

Air Indiana Flight 216

THE PURPLE ACES ARRIVED at Dress Regional Airport on December 13, a foggy, drizzly afternoon, with the temperature hovering near fifty degrees. Recent rains had left the hilly and remote landscape surrounding the airport a muddy mess, and bad weather in Indianapolis had delayed UE's flight, leaving the team to wait in the lounge at Tri-State Aero, a charter company at Evansville's shoebox of an airport. The Aces had been scheduled for a 4:00 p.m. flight to Nashville, followed by a forty-minute bus ride to Murfreesboro. Now it was approaching 7:00 p.m., and UE had already called the Middle Tennessee athletic department twice to explain the delay.

Late that morning, Bobby Watson had sat in his Carson Center office with Anne Harter, a young reporter for the *Evansville Press*. Watson was in an expansive mood, unguarded and frustrated, returning again to the theme that had occupied his mind in recent days. Succeeding in Division I required guts, grit, and perseverance, summoned from the depths of a man's character. He talked about the dire challenges he faced in Vietnam, where he carried the burden of other men's lives while risking his own in those few perilous moments when his helicopter descended under enemy fire. Those experiences had shaped his coaching philosophy, and he wanted to pass on the lessons he learned to his struggling young team.

Watson had expected more from the Aces in the first weeks of the season. He'd hoped that his team would be 2–2 by this time, with victories over Western Kentucky and Pittsburgh and losses to DePaul and ISU. Instead, UE had lost three games by an average margin of nearly twenty points and several key players were clearly in over their heads. John Ed Washington, the leading scorer during the previous season, had regressed, shooting less than 30 percent from the floor and scoring fewer than eight points per game. The four guards averaged twice as many fouls as field goals. Tony Winburn found himself banished to the end of the bench. And now Bryan Taylor was hobbling around on an ankle he'd sprained in Terre Haute, leaving his status in doubt for the next game. Watson had told Stafford Stephenson and Ernie Simpson, his assistant coaches, that by Christmas they'd have a better idea of who was up to the challenge of Division I ball and who wasn't. Christmas was less than two weeks away and an air of uncertainty hovered over the Aces like the dark cumulus clouding the airport runway.

But there was hope. UE had emerged from the most difficult stretch of the schedule and headed into the second half of December with a chance to turn their season around. Their next four opponents—Middle Tennessee State, Austin Peay, Ball State, and Morehead State—had a combined record of 4–9. The rest of the season included matchups with the likes of DePauw and Indiana Central, small schools with lesser programs. Steve Miller was much improved, and Warren Alston had shown great promise, scoring seventeen against Indiana State. Mike Duff had played exceptionally well, averaging twenty points and nearly ten rebounds per game. The season was less than two weeks old. All was not lost.

That afternoon, Watson made some calls from the airport to kill time. About 4:30 p.m. he called Tom Collins, the Aces beat writer at the *Evansville Courier*. They had made plans to talk once the Aces arrived at their hotel. But it was clear by late afternoon that the Aces wouldn't arrive in Murfreesboro until later that night.

"We're still out here at the airport, fogged in," Watson told Collins. "Everything has been moved back. You wouldn't have been able to reach me so I figured I'd call you now."

Collins rolled paper into his typewriter, the keys clacking as Watson told him about Taylor's ankle, Miller's development, and Duff's first four games. Collins planned to use the interview for a story in the next morning's paper, previewing the Middle Tennessee State game.

Watson also called Al Dauble, a local florist and influential supporter of the basketball team, and asked him to deliver a dozen red roses to Deidra the next day. It would be their fourth wedding anniversary. Dauble promised he would.

Arad McCutchan's teams had mostly traveled by bus. The drive to Nashville was only 150 miles. But Watson wanted to compete with the top schools for the best recruits, and the top schools flew on chartered jets. So the Aces would, too. The UE travel party that day included twenty-four people: Watson and his fourteen players, three university officials, three student managers, and radio play-by-play man Marv Bates. Two devoted boosters—Maury King and Charles Goad—had snagged the final empty seats on the flight.

Marv Bates had achieved a rare celebrity in Evansville: he was a local icon with a national reputation. Bates had mastered the art of re-creating live Minor League Baseball games—played anywhere from Denver to New Orleans—from the WGBF radio studio in Evansville. As the voice of the Evansville Triplets, the top farm team for the Detroit Tigers, Bates called the action for home games perched in the press box above Bosse Field. But when the Triplets went out of town, he stayed behind and did the broadcast from the studio, using more than seventy-five individual sound effects to simulate live baseball. And not just organ music or the murmur of the crowd. Bates traveled with the team early in the season to capture unique sounds from each ballpark.

For games in Denver, he recorded trucks zooming along the nearby interstate. In Tulsa, he captured the sound of local stock car races. He used siren sound effects, crowd laughter, the muffled voice of a public address announcer, and the clack of bat on ball. For play-by-play details, he relied on a sportswriter at the game who provided a summary of each pitch.

"Hello again, sports friends," Bates said at the top of each game. He always acknowledged that he was reconstructing the games from the studio, but otherwise tried to make the broadcasts as authentic as possible. He demonstrated his skills on *The Tomorrow Show*, with Tom Snyder, and on *The Baseball World of Joe Garagiola*.

Tall and bespectacled and balding, even as a young man, Bates grew up in Evansville and met his wife, Edie, when they were students at Evansville College. Marv was a decent athlete, a two-way lineman on the Aces football team, and later a legendary softball pitcher known for his underhanded windmill windup. His friends called him "the Bomber." He practiced obsessively, grabbing his glove after dinner in the summer so he could spend a few hours at a nearby elementary school diamond. Neighborhood kids would knock on the back door and ask Edie whether Marv could come out and play and then argue with each other over who would be his catcher.

Marv had initially wanted to be a football coach, but changed his mind after taking a broadcasting class in college. When Marv started out in radio, Edie taught elementary school. But Marv asked her to quit and soon she sat next to him at the broadcast table, knitting, keeping him company, and sometimes keeping stats. Marv and Edie didn't have children. But the local sports community was their extended family. Like Mike Blake and Arad McCutchan, Marv somehow seemed to be at every game, event, and banquet in town. He called Aces football, horse racing, high school football, and high school basketball. He was a busy master of ceremonies, acted in local theater, and served as a deacon at his church, a position he voluntarily resigned when his radio show added a brewery as a sponsor. Broadcasting didn't pay the bills, so Marv worked day jobs. He might spend eight hours selling advertising for the radio station or teaching social studies to high school kids, and then spend another eight that night doing play-by-play at an Aces game. Broadcasting was not a career for Marv. It was a calling. And he had big-city ambitions.

Marv wanted more than anything to broadcast Major League Baseball games. He nearly got a job with a big-league club in the early 1960s. But then his father passed away and Marv stayed in Evansville to look after his mom. He caught a break in 1976, when Harry Caray invited him up to Chicago to help out on White Sox broadcasts as the team looked to expand its broadcast crew. It looked as though Marv's time had finally come. But the White Sox passed him over in favor of a former player, and Marv gave up on his hopes for a big-league job.

But he still had Aces basketball. Marv narrated the biggest moments in Aces history with a clipped and friendly formality that embodied both his hometown allegiance and his professionalism. His finest moment came at the end of the 1965 championship game against Southern Illinois University at Roberts Stadium. When Jerry Sloan calmly sank two free throws at the end of overtime to complete Evansville's perfect season, Bates responded with a call that would define his career.

"There it is, one second," Bates said, his voice rising. "Aces! National champions! National champions! Undefeated! Aces! Aces! The Aces!"

Only later, as the postgame ceremonies unfolded in front of him, did Bates allow himself a moment to express all that Evansville College meant to his hometown.

"This is something you probably see once in a lifetime," he told his listeners. "So enjoy it and have a good time and be proud of our community."

Jeff Bohnert watched the gray afternoon sky darken as he waited at the airport for the chartered jet, nervously anticipating his first ride on an airplane. Jeff was a student manager, a quiet kid with thick glasses and a soft, round face. He didn't want to go to Tennessee, not on an airplane, not in December, and not with finals looming. A biology major considering medical school, he much preferred studying or working in the lab. But Bobby Watson wanted film of the Middle Tennessee State game and, after shooting football games that fall, Jeff knew how to use the camera. Jeff had been a student manager with his friend Mark "Sneezy" Kniese at Harrison High School in Evansville and then joined Mark at UE, schlepping laundry at all hours and rolling out of bed before sunrise to prepare for practices and games. He earned a scholarship for his work and enjoyed the camaraderie he shared with Kniese and Mark Kirkpatrick, another student manager. That evening, the three of them sat in the lounge at the airport, loaded down with uniforms, gear, and other game-day necessities.

Jeff had enjoyed a sheltered childhood, growing up as the oldest child in a close family. He lived with his parents—Don and Dolores—even after he enrolled at UE. The Bohnerts were a deeply religious family and Jeff took his faith seriously, studying the Bible and worshipping each weekend at Holy Rosary Catholic Church. Jeff was especially close with his brother Craig, a year younger. They shared a bedroom and dressed like twins when they were little boys because their mom bought them the same outfits at the same time. When Jeff was in high school, he ran with a big group of kids, girls and boys, who'd meet up at McDonald's or go to the movies, driving back and forth past the malls and fast-food joints along Green River Road, where teens liked to cruise on the weekends. Jeff wasn't like a lot of boys his age, goofing off and making noise to draw the attention of the girls in their orbit. Just the opposite. He exuded calm. Sometimes, while his friends were cracking jokes and horsing around, he seemed to be observing it all from a distance, even as he sat with them in the same car. That's what

Debbie Lankford liked about him. Debbie ran with the same pack of kids at Harrison. Jeff took Debbie to the junior prom and harbored a secret crush on her, even after he graduated high school and went to college. He carried their prom picture in his wallet, but they didn't date. In fact, Jeff told Debbie he had a girlfriend in Florida. "Oh really?" she'd say. "What's her name? What's she like?" Jeff never said, but it sounded like pure fiction.

Debbie went to UE, too. She played in the pep band and sometimes saw Jeff at basketball games. But they didn't reconnect until the fall of 1977, when they found themselves in the same class. One day in December, they lingered in the hallway outside the classroom, chatting about their plans for Christmas break. Maybe, Jeff suggested, he could give her a call after the Aces' annual holiday tournament. Like, for a date. Debbie told him that would be great. Jeff tried to play it cool. But as he turned to walk away, his face lit up with a broad smile, bashful and excited at the same time.

———

Finally, at 7:00 p.m., a Douglas DC-3 descended from the clouds and rolled down the runway, past the main terminal, and stopped in front of Tri-State Aero. Both engines were shut down. The UE traveling party emerged from the lounge and walked into the misty evening with their luggage, equipment, and dinner: hamburgers, fries, and shakes. Eager to make up for lost time, the flight crew worked quickly to load the baggage and restart the engines. There were twenty-nine people aboard, including three crew members and the president and general manager of National Jet Service, the plane's owner. Once the passengers buckled themselves in, the crew closed the doors and the pilots readied for takeoff. The plane, operating as Air Indiana Flight 216, had been on the ground for twelve minutes.

The jet taxied to runway 18 and asked the control tower for permission to take off. An air traffic controller warned the pilots about turbulence in the wake of a recently departed Delta flight and cleared Air Indiana Flight 216 for takeoff. Slowly, the jet rolled down the runway, dragging its tail and swerving back and forth in the moments before liftoff. From the moment the plane finally went airborne, it was clear that something was horribly wrong. With its nose pointing skyward, the plane made a steep left turn, struggling to gain altitude as it crossed over airport property and a single line of railroad tracks. At first, the roar of the engines led air traffic controllers to think the jet was heading straight toward the tower. A controller who asked the pilot to clarify the jet's status received a two-word reply muffled by engine noise: "Stand by." With that, the tower lost contact with the cockpit. The jet flew so low over a subdivision called Melody Hills that it clipped trees, leaving branches in a yard below. With engines roaring and the aircraft wobbling from side to side, the jet reversed course and headed back toward the airport. Air Indiana Flight 216 had been airborne for less than ninety seconds when it dropped, nose down, and landed with a thud along the railroad tracks. Two explosions followed, and the plane burst into flames.

In the tower, a panicked air traffic controller sounded the alarm and screamed to his colleagues: "Oh he crashed! It crashed! Crash! Crash!"

At first, Stephen Troyer thought the plane was headed for his house. He heard the engines rev and then the explosion. Suddenly flames filled the entire picture window in the family dining room. Troyer, a thirty-four-year-old oral surgeon, leaped out of his seat at the dinner table and bolted outside to make sure the house wasn't damaged. Lois, his wife, called the fire department. Troyer changed shoes, grabbed a ski jacket, and ran to his next-door neighbor's house. He pounded on their patio door, asking John and Mary Jo Schymik for help, and then raced

through the woods west of his house, toward the flames. After about
two hundred yards, Troyer came to a ravine and saw, through the fog,
the tail of the plane in flames, sheared from the cabin.

"Is anyone here?" he shouted, hoping to find passengers who were
still alive. He was met with an eerie silence. Troyer scrambled down
the embankment and stumbled into a surreal and ghastly scene: mud-
spattered bodies were strewn across the railroad tracks, some piled on
top of each other, limbs askew, with many still strapped into their seats.
He heard labored breathing and came upon an unconscious young man
with a massive skull fracture. To clear his blocked airway and aid his
breathing, Troyer turned him to the side. He found a second survivor
lying on top of another passenger, struggling to breathe. Troyer removed
the seat belt and the seat and turned him on his side as well. Then he
aided the breathing of a third surviving passenger nearby. About halfway up the other side of the ravine, closer to the tail of the plane, he
found another group of bodies in a pile, parts of their clothing torn
away. He couldn't hear any breathing, so he climbed to the top of the
embankment, where he found a fourth survivor, on top of another
passenger. Because he was closer to the plane and the light was better,
Troyer raised the young man's eyelids and found his eyeballs caked with
dirt. He moved the young man to his side and hurried to the tail of
the plane, searching for other living passengers. When he couldn't find
any, Troyer returned to the railroad tracks. Soon, John and Mary Jo
Schymik arrived. Troyer asked them to clear the airways of two survivors
by elevating their chins and pulling their tongues out. He directed a
young man who'd shown up a few moments later to do the same for a
third passenger. Troyer cared for the fourth.

When Lois Troyer scrambled down the embankment, John
Schymik, a dentist, shouted that they needed flashlights and a helicopter ambulance. So she turned around, climbed back up the steep,
muddy embankment, and ran back through the underbrush in the
woods. When she got home, she called Deaconess Hospital. Lois, a

registered nurse, relayed details of the crash, requested a helicopter, and
warned the hospital to prepare.

"Get your emergency room ready," she said. "We do have survivors."

———

Sirens sounded in the distance as a caravan of firefighters, police officers, civil defense volunteers, sheriff's deputies, and state police troop-
ers rushed to the airport. Stephen Troyer heard the sirens and looked
toward the control tower, hoping to see fire trucks or ambulances heading his way. But there was nothing. Eventually, it dawned on Troyer just
how far out the plane had crashed, how alone they were on the edge
of the ravine.

There was no direct access to the crash site from roads around the
airport. One rescue truck was blocked by traffic and then got lost. An
airport vehicle slid off the road and got stuck in the mud. None of the
Evansville Fire Department engines made it to the site because their
drivers didn't know how to get there. Sheriff James DeGroote got stuck
in traffic, ditched his car in somebody's front yard, and flagged down
one of his deputies in a four-wheel-drive truck. But the four-wheeler
couldn't travel in the mud either, so the deputy hit the gas and barreled
down the railroad tracks toward the wreckage.

Finally, about twenty minutes after the plane went down, the first
firefighters pulled up. They sprayed foam and water to extinguish fires
near an engine and a wing. More firefighters and police officers arrived.
Troyer shouted for stretchers. But the firefighters had left them on their
trucks. When he saw a fire engine racing down the railroad tracks, he
figured it could transport survivors to the hospital. But then the truck's
battery died.

Two of the survivors had stopped breathing. The third was placed
on a makeshift stretcher that John Schymik had fashioned out of a luggage rack and a purple UE banner. But that survivor stopped breathing

as he was carried to the railroad tracks and didn't respond after several minutes of CPR. That left a single young man, out of twenty-nine people on the plane. When a rescue worker returned from his ambulance with a stretcher, a half dozen people carefully lifted this final, unidentified passenger, supporting his broken neck and turning him to his side. It required nearly twelve people to carry him up the embankment and through the woods, Lois Troyer leading the way with a flashlight.

By now, chaos and confusion had replaced the ghostly solitude that Stephen Troyer found when he arrived at the ravine. The crash site had grown crowded with so many rescue workers wearing identical heavy black raincoats that it was difficult to tell who was giving orders and who was taking them. The mayor and the police chief joined the sheriff. Truck drivers showed up to volunteer their services and spectators showed up to watch.

"The best way for you to help is to leave," one rescue worker told the crowd. "Don't make me stand here and keep asking you to leave. We have a lot of work to do."

Spectators walked solemnly from the crash site, warning other sightseers to keep their distance.

"Don't go in," one said. "It's awful."

——————

At the University of Evansville, President Wallace Graves sat in the dark near the back of Wheeler Concert Hall, enjoying a string quartet performance by the music faculty with his wife and mother-in-law. Around 8:00 p.m., shortly after the concert began, UE vice president Thornton Patberg appeared at Graves's side. They spoke briefly before hurrying into the hallway. Details were vague, Patberg said gravely, but there were reports of a plane crash at the airport. It might be the basketball team. The two men rushed to Patberg's house, about two blocks away, where they were joined by Arad McCutchan and the athletic director,

Jim Byers. At first, they thought the reports were wrong. After all, the team had been scheduled to fly out at 4:00 p.m. But the television and radio stations had begun reporting the details from the crash site, leaving Graves and his colleagues to face the grim reality that the UE basketball team, a civic cornerstone, was gone.

McCutchan volunteered to go to Deaconess Hospital to check on the lone survivor. Patberg and Byers would head to the community center downtown, where a makeshift morgue had been opened. Graves wanted to call the families of the passengers, to let them know what had happened and to provide the few details he could. But the police asked the university to refrain from confirming any deaths, even to the families of the victims, until each of the bodies was officially identified by the coroner. It was standard operating procedure for police and fire departments. The potential for a traumatic mistake, notifying the family of someone not on the plane, was too great a risk. Graves reluctantly agreed to hold off and headed for police headquarters, next to the community center. Once he arrived, he was led to an office, given a cup of coffee, and asked to wait. He spent an agonizing interval there, alone, eager to go to the community center, uncertain why the police wanted him to stay, and unwilling to leave of his own volition. There was no disaster plan to prepare Graves for a tragedy like this, nothing to guide him. So he waited until the police told him he was needed at the morgue, where he would endure the most excruciating moments of the evening.

———

Valery Kingston, Kevin's fifteen-year-old sister, heard the news on the pep squad bus after an Eldorado High School basketball game in Norris City. Valery, a junior varsity cheerleader, didn't understand at first. She thought the UE team had been in a bus crash. But slowly, on the fifteen-minute ride home to Eldorado, she realized it was more serious than that. The girls in front of her whispered to each other. The rest of the bus was silent. When it arrived in front of the high school, Valery stopped at the door, where she found her father waiting for her.

"Is he dead?" she asked.

Don Kingston nodded his head, enveloped his only child in his arms, and walked her to the car. Wanda, Valery's mother, sat weeping in the passenger seat. The Kingstons headed to Wanda's parents' house, a few blocks from the high school, because Wanda didn't want them to hear the news on TV. Then Don drove Wanda and Valery home to their house on Old Broughton Road. They walked in the back door to find the kitchen already filled with friends making coffee and getting the house ready for mourners. Lou Beck, the town pharmacist, hugged Valery. So did the pastor's wife from First Baptist Church. Relatives and neighbors streamed in and out. Valery's friends joined her on the porch to get away from the commotion. No one—not the university or the coroner—had contacted the Kingstons to confirm details of the crash, who had died, and who had survived. But for Don, Wanda, and Valery, the mourning had already begun. TV and radio stations were reporting that there was only one survivor, leaving them certain that Kevin was dead. When Valery came inside for the ten o'clock news, old footage of Kevin appeared on the television and Don Kingston broke down in tears.

But across town, at Kay Barrow's house, the mood was different. Kay and John wanted to believe that the lone survivor was Mike. They had been listening to the Eldorado game on the radio when the news broke. Soon, family and friends crowded into their house on Organ Street. Kay's parents came up from Shawneetown. Bob Brown, Mike's high school coach, arrived after visiting the Kingstons. Mike's friends came over. The TV was on. Guests paced the floor, smoking cigarettes, waiting for good news. Kay and John were on the phone, trying to reach someone who would tell them that Mike was alive.

———

In his dorm room at Purdue, Craig Bohnert watched the end of the Purdue-Louisville basketball game with friends and changed the channel to *Soap*. Craig was a sophomore, thinking about a career as a veterinarian. But organic chemistry gave him fits and he wondered about returning to Evansville and earning a scholarship as a student manager, just like his brother Jeff.

The guys who lived on Craig's dorm floor knew that he and his roommate were from Evansville. So, about fifteen minutes after the Purdue game ended, one of their neighbors stuck his head into the room.

"Hey," he said. "Do you know anyone on the Evansville basketball team?"

———

Rescue workers unbuckled bodies from airplane seats, placed them in rubber bags, and carried them through knee-deep water and down the muddy embankment to a train that would transport them to the makeshift morgue. Federal investigators on their way to Evansville asked the workers to cover the bodies and leave them at the site until they arrived the next day. But the sheriff and police chief decided, in deference to the families, that they couldn't abandon the dead amid the wreckage in a desolate field on a wet night.

When the train pulled up behind the morgue, hundreds of people stood in the rain along the railroad tracks in a silent vigil. Dozens more waited in the lobby. They could see into the gym, with basketball hoops at each end, where the bodies were cleaned, examined, and photographed. Fingerprints were taken, and each body was covered with a white sheet and placed on the floor. The heat had been turned off. From outside, as columnist Rod Spaw later described it, the gym looked as if it had been covered in snowdrifts, with white-coated medical examiners moving among white-covered tables that held white-covered bodies. As families arrived, they were led in one by one to identify the bodies. A medical examiner showed them wallets and driver's licenses that had been found at the site. They didn't have to view the bodies if they didn't want to, he said. Some just wanted to see an arm or a leg. One boy's mother entered the gym supported by men on each side. They led her to a table, she covered her face with a hand, her knees buckled, and they helped her away.

"Oh God no," another woman cried. "Not him. Not him."

UE assistant coach Ernie Simpson, who had been scouting a high school game in Kentucky, joined athletic director Jim Byers and a group of priests and ministers to console the relatives. Simpson gently took the arm of Freida Taylor, Bryan's mom, and led her in to identify her son's body. When they pulled back the sheet to reveal his face, Freida noticed that his hair was mussed, as if he had just stepped off the court after practice. His nose was broken, too. Then she saw blood spattered on the sheet, and the medical examiners wouldn't let her see the rest of Bryan's body.

Arad McCutchan moved through the hallways, from one family to another, still dressed in the red V-neck sweater and white shirt he'd worn to class that night, tie knotted at his neck but slightly askew. He consoled the parents of boys he'd recruited, boys who'd sat at his kitchen table, books piled high, as he tutored them in algebra. His famous reserve served him well, a helpful counterpoint to the grief that engulfed the gym.

"At times like this," he said, "you must turn around and face things. But I've never had to face anything like this."

At midnight, Wallace Graves sat in a folding chair with a bare white cinder-block wall as a backdrop and microphones arrayed on a table in front of him. He faced a crowd of local reporters, looking pale and drawn, as if the blood had been drained from his face.

"This is a tragedy that defies description," he said. "We're all quite numb at this point. But we know that the victims of this crash were all fine people, a great bunch of student basketball players and coaches and friends. The university will suffer their loss for the rest of its life."

———

Craig Bohnert ran to a phone in the hallway of his dorm floor and called home. Don Bohnert had just gotten home from a meeting and told Craig he hadn't heard anything about a crash. But Don promised he'd make some calls and get back to him.

After they hung up, Craig threw clothes into a bag. A guy who lived down the hall offered to drive him to Evansville, more than four hours south of West Lafayette. But after ninety minutes on the road, a state trooper pulled them over, walked to the driver's side, and told them he was looking for Craig Bohnert. Craig identified himself and asked the trooper whether he had news about the crash. The trooper told them he didn't know anything about a crash, but was ordered to direct Craig back to West Lafayette. Don Bohnert had called state police because he worried about Craig traveling to Evansville in bad weather.

Once he returned to his dorm, Craig's mom called. As soon as he picked up the phone, she said, "He's gone."

———

Stephen Troyer and John Schymik helped load the last survivor into the ambulance and then climbed in for the ride to Deaconess Hospital. They suctioned his throat, inserted a tube to aid his breathing, and put an oxygen mask on his face. As the ambulance sped downtown in light traffic, a paramedic placed splints on the young man's broken ankles and wrists. A nurse and several technicians met the ambulance in the parking lot with a stretcher. Inside the hospital, an IV was inserted and a blood transfusion was administered. The hospital staff had prepared for mass casualties, filling a hallway with a long line of cots on wheels. Five additional doctors were called in to help and about thirty workers from the day shift returned from a nearby holiday party. But with only one survivor, there was little for them to do.

Around midnight, the phone rang in the emergency room's registration office. It was Kay Barrow, calling from Eldorado. She'd been on the phone for three hours, trying to confirm that her son was still alive. A hospital spokesman came on the line and broke the news: Mike Duff, Eldorado's favorite son, the sweet-faced boy with so much potential, was dead.

Art and Carolyn Smith, Greg's parents, drove ninety minutes from West Frankfort to Evansville after the news director at Art's radio station stopped by their house that night to ask whether they knew anything about the crash. Greg had played sparingly that season and had been left at home for the DePaul game to make room on the team plane for a booster. But the mere fact that he had made the team brought him such great joy. Greg joked after the loss at Indiana State that Larry Bird went to the bench only after Greg entered the game because Bird, obviously, was afraid of him.

After talking to his news director, Art immediately called Greg's room, hopeful that for some reason he had been left behind again. Maybe that booster had wanted to see the Middle Tennessee State game, too. But there was no answer. Then they saw a news alert on TV.

"Greg's dead," cried Doug, his little brother.

Carolyn wouldn't have it. She looked him straight in the eye. "Doug," she said firmly, "don't say that."

Art called the Evansville Police Department to confirm that the team had been on the plane that crashed, and piled into the car with Carolyn and the principal and basketball coach from West Frankfort High School. They headed straight for the community center, but still held out hope after hearing on the radio that there were survivors. Amid the chaos at the morgue, someone from the university told them that Greg was alive and had been taken to Deaconess.

"If he's alive now," Art told Carolyn, "he's going to make it."

They got to the hospital at 12:30 a.m., four hours after Greg had arrived, and rushed inside.

It was five minutes too late. Art was ushered alone into the intensive care unit to identify his son. The doctors told him he could stay with Greg as long as he'd like, and Art didn't want to leave. Art stared at Greg's face, noting the scratches and his swollen lips, the bandage on his head. Finally, he left Greg's side and returned to his wife.

"Carolyn," Art said, "that is Greg. And he is dead."

Then Art and Carolyn Smith stepped away and walked to the hospital chapel, where they sat together, pleading in silence for the wisdom to understand the most horrific day of their lives.

EIGHT

A Feeling of Death

THE FOG LIFTED AT dawn, revealing a crash site that looked like a moonscape: flat, gray, otherworldly, cratered, and nearly impossible to reach. Debris was strewn around the wreckage and in a trail leading down to the ravine: A UE letter jacket. Broken seats and belts. First aid kits and luggage. The purple banner with call letters WUEV that Marv Bates draped over his broadcast table was submerged in a muddy puddle. Bags filled with clothes, shoes, and equipment lined the railroad tracks. Great chunks of the jet were scattered across the field, a wing here, the fuselage there. The nose of the plane was buried so deep in the soft turf that it had to be pulled from the muck with earth-moving equipment. The stench of charred human flesh hung in the air. Investigators sifted through the remains of the jet, from big sections that remained intact, like the tail, to the miniscule components of the wings. Once the last remnants of the fires had burned out and the threat of explosion subsided, the investigators climbed gingerly into what was left of the blackened cockpit, where they found the last two bodies: pilot Ty Van Pham and James Stewart, the owner of National Jet Service. Van Pham, who had flown in the South Vietnamese military before immigrating to the US, was burned beyond recognition. The bodies were dragged from the wreckage, placed in black rubber bags, and transported to mortuaries, first by railcar and then by hearse.

Classes had been canceled at the University of Evansville. The student union was empty. Signs at Carson Center, where Bobby Watson had ended practice in disgust less than forty-eight hours earlier, advised that wrestling practice was postponed, the gym was closed, and the building was locked. The previous night, hundreds of students had filled Neu Chapel, the university's neo-Gothic cathedral, consoling each other with hugs and praying silently at the altar. Some stayed up till the first slivers of muted daylight appeared, watching the news and holding vigils in dorms and fraternity houses. At 6:00 a.m., a group of bleary-eyed boys sat dumbstruck in the lounge at Moore Hall, where they'd spent the whole night in numb confusion.

"You just can't take something like that to bed," one said.

By 11:00 a.m., students, faculty, and townspeople began lining up on the yellowed grass outside the slate-and-limestone chapel for a memorial service that wouldn't start until noon. More than a thousand people, twice the chapel's capacity, came to mourn. They passed through the vaulted entrance and filed into pews, some carrying wreaths of flowers. They sat under the high-arching wooden ceiling, filling every row. When the pews were full, they stood in the aisles, and when the aisles were full, they squeezed into the lobby or waited outside on the steps. Inside, a choir dressed in purple robes stood high up in the loft at the back of the chapel, accompanied by the mournful music of a pipe organ. Ministers of all faiths took turns at the pulpit, leading the stunned and sobbing congregation in prayer. Wallace Graves looked as if he hadn't slept. Arad McCutchan's face was a portrait of grief. Thornton Patberg, who had stayed on campus long after midnight to call the families of the dead, encouraged listeners to remember all that the team had done for the university.

"These men," Patberg said, "were instilled with pride and a sense of Christian worth that permeated the entire institution."

Classes resumed two days later. But the funereal mood had emptied the campus, and the lecture halls were less than half full. The energy and anxiety that typically marked final exams were absent. Professors set aside lesson plans and mundane exam prep to address the existential questions. In a business class that had included three of the players, the instructor showed a film about the fear of the unknown. Faculty called for the cancellation of finals. But it didn't matter. Many students had already left, skipping classes to go home to their families. An economics professor compared the campus to a morgue.

"There's a feeling of death here," one student said. "I think we should get away as quickly as possible and try to begin again after the holidays."

The hearse carrying Mike Duff's body slowly made its way through the narrow streets of Eldorado on a bright Friday afternoon, passing shuttered businesses and flags flying at half-staff, past the town drugstore, not far from the outdoor court where he'd played in the summer. Finally, it pulled up to the gymnasium where the most memorable moments of his brief life had unfolded. This is where he dropped thirty-seven on Metropolis High School, breaking Eldorado's season scoring record the night Joe B. Hall came to town. This is where he'd signed autographs for the elementary school kids, where everyone in the city came to see his wondrous skills and speculate on where they might take him someday. Friends carried his casket inside and placed it along the sideline, near midcourt. It was 1:00 p.m., an hour before the funeral, and already nearly three thousand people filled the stands, a great cross section of family and friends, coaches and players from other schools, and mourners who only knew Mike and Kevin from the newspapers. Kevin's casket arrived a half hour later, carried by former Eldorado High School teammates. The Duff and Kingston families sat in folding chairs on the court, near the caskets, each of which was decorated with vases of flowers, wreaths of chrysanthemums, and a basketball. Players from the current Eldorado team, dressed in purple and gold jackets, sat behind the families. At midcourt, Ernie Simpson sat stone-faced next to Bob Brown, who wept throughout the service. Children who once sat on the gym floor to watch Kevin and Mike play, took seats in the stands, fidgeting in their church clothes, sad and confused.

The funeral commenced at 2:00 p.m. and included hymns by the Phelps Brothers Quartet: "O What a Sunrise" and "How Great Thou Art." Father Clyde Grogan, who had been the priest at Mike's church, urged mourners to consider all that the two young men had given them, rather than what had been taken away.

"We gather here not just because they are dead, but because they lived," he said. "They've been part of us. Helped us to laugh, to have dreams, and even to get into arguments, all the complexities that we call life."

When the service ended, pallbearers carried the caskets outside and placed them in the waiting hearses. A dual procession several blocks long snaked through downtown until the hearses reached the intersection of State and Locust, where they separated, taking Mike and Kevin to different cemeteries.

Bob Brown stayed behind, inconsolable, lingering near the Eldorado locker room. Two of his former team managers stood with him, holding him up. The two young men had been so close to Mike and Kevin that, rather than having to choose between one burial service or the other, they skipped them both altogether.

———

Bobby Watson was laid to rest at Forest Lawn Gardens, a rural cemetery near Pittsburgh. Seven men lowered his flag-draped casket into the ground on a sunny hillside next to his father's. Deidra Watson wept quietly as the minister delivered a eulogy to 175 mourners.

"God has hold of his hand," the minister said, "and He will never let go."

But it was Weenie Miller, Watson's coach at VMI, who asked the question that hovered over every memorial service, every funeral: "You've just got to wonder," he said, wiping tears from his eyes. "Why?"

It was a question with no answer. In a deeply religious community like Evansville, faith informed our understanding of a confusing world, the mysteries we confronted every day, and the existential questions of life and death. When we couldn't grasp the answers to these questions, we attributed them to God's plan because we believed that He had a plan for all of us. And yet, in the days after the crash, it felt as if God had abandoned us. We couldn't understand the horror, couldn't fathom the random brutality, the infliction of unendurable pain and suffering. Hadn't we been faithful? Hadn't we tried to live by the virtues of kindness, humility, sacrifice, and all that He asked of us? How could a merciful God allow this?

The ministers tried to make sense of it, at dozens of funerals that stretched from Evansville to Indianapolis; Colorado Springs; Cincinnati; Goldsboro, North Carolina; and small towns throughout Indiana: Tell City, New Albany, and Munster.

On the same day that Mike and Kevin were laid to rest, Bob Hudson was buried at Park Lawn Cemetery in Evansville. After a graveside ceremony, mourners returned to their cars and drove across the street to Holy Rosary Catholic Church for the funeral of Jeff Bohnert. The church would host a service for UE comptroller Charles Shike later in the day. At Alexander Funeral Home on Evansville's east side, hundreds turned out for separate services to celebrate the lives of Marv Bates and Mark Kirkpatrick. Bates was buried at Oak Hill Cemetery. An hour later, Kirkpatrick was buried a few yards away.

University officials and the three assistant coaches fanned out across the country to attend funerals and comfort families. Stafford Stephenson attended services for Bryan Taylor in Tell City, Mark Siegel in Indianapolis, and Kraig Heckendorn in Cincinnati. He joined more than sixteen hundred people at a Goldsboro auditorium for the joint funeral of Warren Alston and Barney Lewis. "There were no eulogies," Goldsboro High School principal Patrick Best said afterward. "Their lives were their eulogies."

Condolences poured in from across the country. Middle Tennessee State hosted a campus memorial service that drew two hundred people. Players wore black armbands with their blue and white uniforms as Head Coach Jimmy Earle read the scouting report on the Aces in tribute to the dead. President Jimmy Carter, who had been monitoring peace talks between Israel and Egypt, sent a note addressed to "Members of the University of Evansville Community":

> Rosalynn and I were saddened to learn of your tragic loss. You have our heartfelt sympathy. May each of you find comfort in the prayers and concern of those of us who share your sorrow.

The athletic director from Marshall University called Jim Byers to express his sympathy. He'd been through this before: a crash in November 1970 killed seventy-five people, including Marshall football players, coaches, and fans, when their plane slammed into a hill as they returned from a game in North Carolina.

In Evansville, striking farmers offered sympathy from the picket line. Members of the American Agricultural Movement stood in the freezing cold not far from the airport with signs that said "Can You Live on Peanuts and Billy Beer?" and "We Want Parity." One striker, bundled up in gloves and a hat, held a homemade placard that said: "God Bless the U of E Purple Aces."

Two weeks after the crash, at halftime of the championship game of the Eldorado holiday tournament, school superintendent Kenneth Walker presented Kay Barrow with Mike Duff's old number 40 high school jersey and then handed her the microphone. The stands were full, but the crowd was hushed and expectant, the silence interrupted only by scattered sobs.

"Mike would be very proud that you have retired his jersey," Kay said, standing straight and dignified. "It makes me very proud, too."

They gave her a standing ovation, and for once she knew how Mike felt on so many nights in that very gym, embraced by the good people of Eldorado, held tight in the cocoon of a small town.

Eldorado enveloped Kay and her family. The school renamed its field house the Duff-Kingston Memorial Gym and hung a plaque etched with the likenesses of Mike and Kevin. A display case in the lobby was crammed with photos, jerseys, and other memorabilia. A scholarship was created in memory of the boys. Sometimes townspeople would stop by John Barrow's doctor's office, at the front of the house on Organ Street, and show Kay their old snapshots of Mike.

But the outpouring was not limited to Eldorado. The loss was so transparently devastating that it moved strangers to reach out to Mike's family. A rival high school sent a check for seventy-five dollars to the Eldorado principal and a note that was passed on to Kay:

> Our students remember Mike from our meeting with him in the semifinals of last year's State 1A Basketball Championships at Champaign. His attitude and performance epitomize what we look for in a student athlete. He was a credit to his family, church, school, and team.

Another letter, just two sentences, was typed neatly and dated December 15, 1977:

> Dear folks:
> I have just read about Mikes [*sic*] terrible death. I don't know if we are related or not, but it strikes home, as we lost a 21-year-old boy about five years ago.
> Sincerely,
> Mr. & Mrs. T. C. Duff
> Beloit, Wisconsin 53511

Kay saved the condolence letters, placing them neatly in the scrapbooks she kept to commemorate Mike's life. On this page, a newspaper story announcing Mike's victory at the Pitch, Hit, and Throw contest for twelve-year-olds in Harrisburg. On the next, a letter from US senator Thomas Eagleton ("Mike, I was delighted to learn of your plans to attend the University of Missouri this fall!"). Certificates from Ed Macauley's Camp for Boys, where Jerry Sloan met Mike for the first time.

In the days after her son perished, Kay sent her own letter to the *Sunday Courier & Press*, expressing her gratitude to everyone who had looked after Mike, before and after the crash: volunteers, ministers, funeral directors, the university, and its students. She thanked the radio and TV stations for handling the crash with such dignity and respect. She thanked the sportswriters by name for the stories they'd written about Mike over the years, the good times they'd preserved. Mike loved Evansville, she wrote, and considered it his home. He would surely want to see a new Aces team carry on UE's long tradition of excellence.

"We always hoped and prayed that Mike would use his God-given talent as a stepping-stone to higher and greater rewards."

Quiet and somber, David Furr slid into the passenger seat of his mother's car outside his dorm early one afternoon for the drive home to Olney, Illinois. He had skipped his math exam after the professor, none other than Arad McCutchan, told him he could take it when he came back in January. But David stayed in town for a few days so he could go to the funerals, as many as he could. Now, with Christmas approaching, there was nothing left for him in Evansville. It was the middle of basketball season but all of his teammates were gone.

The drive from Evansville to Olney was ninety minutes, a straight shot on flat blacktop, nearly seventy-five miles north. David didn't say much on the trip home. But when his stepfather met him at the front door, they hugged and David wept, briefly and quietly.

Christmas was bleak. A quiet anguish hung over the whole family. It was too early for David to appreciate the wonder of his own survival, the great good fortune of his ankle injury. Making the team, it turned out, was not the life-altering accomplishment that it had once seemed. The injury is what saved his life.

But David didn't want to talk about it, at least not to Elisabeth. After he was hurt, she wanted to drive down to Evansville to comfort him. It was the purest maternal instinct. She had felt the same impulse after the crash. He was her son. Just eighteen years old. Not yet a grown man. Who could blame her? But she knew he wouldn't want her hugging him and making a fuss around all of his friends. He had always been like that, a stoic kid, holding everything inside. Byron, his little brother, was different, voluble and carefree, more comfortable opening up to their mother. Byron was smaller than David and labored in his brother's shadow before he finally decided to give up basketball. But it didn't faze him. Byron took up golf and mastered the public course in Olney. He'd play all day if he could, hanging around, shooting the breeze with the course pro. During the summer, his mom had to call the tiny clubhouse to remind Byron to come home for supper.

Byron and David were polar opposites and yet, just fourteen months apart, they were especially close. Byron understood David in ways their mother never could. They liked to hang out, unless David's friends were around. Then he'd leave Byron behind and head off with his buddies. But on December 27, when the cleaning lady arrived, they decided to get out of the house and head to Charleston, Illinois, where Olney High School would play Pana that afternoon in the holiday tournament. It would be a helpful distraction for David and, at the same time, a potent reminder of what he *hadn't* lost when Air Indiana Flight 216 went down: his brother, his friends, and basketball.

That night, Larry took Elisabeth and his sons Tim and Bob to dinner at the Elks Lodge in Olney. Not long after they were seated, a waiter approached and told Larry he had a phone call. Then Elisabeth was called from the table and she followed him. She heard the news, before Larry could get to her, when she walked into the foyer at the lodge entrance: David and Byron had been killed in a car crash.

The boys had been about twenty miles from home at 6:30 p.m. when David's car hit a patch of ice and skidded into the northbound lane of a state highway and collided with a pickup. They died instantly. The rescue crew didn't even take them to the hospital, opting instead for a basement morgue at an Olney mortuary, where Larry made the official identification. Elisabeth couldn't bear the thought of it.

She had wanted, all her life, to be a mother, to watch her sons grow up and raise families of their own. And now they had been snatched away and left to die on a cold and desolate stretch of blacktop, two good boys who would never grow into men.

───────

A team of investigators from the National Transportation Safety Board flew into Evansville within hours of the crash and traveled by train to the sodden field where Air Indiana Flight 216 had gone down. The seven investigators were members of the agency's "go team," on call 24-7 to unravel the mysteries of plane crashes across the country. They would study the plane's engines, examine the wreckage, search the site for microscopic clues, and review the work of the flight crew from the moment the plane landed in Evansville to the moment it crashed. Witnesses would provide crucial details about what they heard and what they saw. One crucial piece of evidence was missing: a cockpit recording device was not required for the flight, which meant that conversations between the pilot and copilot were lost to history.

Still, investigators had plenty of evidence to consider and quickly ruled out the most obvious causes. The crash had not been caused by the wake of the Delta jet. Neither the weather nor the performance of air traffic controllers was to blame. An autopsy of pilot Ty Van Pham showed he had been in excellent health. Investigators concluded that no one could have survived the impact of the crash, even if police and fire agencies had arrived at the site immediately. An analysis of the engines and other mechanical systems found that the thirty-six-year-old DC-3 was in top shape, despite its advanced age. National Jet Service, which bought the aircraft in 1976, had a sterling safety record.

The first crucial clue turned up just five minutes after investigators arrived at the site. After sloshing through the muck, one investigator stepped up to the right wing, which had been torn from the rest of the plane. Amid the wreckage, he spotted a small piece of equipment called a gust lock in the mud. On DC-3s, pilots had to manually insert gust locks on the right wing and the tail to hold them in place and steady the aircraft while it was on the ground. But if pilots didn't remove the locks before takeoff, the plane would be nearly impossible to steer safely. Witnesses who saw the plane lift off provided another important clue. The jet's unusually slow takeoff, with its nose pointed skyward, suggested a weight imbalance.

After tests on the gust lock and an analysis of the jet's contents, investigators pieced together a series of mistakes that doomed the flight even before it got to Evansville. Because the aircraft was three hours late, the crew hurried through the boarding process and tossed nearly all of the bags and equipment into the back of the plane, leaving the tail dangerously overloaded. First Officer Gaston Ruiz also miscalculated the weight of the passengers by two hundred pounds, which meant the plane nearly exceeded the maximum weight for takeoff. The gust locks that were placed on the right wing and rudder when the plane landed weren't removed before it took off. This limited the flight crew's ability to safely maneuver the plane. The roaring engines that witnesses heard shortly before the plane went down indicated that the pilots may have been trying to guide the aircraft by revving one engine and then the other. That tactic, however, would have limited the plane's power to accelerate and remain airborne. So the pilots changed direction and headed back toward the airport, perhaps for a crash landing. But because the plane didn't have enough power to make the turn, it stalled in midair and crashed into the rain-soaked hillside.

The final investigation report, released in August 1978, included an analysis of similar crashes and detailed measurements to determine the plane's speed, weight, and flight path. But one calculation served as a concise summary of the doomed flight: investigators concluded that Air Indiana Flight 216 had been airborne between 72 and 82 seconds.

On a Sunday afternoon, Wallace Graves stood at a podium draped with ferns, surveying a crowd of four thousand at Roberts Stadium. In a dark suit, bending slightly toward the microphones, Graves slowly recited the names of the passengers who had died five days before.

"They are now with God."

Amid the funerals and memorial services, the thoughtful and deliberate pace of campus life was replaced by a raw anguish. Sleepless, Graves hopscotched from one crisis to the next, huddling with alumni, students, and administrators to address questions unfathomable just a week before. How does the university prepare its budget now that its comptroller is gone? Should the holiday tournament be canceled? How do you replace Bob Hudson, the very heart of the athletic department?

But the most daunting question of all, the one with no simple answer, enveloped the city in a bleak uncertainty: Where do we go from here?

The future of the basketball program was the most pressing issue. There was some discussion of creating a new team, featuring current UE students, to play out the rest of the schedule. But after discussions with the assistant coaches, Graves abandoned that idea and the season was canceled.

"We didn't want to do anything that would be a travesty—without dignity—an embarrassment to the university or anyone else," Graves said later. "To think about being supported game after game after game by sympathy seemed almost too horrible to contemplate."

Instead, Jim Byers dusted off the résumés of coaches who had initially applied to replace McCutchan and reassembled the hiring committee. Stephenson and Simpson added their names to the list. With this, the University of Evansville took the first tentative steps toward putting all of the pieces back together.

The solemnity at Roberts Stadium that day contrasted so sharply with the spontaneous celebrations that had erupted there over the years. Black-robed ministers sat behind Graves on the dais, alongside the mayor, the governor, and members of Congress. The scoreboard was turned off, the locker rooms were closed, and the hardwood basketball floor was gone, replaced by row after row of folding chairs.

Graves had experienced a fair share of suffering and sorrow in his life. In September 1944, after graduating from the University of Oklahoma and joining the army, he was taken prisoner in France by Nazi soldiers. For more than five months, he wasted away, subsisting on a bowl of soup each day. He escaped in early 1945 during a forced march and ultimately made his way back to Texas. He was twenty-three years old.

Now here he was, a few pounds heavier, his hair gone gray, peering out at friends, neighbors, and colleagues, offering words of solace and determination. Graves lacked the sweeping eloquence of the ministers and politicians behind him. But his words rang true when he vowed that the University of Evansville would emerge from the crash of Air Indiana Flight 216 better and stronger, like iron tempered into steel. A new basketball program would be built as a living testament to the legacy of Bobby Watson and his team.

"Out of the agony of this hour," Wallace Graves declared, "we shall rise."

PART II

THE RETURN OF THE ACES

NINE

Memorial

LATE ON DECEMBER 13, 1977, Dick Walters and a small entourage of family and friends commandeered several tables at Alfie's Inn, a neighborhood hangout not far from the College of DuPage in Chicago's sprawling western suburbs. Walters was the head coach at DuPage and his team had just won its ninth straight game, routing the Harper Hawks by nearly forty points. Walters was only thirty years old, with a boyish face framed by feathery brown hair, high and delicate cheekbones, and a smile so white it nearly glowed. In the previous six years at the college, he'd won nearly 140 games and a state championship. He wore the finest suits, drove a flashy courtesy car from a local dealership, and gave his players a handbook titled *P.R.I.D.E.: The Winning Edge*, an acronym that stood for pride, respect, intelligence, desire, and enthusiasm. Walters ran his two-year program like he was coaching on the hallowed ground at Kentucky or UCLA. He craved a Division I head-coaching job and he'd grown tired of waiting. Despite everything he'd accomplished at the College of DuPage, Walters watched as other young coaches took jobs he wanted for himself. Just a few weeks before, Walters had spent an evening with Bobby Watson. Watson visited the DuPage gym to scout transfers, taking a seat in the bleachers to check out Walters's players. After practice, Walters invited him to the modest little two-story bungalow on Coolidge Avenue that his parents had bought him. He introduced Watson to his wife, Jan, and the two men settled in to talk basketball near the big picture window that overlooked the front yard. It was a pleasant, if uneventful, evening. Walters had never met Watson. He liked him, though. Decent guy, eager to start a Division I tradition in Evansville.

The thing is, Walters had wanted that job. He knew it would be difficult to jump from junior college to Division I. He figured his only chance would be at a small college that hadn't won much or at a school moving up from Division II. So, before UE hired Jerry Sloan, Walters called Arad McCutchan. Mac was polite, but blunt: "There is no way," he said, "that UE will hire a junior college coach." Walters sent a résumé anyway, custom-printed on the thickest, most expensive paper he could find.

Rumors about big-name schools chasing after Walters were a rite of spring, as certain as the green buds on the sugar maples. Walters often fanned these rumors himself. It was a pattern he'd use throughout his coaching career. He'd pursue a new job, tell the media that a big school was pursuing *him*, and almost in the same breath, say he couldn't bear to leave the job he had. In March 1975, at the age of twenty-seven, he told a reporter from the *Courier*, the College of DuPage's student newspaper, that he got offers every summer from major college basketball programs. He wanted to be a head coach at a big school by the time he was twenty-eight, he said. And then he pivoted nimbly, professing his love for the college.

"I'm very happy here," he told the young journalist. "I feel I will never have a better coaching job than the one I have at DuPage."

But now he'd fallen behind his ambitious schedule. Like Watson, coaches from Division I schools visited the DuPage gym all the time, looking for kids prepared for the physical and emotional rigors of big-time college basketball. For Walters, these visits were networking opportunities. He brought the coaches home or took them out to dinner, invited them to speak at his summer camps, and encouraged them to recruit his players. In fact, the only guys he promoted more than himself were the kids on his team, sending them on to big programs and happily taking credit for their success. He worked the phone, every day, calling coaches at Michigan and Illinois and elsewhere, tipping them off about young men who'd fit their program and looking for leads in his never-ending search for a better job at a bigger school with a nicer gym. When he wasn't calling coaches, he was calling reporters. The Chicago media loved him, and Walters loved them back, always happy to oblige with interviews, sound bites, whatever they needed. In a major media market with big-league competition from the Cubs, White Sox, Bears, and Bulls, Walters drew attention to an otherwise-anonymous junior college program. He befriended reporters at the *Chicago Tribune*, the *Sun-Times*, and WMAQ-TV, young guys like Greg Gumbel who were on their way up and didn't mind devoting a few minutes to the telegenic young coach in the suburbs.

That night at Alfie's, Walters sat with Jan, his parents, and a group of boosters. The TV in the bar was tuned to the news, and Walters glanced over to check the scores. That's how he heard: a plane crash had killed Bobby Watson and his team. Amid the low hum of the busy restaurant, Walters stared at the screen in disbelief, while the people around him continued to eat and drink as if nothing at all had happened.

For the third time in less than a year, the University of Evansville went looking for a new basketball coach. As ever, Aces fans harbored high expectations, forcing the university to swat down pie-in-the-sky rumors about who would replace Bobby Watson. John Wooden? Al McGuire? Even Jerry Sloan was asked by a reporter whether he'd return to his alma mater.

"I made that mistake once," said Sloan, an assistant with the Chicago Bulls. "I see no reason to make it again."

But UE wasn't looking for a star. Fifty-five coaches applied for the job, and the eight finalists were not exactly household names. Coaches from Dodge City Community College, Southwest Texas State, Alabama–Birmingham, and Western Kentucky were among those who made the cut.

Stafford Stephenson and Ernie Simpson were interviewed for the job, and both enjoyed a measure of support from Aces fans and sportswriters. Simpson had been a brilliant high school coach in Kentucky, winning 166 games in seven years and sending top-notch recruits to Joe B. Hall at UK. Stephenson had been a graduate assistant at Wake Forest with Bobby Watson, and later coached at Wingate College, a two-year school in North Carolina. He'd grown up in small-town Marion, Virginia, the youngest of three. Now he was thirty years old, friendly, and ambitious, with a subtle southern drawl and a receding hairline that belied his youthful face. As Watson's top assistant, he knew the campus community—the administrators and the boosters and the sportswriters. He also understood what the basketball program meant to the city. He would be a sentimental choice in Evansville, a young coach who had mourned alongside everyone else. Stafford and his wife, Tess, had gone through the motions that Christmas, for the sake of their two little girls. Thornton Patberg dressed as Santa and visited their house, as he did for UE faculty and staff every year. But the holidays weren't the same. Stephenson had never suffered such a devastating loss.

Then, mercifully, December passed and the university sent Stephenson, Simpson, and graduate assistant Mark Sandy out to resume recruiting. They spent each week traveling to high school games and holiday tournaments, touching base with players and coaches who'd been on their radar before. They wanted recruits to know that UE was committed to having a competitive Division I basketball program again.

Just like before, they listed everything that UE had to offer: a storied history, a rabid fan base, and a packed arena.

Those very same assets made Evansville an attractive destination for the coaching candidates. But the job also came with twin burdens unique to UE: The next coach would have to build a team from scratch, recruiting a dozen or so players, most likely total strangers who had never played a minute of basketball together. Molding a cohesive team out of such disparate parts required patience. The bigger challenge, by far, was whipping up enthusiasm for a new basketball program while respecting the one that was lost in the fog at Dress Regional Airport. The new coach would speak at the same Kiwanis Club lunches and Jaycees meetings. He'd schmooze with the same car dealers, flower shop owners, and alumni. And he'd have to win over several thousand students on a small campus where John Ed Washington, Bryan Taylor, and their teammates had lived in the same dorms, gone to the same parties, and eaten at the same dining hall as everyone else. Bridging the gap between the Bobby Watson era and whatever came next required a deft touch and sincere humility. As it turned out, striking that balance was nearly as difficult as building a winning basketball program.

When Arad McCutchan recounted the story of that horrific December night, it began with the redheaded girl in the hallway.

At 9:15 p.m., McCutchan dismissed the students in his class on the fundamentals of basketball coaching and gathered his things, getting ready to head home. It had been an unremarkable day on campus for the old coach, like so many hundreds before.

Until he heard that redheaded girl: "Does he know?"

"They sat me down in a nearby room before telling me," he said, reliving that night for a reporter from the *St. Louis Post-Dispatch*. "But all those poor young kids—they just blurted it out."

He bounced that night from Thornton Patberg's house to Deaconess Hospital to the makeshift morgue and then, finally, home. It was 4:00 a.m., only nine hours since the crash. The chaos had turned to quiet and the depth of his loss was clear: The kids he'd recruited. Marv Bates. Bob Hudson. No one at the university knew the dead like Mac. He'd taught them or coached them or worked alongside them in the athletic department. He'd been retired from coaching for nearly ten months, but it was still his basketball program, the tradition he'd built over three decades, and now it was all gone, his life's work, scattered in a cold muddy field.

McCutchan had bumped into Hudson a few hours before the crash, and they chatted a bit about an upcoming golf trip. They'd known each other since the '30s, when they were students at Bosse High School. They'd worked side by side for decades. As athletic business manager, Hudson handled the athletic department budget and organized the annual College Division national championships at Roberts Stadium. He also coordinated travel for UE teams and often accompanied them on the road.

"I don't know of anyone who so completely worked for the good of the University of Evansville as Bob Hudson," McCutchan said.

He'd also known Marv Bates forever, since Marv was a student at Evansville College. How many times had Marv interviewed Mac? How many road trips had they spent together, whiling away the time until tip-off, talking about everything but basketball? And the players. Oh Lord. He'd promised their parents that if they turned their sons over to him, he'd take care of them like they were his own. And he did, with the haircuts, the tutoring, the popcorn, and the big sugary sodas he gave them each time they came over. But he couldn't protect them from this, and seeing their parents at all of the funerals, whispering to them with an arm around their slumped shoulders, was excruciating, the parade of pallbearers, day after day of bottomless grief.

McCutchan talked about the aftermath with his family, the horror of it. But once the initial shock wore off, he didn't wallow, not in

The riverfront in Evansville, Indiana, 1907. Courtesy of the Library of Congress

Evansville College changes its name to University of Evansville, 1967. Courtesy of the University of Evansville / Indiana State Historical Society

Future Aces coach Arad McCutchan, as a player, 1934. Courtesy of Joe Atkinson and the University of Evansville

Coach McCutchan on the sidelines, 1973. Courtesy of Joe Atkinson and the University of Evansville

Larry Humes, Arad McCutchan, and Jerry Sloan (L-R), c. 1964. Courtesy of Joe Atkinson and the University of Evansville

Jerry Sloan announces his acceptance of the Aces coaching position. Courtesy of Joe Atkinson and the University of Evansville

Bobby Watson on the sidelines with the Aces, 1977. Courtesy of Joe Atkinson and *Courier & Press* Archives / Imagn Pictures

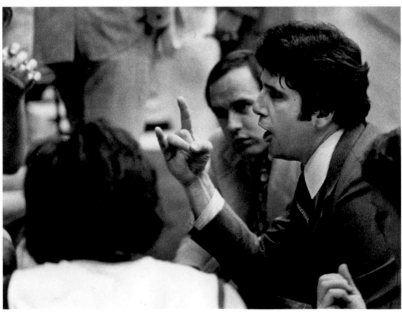

Mike Duff dominates smaller opponents for the Eldorado High School Eagles. Courtesy of Joe
Atkinson and Kay Barrow

Mike Duff rises for a shot against Western Kentucky, 1977. Courtesy of Joe Atkinson and the University of Evansville

Kevin Kingston leads the fast break at Roberts Stadium, 1977. Courtesy of Joe Atkinson and the University of Evansville

Aces guard Mark Siegel heads for the basket at Roberts Stadium, 1977. Courtesy of Joe Atkinson and the University of Evansville

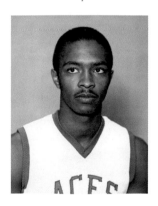

Aces guard John Ed Washington. Courtesy of Joe Atkinson and the University of Evansville

University of Evansville president Wallace Graves. Courtesy of Joe Atkinson and the University of Evansville

Tony Winburn (22), Mike Duff (40), and Steve Miller (42) during Evansville's loss to Western Kentucky. Courtesy of Joe Atkinson and the University of Evansville

Larry Bird can only watch as Mike Duff scores against Indiana State. Courtesy of Joe Atkinson and the University of Evansville

Rescue workers drag a body bag from the crash site. Courtesy of Joe Atkinson

The tail of the plane that carried the Aces. Courtesy of Joe Atkinson and the Evansville Police Department

One of many services for the fallen. Courtesy of *Courier & Press* Archives / Imagn Pictures

Retired Aces coach Arad McCutchan, in white overcoat, attended many of the funerals after the crash.
Courtesy of Joe Atkinson and the University of Evansville

The 1977 University of Evansville Purple Aces in the parking lot at Roberts Stadium. Courtesy of
Joe Atkinson and the University of Evansville

Aces walk-on David Furr (left) wasn't on the plane that crashed but was killed in a car accident two weeks later. Byron Furr (right) was killed in the same car crash that killed his older brother, David. Both photos courtesy of the author

(L-R) Theren Bullock, Eric Harris, Steve Sherwood, and Brad Leaf were among the first recruits after the crash. Courtesy of Joe Atkinson and the University of Evansville

Brad Leaf on the court, c. 1982. From UE Athletic's Twitter: "Brad Leaf lettered at UE from 1979 through 1982. He scored 17.6 points a game, leading UE to its first Division I tournament in 1982. 8th in UE history with 1,605 points, Leaf was a 3-time All-MCC First Teamer." Courtesy of the University of Evansville

Aces coach Dick Walters rebuilt the basketball program. Courtesy of Joe Atkinson and the University of Evansville

From the 1982 Evansville LinC yearbook: Eric Harris (L), Brad Leaf and Theren Bullock (T-R), and a crowd greeting the Aces after a win (B-R). Courtesy of the University of Evansville

Larry Olsthoorn and Theren Bullock greet Ace Purple. Courtesy of Joe Atkinson and the University of Evansville

Ed Siegel, whose son Mark was killed in the plane crash, in January 2014, in the documentary From the Ashes. *Courtesy of Joe Atkinson*

Kay Barrow, mother of Mike Duff, in 2015, in From the Ashes. *Courtesy of Joe Atkinson*

Lois Ford, Bobby Watson's sister, in January 2014, in From the Ashes. *Courtesy of Joe Atkinson*

Stephen Troyer, one of the first rescuers at the scene of the crash, in 2014, in From the Ashes. *Courtesy of Joe Atkinson*

public and not at home. The crash did not change him. He didn't fall into depression. He was a resilient, stoic man, farm-bred, even-keeled in every way. He leaned on his faith, talked about it with friends who'd previously considered Christ a topic fit only for church. This is how they coped, Mac, his friends, and everyone who'd been swept up in the horror of that night. This was their test and the church was their refuge.

"You know," McCutchan said softly one day, "you find when something like this happens, you realize a strength you never knew you had."

At first they seemed like an odd couple. Dick Walters was a talk-first, explain-later kind of guy, a hustler, always moving, never content. Wallace Graves made his way in the world at a more deliberate speed, as befitting a lifelong academic who was twenty-five years older.

But in the beginning, at least, they got along quite well. Walters had impressed Graves with his energy and ambition, the way he talked about recruiting and rebuilding. Junior college coaches put together a new team every season, and Walters was a master recruiter with deep contacts among high school coaches in Chicago and community college coaches throughout the Midwest. He was also young and articulate and clearly willing to pour every ounce of himself into the job. Graves knew that rebuilding would require workaholic intensity and harbored no doubt that Walters felt the same way.

UE offered Walters its coaching job in late February 1978, and he agreed to the terms of the deal over the telephone, with no agent and no negotiation. It wasn't a long conversation. He'd wanted a job at a Division I school, and now he had it. Finally, at the age of thirty.

Walters came to Evansville on February 28 and signed the contract the next day—for three years and $25,000 annually. Then he met the media for the first time, nattily attired in a tan pin-striped three-piece suit. His hair was perfect.

"I have a monstrous rebuilding job ahead of me," Walters said. "But with a great recruiting effort and the help of the Evansville community, I see no reason the program couldn't be rebuilt quickly."

Walters lacked McCutchan's hometown familiarity and Watson's military gravitas. But at that moment, he embodied everything Evansville wanted. And he said all the right things on that first day. He was a winner with an old-school coaching philosophy built on discipline and defense. He would not tolerate tardiness. When his leading scorer at DuPage was late for the team bus before a road game that season, Walters left without him and his team lost. He promised reporters that his teams would play suffocating defense and run a fast-break offense. He accepted neither long hair nor beards during the season. A young man's jersey was meant to be tucked in, even during practice. He wanted a close-knit team culture and demanded his players spend nearly every hour of every day together, in the same apartments, at meals, and at study tables.

"That's what Bobby was building and what I'll continue," he said.

Walters promised a roster with an equal mix of high school players, transfers from major colleges, and junior college recruits, including some from the College of DuPage. Bringing in his own players would give Walters a head start. They understood his expectations, his offensive strategies, the way he ran practice. Transfers would also be an immediate help. To aid UE, the NCAA waived its rule requiring Division I transfers to sit out a year once they arrived at a new school, creating an appealing opportunity for upperclassmen who'd been stuck on the bench elsewhere. In his first months on the job, Walters signed transfers from Kansas, Arkansas, and Iowa. But to build a program for lasting success, Walters knew he had to attract high school kids he could work with and develop for four years.

Walters announced at that opening press conference that he would retain Stafford Stephenson and Ernie Simpson. Stephenson was disappointed but not bitter about being passed over for the head-coaching job and soon returned to recruiting. Once his final season at the College of DuPage ended, Walters hit the road as well.

———

But after less than two months on the job, Walters stumbled upon an obstacle he hadn't considered when devising a recruiting strategy: Evansville's checkered history of race relations, its proximity to the South, and the lack of black students on campus. A Chicago-area recruit turned down a scholarship to Evansville, in part, because of low African American enrollment at the university and the city's small black population, which was about 9 percent.

In an interview with a Chicago journalist at about the same time, UE's director of admissions blamed the lack of diversity on the fact that Kentucky was just across the river and "there's still a lot of rednecks there." This assertion deeply wounded an Evansville sports columnist, but not because he felt it discredited Evansville. He found it insulting to Kentucky.

The reluctance of African American recruits to play in Evansville reflected a hard truth about the university and its hometown: more than a half century after the first black student was admitted to Evansville College in the mid-1930s, and despite a concerted effort by the UE administration, black enrollment represented a miniscule fraction of the student body.

More than a dozen black players suited up for the Aces in the quarter century before Walters took over. Black students, however, remained a small minority on campus even after Graves arrived in 1967 and promised to make changes. Graves envisioned a university that admitted students from all backgrounds and prepared them to live in a world that stretched far beyond Evansville's city limits. In the first years after Graves was hired, UE created an urban affairs program. Black professional development scholarships were given to students interested in careers in law, medicine, business, and engineering. The university said it would try to recruit seventy-five black students in 1968 and three hundred in 1969. These were ambitious goals. In 1968, enrollment included about fifty black students out of three thousand. Despite these promises, the university could never achieve the enrollment targets Graves had set. Recruiters from the admissions office found it difficult to convince black teenagers to move to southern Indiana.

Evansville's reputation almost cost Walters a second recruit that spring. Theren Bullock was a slashing forward from Blue Island, Illinois, just south of Chicago. When it came time to decide between UE and Northwestern, he worried about the lack of black students on campus in Evansville. Upon hearing Bullock's reservations, Walters asked the university's most venerated alum to reassure his recruit that basketball players, no matter their race, were treated as royalty in Evansville.

"I was happy when Jerry Sloan called me and told me that in his time there, blacks and whites were treated the same," Bullock said after he had chosen UE. "He said there may be some people who get out of hand, but no more than anywhere else."

The irony—that it took a white alum to convince a black recruit to choose UE—went unmentioned. But Bullock's commitment was a boon for Walters's fledgling program. For the next four years, Theren would be a cornerstone of Aces basketball.

———

As Walters assembled his team and prepared for the coming season, the university scrambled to contain growing resentment among the families of players who died in the crash.

An unexpected by-product of the condolences that poured in after the crash was a pile of checks and cash that accompanied the sympathy cards and letters. The university didn't ask for a penny. But fans, students, and boosters began raising money for scholarships, a memorial plaza on campus, and other rebuilding expenses. The student association collected money from the sale of bumper stickers. Indiana fans contributed $5,100 when the Hoosiers played Alabama in Bloomington. St. Joseph's College, in northern Indiana, collected $341 at its game against Montana State. Ross Theater in Evansville pledged proceeds from a showing of *The Billion Dollar Hobo*. Total strangers from across the country sent checks. Within two weeks, the university had collected nearly $60,000. Ultimately, the memorial fund totaled more than $330,000. The support was heartening for a university faced with rebuilding its basketball program from scratch.

In the year after the crash, Graves convened families of the victims for their input on how the money should be spent. But the parents of six victims—Bryan Taylor, Ray Comandella, Mark Kniese, Mark Kirkpatrick, Mark Siegel, and Jeff Bohnert—later accused the university of paying their wishes little heed. These parents hired an attorney and demanded an independent audit of the fund. It was a nasty dispute, played out in public and fueled by Graves's uncharacteristically tone-deaf argument that UE was a private institution that wasn't required to open its books to the community. Donald Moon, whose son Keith was a sophomore forward, eventually asked the university to give him the money donated in Keith's name so he could grant his own scholarships in his son's honor. UE agreed, but told Moon it required permission in writing from each donor who had given in Keith's name. Moon felt UE's letter to these donors portrayed him unfavorably. After he received about $3,000 given in his son's name, he told a reporter that UE's actions reflect a "tragic lack of sensitivity on the part of the university, particularly Mr. Graves."

Ultimately, after investigative stories about the fund-raising appeared in the *Evansville Courier* in late 1978, Graves agreed to release a breakdown of how the money was spent. It included more than $110,000 for construction of a memorial plaza on campus and only $26,000 for scholarships. The bill for the funerals was $58,000 and the cost of stadium renovations was $5,600. The university spent more than $17,000 on a bus to ferry the team to road games. But it was too small and thus used mostly to impress visiting high school recruits. Seven-foot beds for the new players and a costume for Ace Purple, the school mascot, each cost $500. Such trifling expenditures seemed disproportionate to the magnitude of the tragedy.

In an editorial, the newspaper criticized Graves for his reluctance to release details about the fund and an attitude that "smacks of imperiousness." It was an unusually public and painful rebuke for a man accustomed to unanimous support from the city's leadership class, support he had carefully cultivated for more than a decade.

Graves lashed out at the *Courier*, writing in a letter to readers that its investigation "inflicted injury to an institution which has for many years faithfully served the educational requirements of its community."

The university's response did little to satisfy some of the families, and hard feelings lingered for decades, to Graves's great dismay. The suggestion that he didn't do enough on behalf of the victims and their relatives troubled him until his death in 2011.

"I did care terribly about it all," Graves said three decades after the crash, sounding as if it had all transpired only recently.

———

The Pittsburgh Steelers touched down at Dress Regional Airport on February 11, 1978, two months after the crash. Greeted by Aces fans and a national TV crew, the Steelers stepped off the plane and climbed aboard a double-decker bus headed for Roberts Stadium, a police escort leading the way.

The Steelers' off-season basketball team, led by all-pro running back Franco Harris, had come to Evansville for a benefit game to support the UE memorial fund. The Steelers, who had won the Super Bowl in 1975 and 1976, represented the sort of gritty, blue-collar ethos that Aces fans could appreciate. Normally, the Steelers played charity games in and around Pittsburgh. But when a local judge who managed the team heard about the crash, he asked Harris whether he'd play and then contacted the university.

The memorial fund grew day by day in the early weeks of 1978, with hundreds of checks from families, civic groups, and businesses stretching from Oolitic, Indiana, to Tasmania, Australia. The Atlantic Coast Conference and the Rose Bowl committee both chipped in $10,000. Benefit concerts by the Oak Ridge Boys and impressionist Rich Little raised $15,000. But the Steelers were the biggest celebrities to lend a hand.

After a pregame meal donated by McDonald's, Harris and his teammates took the court. Their opponents: alumni from Arad McCutchan's old squads. But it was more like a circus than an Aces game, with musical guests, dancers, and trick-shot artists taking their turns on the court. The Big Red Line, cheerleaders for the NFL's St. Louis Cardinals, performed with the UE pep band. Then came a free throw competition, a Ping-Pong exhibition, and a nine-year-old dribbling whiz.

The shock that had gripped Evansville in the weeks after the Aces' plane went down had begun to subside. Classes resumed. A blizzard at the end of January paralyzed the city and provided a welcome distraction. The crash no longer dominated the evening news or the front pages of Evansville's newspapers. But the empty parking lot at Roberts Stadium on Saturday nights was a painful reminder of December 13. The buses no longer idled outside the Oak Meadow Country Club, waiting to whisk well-heeled UE fans to games. There was no socializing at halftime in the courtside seats. Fathers and sons who'd tuned in to Marv Bates's radio broadcasts had to look elsewhere on the dial.

High schools still played at Roberts Stadium, and UE hosted its annual holiday tournament at the end of December, after Southern Illinois rearranged its schedule to serve as a substitute for the Aces. But it wasn't until the Steelers arrived that the cavernous old arena felt alive again. Nearly eleven thousand fans braved deep snow, filling row after row all the way up to the bleachers. The exhibition they saw was so awful, it was entertaining, more like comic relief than a basketball game. Paunchy Aces stars from the old days huffed and puffed up and down the court in an old-timers' game featuring two alumni teams. Then, Arad McCutchan came out of retirement to lead a team of middle-aged Aces all-stars against the Steelers, a game that no one took seriously. Harold and Clyde Cox, brothers who played at Evansville College back in the day, wore Halloween masks that made them look like elderly gentlemen who'd wandered away from the nursing home. Franco Harris mingled with fans. He and his teammates, professional athletes and recent Super Bowl champs, took it easy on the home team. Final score: Aces 42, Steelers 38. Afterward, the alumni team gave each other awards for poorest sport, oldest old-timer, and least valuable player. Hundreds of kids crowded the hallway outside the Steelers' locker room, collecting autographs from Harris and his teammates. Stafford Stephenson led the young son of booster Maury King, who died in the crash, into the locker room to meet his heroes.

UE raised about $50,000 that night. But the true impact of the evening couldn't be quantified by donations or ticket sales. As Aces fans filed out of the stadium and drove home on snowy streets, it felt as if a great burden had been lifted, as if all of Evansville had taken its first steps forward.

Edie Bates, who'd spent so many nights at Roberts Stadium with Marv, soaked in every joyous moment. "Wasn't it wonderful?"

TEN

Edie

IT DIDN'T TAKE LONG for construction crews to fill up the big suburban lots around Bobby and Deidra Watson's house on Bunker Hill Court, five miles east of campus. Within months, a dozen homes were built on the flat treeless lots, two-story houses with two-car garages, long sloping driveways, and lawns so perfect and green they looked like an artist's rendering. Deidra and Bobby had planned to raise their three daughters on Bunker Hill Court, among the pioneering families that had joined them in the rural landscape of Warrick County.

But Bobby was gone, leaving Deidra and the girls to stumble along in shock and uncertainty. Deidra had enjoyed a traditional family life with Bobby. She didn't love basketball. She loved him and considered his career central to everything they did. She invited players and their girlfriends over for cookouts and holidays. She ran the house and raised the girls, especially with Bobby on the road so much. She had a daughter before she met Bobby, and making all of the decisions had weighed on her. Once they met, Bobby had eased that pressure. He was so strong, a natural leader. He filled up the house every time he walked in the door. Now, here she was, a single mom again, lonely and on her own. Deidra had appreciated the outpouring of support, from

Evansville and across the country. Nearly every day, she received letters from coaches Bobby had met over the years, veterans who had served with him in Vietnam, and former teammates at the Virginia Military Institute. It was comforting. But most of these people were strangers to her. Deidra's mom and sister—her nearest family—lived two hours away in Louisville. Deidra was private, not as naturally outgoing as Bobby. They'd lived in Evansville for less than a year, hardly enough time to develop deep, lasting friendships.

Then, early on New Year's Eve, less than three weeks after the bodies were pulled from the mud, Edie Bates called. Edie was fifty-six, gracious and warm, with steel-gray hair that framed the soft features of her face. She wore big round eyeglasses, ruffled blouses, and hemlines below the knee. Edie missed Marv desperately, mourned his loss and the end of the life they'd built, the nights she'd spent with him at the broadcast table. She had no children or grandchildren, but assumed a maternal role with Deidra and her girls.

Edie knew the holidays would be especially difficult for Bobby's family and wanted Deidra to know she'd been thinking of them. Not long after, Deidra invited Edie to her home for dinner. Later, she invited Jennifer Kuster to join them. Jennifer, Bryan Taylor's girlfriend, had stayed in Evansville to finish her nursing degree. Their dinners were sporadic and tearful at first. But the mood lightened as their gatherings evolved into a weekly tradition. The three women usually met at Deidra's house, because she loved to cook. Then she bought a piano, and Jennifer led the women—and Deidra's girls—in sing-alongs. Edie and Deidra traveled to Tell City—where Bryan and Jennifer had grown up—to celebrate Jennifer's twenty-second birthday. And when Edie was whisked to the hospital with a heart ailment, Deidra and Jennifer sat with her in the intensive care unit, an area reserved only for immediate family, holding her hands.

"I knew they would come," Edie said.

Doctors had diagnosed Edie with chronic heart disease before the crash, suggesting that she would eventually need a transplant. She and Marv had been making plans to see a specialist in Houston, and her friends feared that his death would weaken her fragile health. But it was just the opposite. Edie felt compelled to live the kind of life that Marv had lived, with the determined optimism and work ethic that drove him each time he sat down behind the microphone at a dimly lit high school football field or a cramped college gym. Marv never made it as a big-league play-by-play man. But in Evansville, he represented more than any single team or school, and Edie assumed this same role in the years after the crash. As the days and weeks passed and the initial shock faded, she drew strength from the public tributes to her late husband. When the Society of Professional Journalists honored Marv, Edie spoke on his behalf. When they unveiled a portrait of Marv during a baseball game at Bosse Field, Edie was there, taking in Marv's image with such transparent joy that it seemed as if he were standing there before her in the flesh. When the reporters needed to interview crash survivors each December, Edie always said yes, patiently answering the same questions over and over again. When the society page editor wrote a story about women challenging the stereotypes of widowhood, she wrote about Edie's transition since the crash. Edie was a fixture at Aces games at Roberts Stadium, as much a link to the program's past as Arad McCutchan and Jerry Sloan. She was elected to the UE board of trustees and joined the alumni board. When critics wondered how she could devote herself to an institution so closely associated with Marv's death, Edie didn't hesitate to put them in their place.

"I look those people squarely in the eye and say, 'Listen, the university didn't want Marv dead any more than I.' That usually ends the conversation."

On an overcast fall day in late October 1979, Edie stood at the lectern in front of the new memorial dedicated to victims of the crash. The plaza was built in the middle of campus on a foundation of bricks laid by students and other volunteers. A cylindrical fountain was flanked by two stone columns etched with the names of everyone on the plane who was associated with the university, plus David Furr. One column paraphrased the eulogy Wallace Graves gave at Roberts Stadium: "Out of the agony of this hour," it said, "we will rise." It was a solemn and fitting reminder of the city's loss.

And here was Edie, standing against a backdrop of bare trees, looking out at two hundred expectant faces. It had been less than two years since the crash, and even after all the speeches and interviews, she knew today would be difficult. This was no Kiwanis lunch. But she had taken on a new role in Evansville. She'd emerged as the walking embodiment of her hometown's resilience. With that new role came new responsibilities.

Edie gathered her strength and leaned toward the microphones.

ELEVEN

The New Aces

THE WAIT WAS EXCRUCIATING, each day melting ever so slowly into the next, anticipation building as the choking humidity of summer gave way to crisp fall days, until a Sunday morning in mid-October 1978 when Dick Walters threw open the doors at Carson Center.

The first day of practice: more than four hundred fans filled the bleachers for two sessions, two hours in the morning and two more at night. Joined by an NBC television crew, they'd come to get their first look at the team Walters had assembled out of spare parts. Sixteen young men, virtual strangers from Chicago, Indianapolis, North Carolina, California, and points in between. They each came for their own reasons. Brad Leaf wanted to start. Steve Sherwood liked the engineering school. Eric Harris appreciated the rigor of the academics. Theren Bullock preferred a small campus. Mostly they came to Evansville because they were a step too slow or a few inches too short for the big, name-brand schools like IU or Purdue, and figured they had a better chance to play. But as they sat before Walters on that first day of practice, with all of those Aces fans who'd skipped church to be there, not one of the new players could truly grasp the enormity of all that lay ahead. Walters had done what he could to shield them from it, to steer the conversation to the future and not the past.

"Today is a new day," he told his players at that first practice. "We're starting over from scratch."

From the very beginning, Walters made clear that he didn't want Evansville to wallow in the misery of the previous December. He opposed a moment of silence before games. A tribute to Bobby Watson and his team was relegated to the very back of the media guide. He ordered a redesign of the warm-up suits and uniforms because he didn't want Aces fans saying, "Oh, that's what so-and-so wore." In a regrettable interview with a television crew, he expressed his wish that something good could come from the crash, a sentiment that didn't go over well with the families whose sons and husbands and fathers had perished on Air Indiana Flight 216. It's not that Walters was insensitive. He was simply in a hurry.

"I've done everything humanly possible to make people forget," he said one day to a reporter from the *Chicago Tribune*. "It's history and you can't change history. No one can. The only thing you can control is the future."

Despite Walters's missteps, Evansville embraced its new basketball team. Season ticket sales grew from three thousand to four thousand. Membership in the Tip-Off Club more than doubled to seven hundred. A new campus group called the Purple Pride Gang signed up thirteen hundred students. An exhibition against the Polish national team—*the Polish national team!*—drew more than seven thousand fans. On Walters's first day on the job, the lead editorial in the *Evansville Press*—"Welcome, Coach Walters"—called the city and the team a true family that had celebrated and suffered together. Now, it added solemnly, Walters must carry on what Bobby Watson had started. It made clear, in so many words, that Evansville needed more than a guy with a whistle and a working knowledge of the zone press. A mere basketball coach was not enough. Evansville needed a spiritual leader, a coach who could piece the community back together, one game at a time. Walters had taken this burden on his slender shoulders, and on some days it seemed as if he might collapse under the weight.

By his own count, in those first six months, Walters lost seventeen pounds—down to 146—and got by on some nights with only a few hours of sleep. He lived like a transient, staying by himself at a booster's experimental solar house next to a country club in a swanky north-side neighborhood, with a half dozen bedrooms and no furniture. Which was fine, because Walters was on the road, three or four cities in a day, hitting the department stores for new underwear because there was no time to do laundry. He gave more than a hundred speeches and rarely ate dinner at home, even after his family moved down from Chicago.

Walters and his assistants had built the roster out of electrical tape and baling wire. They brought in a group of unheralded freshmen with long-term potential and two kids from the College of DuPage. He also poached five veterans from Kansas, Arkansas, and Iowa, making a few enemies in the process.

Iowa coach Lute Olson released two little-used subs from their scholarships so they could transfer to Evansville. But his generosity was limited. He wouldn't let go of Larry Olsthoorn.

Olsthoorn was a 6'10" center who'd started for Iowa throughout most of the 1977–78 season. He seemed like a perfect fit for the Hawkeyes, a big blond kid from Pella and a high school all-American who'd played particularly well when Iowa faced Big Ten rivals like Minnesota and Purdue. But he was also hulking and slow and handled the ball at times like he was wearing concrete gloves. When Olson banished him to the bench late in his sophomore season, Olsthoorn decided to follow his two teammates from Iowa City to Evansville. Walters desperately wanted a big kid like Olsthoorn, someone who could rebound, clog the lane on defense, and drop in a few short jumpers when the opportunity arose. But when Olsthoorn called UE to say he wanted to transfer, Walters told him to request a release from Iowa so Aces coaches could meet with him. That's when Olson got testy. Taking two reserves was one thing. But swiping a potential starter? No way. Olson was angry. And adamant, telling Olsthoorn, in no uncertain terms, to reconsider. Iowa athletic director Bump Elliott then offered a friendly reminder to Jim Byers, his counterpart at Evansville. "I only called to remind him that a school can't visit with our players unless we give permission," Elliott said. "I didn't threaten anything."

Still, he left the impression that Iowa might file a complaint with the NCAA, accusing UE of recruiting violations. So Olsthoorn—and Walters—had to wait. Two weeks passed before Olson relented, publicly questioning Olsthoorn's fortitude as he kicked him out the door.

When Olsthoorn moved to Evansville, Walters rejoiced, calling his new center "potentially the best pivotman ever to play for the University of Evansville."

It was classic Walters, a shameless mix of optimism and overstatement, and Aces fans wanted to believe every syllable.

———

On November 29, Ray Meyer brought his DePaul Blue Demons to Roberts Stadium for the home opener. Meyer was an aging huckster with a cauliflower face and a gray brush cut, the winner of 571 games in thirty-six years, and a reliable dispenser of bluster and charm. The Blue Demons had finished the previous season 27–3, and their visit made for a high-profile coming-out party for Evansville's new basketball program. The Aces lost their first game on the road to Southern Illinois by twelve. But for UE fans, that loss was like a dress rehearsal, a chance for this new collection of strangers to shake off their nerves before a proper introduction at Roberts Stadium.

The national media converged on Evansville, with more than sixty writers, broadcasters, and camera crews filling the press box and camped out courtside. But there was only one true superstar among the dozens of journalists who'd come to the stadium on that Wednesday night.

Frank Deford returned to Evansville thirteen years after he had chronicled Arad McCutchan, Larry Humes, Jerry Sloan, and their undefeated national championship season for *Sports Illustrated* back in 1965.

In the years since, Deford had established himself as one of the greatest magazine writers in the country. He didn't hang around ballparks and arenas, interviewing half-naked athletes about their batting streaks or free throws. Instead, he spent weeks and weeks with his subjects, probing their fragile psyches, searching for the soft spots, conducting dozens of interviews with family and friends. He wrote sweeping, highly stylized stories, some nearly ten thousand words long, and the writing was ambitious, almost grandiose. Three months before he came back to Evansville, Deford opened a seven-thousand-word profile of tennis star Jimmy Connors with a quote from Freud followed by a reference to "Alexander astride Bucephalus astride the globe."

"Evansville symbolizes college basketball," Deford said that night. "This may sound like a terrible thing to say because any plane crash is a tragedy. But Evansville's comeback has a little more meaning than if it had been any other team."

Deford spent many hours with the Aces and their coach, sizing up Walters as the antithesis of his predecessors at UE. Walters was a generation behind McCutchan, and several years younger than Sloan and Watson. He fit squarely within a wave of emerging young coaches who were media savvy, dressed for success, and eager to jump from one school to the next, with a detour or three in the NBA, all in search of a better job, a bigger challenge, and more money. As Bob Knight and Joe B. Hall enjoyed the best years of their careers, little-known young coaches like Walters, Rick Pitino, and Jim Valvano waited in the wings.

"College basketball coaches tend to be brash front men—vain, often foppish," Deford wrote. "And no one is more stylish than Walters:

contained, slick, earnest, handsome, and absolutely sure of what he wants . . . He knows himself. Every hair is in place, every color coordinated, everything about him is impeccable—except for one. His nails are bitten to the quick."

It had been difficult, Walters told Deford, to establish a unique identity for himself and his team in Evansville. The history of the program, memories of the crash, and the presence of two sainted coaches before him made rebuilding even more difficult than it appeared.

"On the one hand," the young coach said, "there's the legend of Coach McCutchan and his five titles. On the other, there's the memory of Coach Watson and the thoughts of what he might have done. That's been almost a JFK kind of thing."

Four hours before the game, Walters and his team gathered in the basement of the Harper Dining Center for a pregame meal of roast beef and baked potatoes. Afterward, he reviewed the DePaul scouting report with his players, the defensive assignments, how to stop the spectacular freshman forward Mark Aguirre. He skipped an inspirational speech in favor of a more subtle approach. He was eager to take his seat on the UE bench that night, excited about their shared future. But he envied his players.

"I'd rather be you," he told them. "I'd rather be playing tonight."

His ballhandling would have helped. The Aces turned the ball over thirty-two times, wilting in the face of DePaul's ferocious full-court press. UE didn't score until two minutes and twenty seconds had elapsed. The Blue Demons led 47–28 at halftime. When the Aces cut the lead to eleven midway through the second half, 9,500 UE fans erupted, hopeful, if only briefly. But Ray Meyer's team was merely toying with the Aces. The final score wasn't pretty: DePaul 74, UE 55.

While Walters was disgusted—"This was the worst I've ever had a team play"—Deford took a more dispassionate view. After all, it was only one game, one step on the long road back to relevance.

"The fans did not appear to be all that dismayed," he wrote. "Evansville has very knowledgeable fans . . . It's a basketball town, in the basketball season."

———

Jerry Leaf grew up amid the rolling hills and limestone quarries of southern Indiana. At 6′1″, he played high school ball in the early 1950s for the Bedford Stonecutters, one hundred miles northeast of Evansville. But Jerry married young and took a job to support his family, leaving behind his hopes for a high-scoring college career. Jerry and Jackie Leaf had two sons, five years apart. Greg was the oldest. But it was Brad who shared Jerry's intensity for the game. And it was through Brad that Jerry channeled all of the ambition he'd once harbored for himself. In the early 1970s, when Brad was in junior high, Jerry told him to give up baseball so he could concentrate on basketball. By then, the Leafs lived on the north side of Indianapolis and Jerry drove a forklift on the overnight shift at a Ford plant. Each day during the summer, while Jerry slept, Brad hopped on his bike and rode three miles to North Central High School, where he worked on his shot and played pickup games from 9:00 a.m. to 3:00 p.m., pausing only for a lunch break at the burger joint around the corner. Then, after Jerry woke up and the family had dinner, Brad followed his dad out to the driveway for another ninety minutes of practice. Jerry instructed Brad to shoot from several spots on the court—say, fifty shots from the right baseline, fifty from the left baseline, fifty free throws. Jerry tracked every shot, keeping detailed written records of each session. For conditioning, he ordered Brad to skip rope and mapped out a four-mile route that Brad ran through the neighborhood. And when the high school kids gathered on the outdoor court at the elementary school across the street, Jerry made sure his boy got to play, even though Brad was only thirteen. He kept an eye on the games from a lawn chair on the Leafs' front porch.

Brad did as he was told, without complaint. He loved Jerry as much as he loved basketball.

By the fall of 1976, Brad was a high school junior, 6'3" and skinny as a pole, a decent leaper with a decent shot and a knack for anticipating the trajectory of each ball as it bounced off the rim. He'd also learned how to get open shots against bigger and faster players, twisting, fading, leaning in, or stepping out to create just enough space to flick the ball toward the hoop. But he needed playing time if he wanted to attract the attention of Division I coaches, and he wasn't getting it at North Central High School. So Jerry and Jackie Leaf made a bold decision: the family would move to an apartment in a neighboring district so Brad could enroll at a new high school with a lousy basketball team.

On the day that Brad walked into the coach's office at Lawrence North High School, Jack Keefer thought, *What the hell? Why not?* He didn't care that it was the middle of the season. The school had opened its doors only a few months before and that first year there were no seniors, forcing Keefer to assemble a team from a small group of athletes with little or no varsity experience. Adding Brad might not help. But it couldn't hurt. The young coach realized soon enough that the skinny kid with the goofy smile and a halo of curly black hair had been an unexpected midseason gift. He didn't start at first. But a few weeks after Brad transferred, Keefer waved him to the scorer's table early in a game against a suburban rival and Brad scored twenty points. The next week he dropped in nineteen and then twenty-three. Keefer's team won six of its final ten games, and Brad was among the leading scorers in Marion County. The following season, the Lawrence North Wildcats finished 22–2 and Brad averaged twenty-five points a game. Coaches from low-level Division I schools started sniffing around. Texas Christian and Nebraska were especially aggressive, and Brad visited both. Evansville didn't get interested until late in the season. But once Aces assistant Gary Marriott saw Brad's gorgeous shot, he was convinced.

Holy shit, Marriott thought, *this guy can play.*

Brad didn't know much about Evansville's basketball tradition or the crash. But it didn't matter. He eagerly accepted UE's scholarship offer. It was too good to pass up. He could play immediately, maybe even start. And it was close enough that Jackie and Jerry could see every home game.

Before Leaf moved to Evansville in June, he assumed his new teammates would include a half dozen or so quality Division I players. But he realized soon enough that Walters and his coaches had put together a big and experienced team. Guys from big-time basketball schools. Two centers who stood 6'10" and two burly forwards who were 6'8". Leaf would compete for playing time against five guards and learned during the pickup games that summer inside the sweltering confines of Carson Center that several of his new teammates were quicker and more agile than he. So, when he returned to Indianapolis later in the summer, Leaf created his own boot camp to prepare for the challenges that awaited him back in Evansville. He worked out for three hours in the morning, starting at 10:00 a.m., honing his shot and jumping rope to improve his foot speed. He worked out again for three hours each night and played on a summer league team. Brad brought the same work ethic back to Evansville. His first day on campus, he wasted no time before getting into the gym.

He played well in preseason practices and scored thirty-four points in the final intrasquad scrimmage. But when the regular season began, Brad seemed to vanish, playing in only five of the first sixteen games for a total of twenty-six minutes. Walters believed he wasn't quick enough to play point guard or tall enough to be an effective shooting guard. Plus, he was a plodding defender on a team defined by its defense. For Leaf, it was a demoralizing start to a season that had once held so much promise. As December turned to January, he thought about quitting. The Leafs racked up triple-digit phone bills to soothe his disappointment. Jerry called Brad nearly every day, encouraging him to stick it out. Jack Keefer assured him that his moment would come.

Brad wasn't alone in his despair. The first two months of the 1978–79 season were ugly. The Aces opened with five consecutive losses, winning their first game by a point at Murray State on December 11. Three players had quit by early January because they didn't get enough playing time. Walters complained bitterly about the referees, claiming officials favored Aces' opponents because they didn't want to be accused by other coaches of being soft on the poor school recovering from a plane crash. He was grouchy at home with Jan and the kids and weary of scrutiny from UE fans who thought they could coach his team better than he. They booed him when the Aces played a four-corners offense and booed him some more one night when he grabbed center Barry Weston and pulled him off the court. They also sent him mail, about thirty letters a day. Some correspondents included diagrams of plays. Others sent hate mail full of vitriol for the young coach from the big city. Walters had little patience for his detractors.

"Somebody ought to throw a bucket of water in their face and wake them up," he said. "Their kind of support we don't need. They can stay at home and watch Bugs Bunny."

Clearly, the honeymoon had ended.

Walters also told a reporter that he got fan mail from young women who didn't know he was married and wanted to meet him. True or not, it was a curious tidbit to share with a newspaper. Walters was a handsome guy, almost pretty, and there had always been whispers about his personal life. The whispers occasionally grew loud enough, Walters says now, that UE boosters pulled him aside and asked him to explain. "Nothing but gossip and lies," he told them.

Jan Walters grew up on a farm outside of their hometown of Chatsworth, Illinois. They started dating in high school, and by the time Dick was hired at Evansville, they'd been married for a decade, with three children under the age of ten. Jan was utterly devoted to

Dick's career and their family. She went to nearly every game, home and away, during his last two years at the College of DuPage. She often brought the kids with her.

"Basketball is Dick's life—the one thing he's always wanted to do—and we try to be part of it," Jan said shortly after UE hired her husband. "I've always told him, wherever you go, we'll go."

But basketball took a toll on Walters's family. Dick's peripatetic work style left the five of them with little time together, especially during the season. Dick was always out recruiting, on the road with his team, or at speaking gigs. He talked often about how rarely he slept at home. When the pace slowed during the summer, Dick and Jan took the kids to the country club on Sundays, where they'd all lounge around the pool before having dinner and heading home. Dick, however, was a big celebrity in Evansville, and it wasn't unusual for UE fans to stop and chat. Walters was gracious and polite to a fault, which sometimes complicated otherwise-ordinary outings with Jan and the kids. To give the family some privacy, he had a swimming pool built in their backyard.

Jan had always been interested in art, ever since she was four, when she used pieces of wood from her father as her canvas. She had little time for herself in her first few years in Evansville. But as the kids got older, she resumed her interest in sketching and painting and enrolled as an undergraduate art major at UE. Her work included still-life pencil sketches and a portrait of Chad, their youngest. Dick was elated when Mark Tomasik, a young beat writer from the *Evansville Press*, began working on a long profile of Jan. Dick supported her passion for art and seemed genuinely proud of her sketches and paintings.

Walters knew Jan never got the credit she deserved. While he traveled on private jets and spent nearly as much time in nice hotels as he did at home, Jan raised their kids in anonymity, taking them to school and helping with their homework.

She was married to the basketball coach at the University of Evansville and, on some days, it was a thankless job.

The future of the University of Evansville basketball program made its debut on a Monday night in late January 1979, when the Aces traveled north to play the University of Wisconsin–Milwaukee.

Brad Leaf finally emerged from the fog that had shrouded his season and soon put the idea of leaving Evansville out of his mind. As the starters struggled early in Milwaukee, Walters sent Leaf to the scorer's table, and he responded with eight points to help turn a ten-point deficit to a one-point lead at halftime. He finished with thirteen, and the Aces left town that night with their sixth victory. Eric Harris scored sixteen, Theren Bullock grabbed eleven rebounds, and Walters finally got some sense of clarity about his lineup. Brad played even better three nights later in a victory over Tennessee Tech, dribbling through the defense and pulling up for short jumpers. He hit all four of his shots from the field and all four of his free throws for twelve points. As the season progressed, Leaf proved his value as a sub, consistently scoring in double figures.

Bullock built his reputation on defense. At 6'6" and 170 pounds, he was long, sinewy, and tireless, with a pterodactyl's wingspan and an intensity that recalled Jerry Sloan in his prime. Bullock grew up in Blue Island, a town of twenty-two thousand about fifteen miles south of downtown Chicago. He learned his work ethic from his father, a construction worker, and earned his nickname—Snow—because he reminded childhood friends of NFL wide receiver Jack Snow. His was the house where every kid on the block gravitated, where he played basketball with his friends for hours in the backyard, pausing only for injuries and his mother's iced tea. Theren gave up football after breaking his shoulder as a high school freshman—"My grandmother made me promise I would quit"—and grew into a star on the basketball team. He was an amiable and outgoing kid, a B-plus student who averaged twenty-one points and fourteen rebounds as a senior at Dwight D.

Eisenhower High School. He turned down a chance to play Big Ten ball at Northwestern, in Chicago's northern suburbs, because he wanted to get away from home and found UE's small campus friendly and inviting. Bullock played regularly almost from the beginning of the season. But he struggled at times. He was no longer the best athlete on the floor. The days when he could get any shot he wanted under the basket had faded into memory, as had the smaller, slower opponents who couldn't stop his ballhandling.

Of all of the freshmen, Eric Harris was the first to earn consistent playing time. He arrived in Evansville shortly after graduating from high school in tiny Washington, North Carolina, and immediately enrolled in summer classes: physics, math, and chemistry. He'd decided on a career in medicine after knee surgery in high school. He liked the doctor and he liked science and mathematics and envisioned his future as a physician. So, in addition to summer school at UE, Harris took a job as a courier at Welborn Hospital, delivering lab reports and X-rays.

"The lab reports list a variety of diseases and I can ask the nurses what they mean," he told the *Evansville Courier* that summer. "Going into different units gives me something of an overall picture of the hospital."

Late in the season, as Leaf, Harris, and Bullock settled in, the bitterness of the previous months diminished with each Aces victory. UE's improvement coincided with the reemergence of Scott Kelley, another refugee from Iowa. Kelley was 6'8" and slow, a frequent target of criticism from Walters. But once Walters stopped yelling at him, Kelley relaxed and led the Aces in scoring in the three games prior to a Valentine's Day matchup against Butler University in Indianapolis. UE had won five of its last seven, a promising streak that eased the anxiety among Evansville fans. Butler was just 9–13. But this was an important game for the Aces, on the road against a longtime rival that had beaten UE the month before at Roberts Stadium. Butler, like Evansville, was a small private school with a sacred hoops history. The Bulldogs played

on holy ground at Hinkle Fieldhouse, a fifty-year-old campus gym that
hosted the state high school basketball championships for many years
and later served as the setting for the climactic scenes in the movie
Hoosiers.

UE led by twelve at halftime. But the Bulldogs surged back, tying
the game at seventy-six with a minute to play. On their final possession,
the Aces went into a stall, whipping the ball around the perimeter, looking for a final basket that would leave Butler with little time to forge
another tie. As Eric Harris dribbled from the top of the key toward the
basket, he made a smart bounce pass to Kelley, who dribbled once and
took two long steps to the hoop along the left baseline.

Mike Blake handled the play-by-play for the television broadcast,
his ragged baritone reflecting the gravity of the moment. "Sixteen seconds . . . We're down to the nitty-gritty . . . Scott Kelley on the drive
. . . And he's got it! Eight seconds. Six seconds . . . The game is over!
Evansville has won the ball game!"

The Aces rushed the floor in a mob, hugging and slapping backs
and palms. Walters raised his arms in triumph, walking toward the
locker room, as if he had shrugged deadweight from his shoulders. Two
weeks later, UE wrapped up its first full season in Division I at 13–16.
It wasn't the .500 record Walters had predicted. But after losing its first
five games, his resilient team of castoffs and transfers had recovered to
give Aces fans hope for the future.

And in Leaf, Bullock, and Harris, Walters had discovered the foundation of Evansville's resurgent basketball program.

TWELVE

Out of the Agony

IN THE WEEKS BEFORE Jeff Bohnert died aboard Air Indiana Flight 216, his younger brother Craig decided to give up on a career in veterinary medicine and transfer from Purdue to the University of Evansville. He planned to move back in with his family during the holidays and stop by the athletic department to talk with Bob Hudson about joining Jeff as a student manager. But Bob Hudson was gone now and so was Jeff. Craig needed his family more than ever. And they needed him.

In the spring of 1978, the Bohnerts met their firstborn son's death with silence. Jeff was the oldest of four, the one Don called "our first miracle" because doctors had told Dolores Bohnert she'd never have children. The void Jeff left was obvious but unspoken. Dolores, known by nearly everyone as Dee, did her best to maintain a sense of normalcy and order for Don and their three sons, sticking to routine, moving forward every day. In an era when mothers stayed home to care for their children, Dee continued working at the phone company. She made sure the boys did their chores, that they kept the house clean, that Craig cleared the table every night after dinner, a responsibility he had once shared with Jeff. When Don decided to build an addition at the back of the house, Craig resumed his role as his father's helper, hanging drywall and sanding rough edges from the lumber, just like he and Jeff used to do. But resuming their old life provided little comfort, especially for Don.

Don was forty-seven when Jeff died, a salesman for a sanitation company who had lived most of his life in Jasper, a small town about an hour northeast of Evansville. He was an affable guy, a talker with a knack for putting even strangers at ease. He'd been doing the news on the radio in Jasper when he got a job as a reporter and weekend anchor at an Evansville TV station. In 1965, he moved the family to the east side of Evansville and joined the Holy Rosary Catholic Church. Don was a US Navy man with high blood pressure who enjoyed a drink now and then and kept his feelings to himself. He also kept his sons in line. If Dee ran the house, Don was the disciplinarian. The weekend after the crash, one of Jeff's best friends brought Craig and his brother Scott to a fraternity party at UE, hoping to provide them a brief respite from the misery of the past several days. But when Don found out, he called the fraternity, ordered his boys home, grounded them both, and dressed them down. He was angry and disgusted: How could they go to a fraternity party just days after Jeff had been buried?

Don was a devout Catholic with a black-and-white sense of right and wrong. He felt, from the very first days after the crash, that the University of Evansville wasn't being honest with the families of the victims. He was among the parents who hired an attorney to find out how the university spent the contributions that flowed in after the crash. Don suspected the money was going straight into UE's general fund. He was also angry about the memorial. He couldn't understand why the university included a globe-like fountain instead of the eternal flame the families had requested. He was angry that the plaza had been built in the middle of campus, behind the dining center, instead of near Carson Center. It seemed to him that the university had used the memorial to beautify an unattractive part of campus rather than constructing it on a spot associated with UE basketball.

Craig shared his father's bitterness, even as he took a job in the athletic department. He started that spring, working with the track team, and then took over Jeff's old job with the basketball team the following fall. He worked part-time in the sports information office and hauled uniforms and equipment back and forth to Roberts Stadium. He also occasionally traveled with the team to road games. Craig felt deeply invested in the program, as if he was carrying on Jeff's legacy.

On game days, Craig climbed up to the press box with the 16 mm camera that Jeff had used and shot game film. It was a nerve-racking assignment. Operating the camera was complex, and he wanted to make sure that Walters and his coaches got the high-quality film they needed. In early December 1978, UE hit the road for a game at Pittsburgh. The first half went smoothly for Craig. He remembered to shoot the game from a wide angle, so the coaches could get a complete view of the action. Once the second half began, however, something happened and the film unspooled, coiling around Craig's ankles. The Aces played a terrible second half and lost by nineteen, their fourth loss to start Walters's first season. Back in Evansville, Craig took the film to be developed and found that he hadn't captured a single minute of play after halftime—when he had opened the camera to reinsert the film, he had exposed the portion he'd already shot. Walters was furious. Decades later, Craig easily recalls the humiliation he felt at the next practice as Walters criticized the quality of the film in front of the whole team.

"I felt about two inches tall," Craig says. "It wasn't just one comment. It was several."

Craig also felt that Walters wanted to have it both ways when he talked about the crash. He preached over and over about the need to focus on the future, yet talked about the difficulty of rebuilding from scratch when the Aces played poorly at the start of that first season.

In early 1979, Walters got wind of Craig's discontent and called him into his office one day before practice. He could tell the young man before him was angry. He wanted to hear him out and ease the tension. Craig agreed that it was important to look forward, to try to move on from the crash. He was also struggling with dual roles, at home and on campus, navigating his family's grief while taking over Jeff's old job. Expressing his frustration to Walters helped. It was a brief conversation, maybe ten minutes, and Craig walked away impressed that the coach took time to make peace with a lowly student manager.

But Craig couldn't make peace at home and Don couldn't shake his anger. It ate at him, even as other parents had begun coming to terms with their losses. Don could no longer watch basketball, in person or on TV—high school, college, or pro. He stopped taking his blood pressure medication, complaining that it slowed him down. He also started drinking more. While Dee forged ahead, holding her family close and relying on her Christian faith, Don seemed to fade. His health deteriorated. In January 1981, he was rushed to the hospital after suffering a stroke. Craig and his family took turns keeping vigil in his room as Don slipped into a coma. He died on February 7, at the age of fifty, having never recovered from the crash of Air Indiana Flight 216, and having never forgiven the University of Evansville.

THIRTEEN

Young Man in a Hurry

AS CHAOS ENGULFED THE court in Salt Lake City, Larry Bird retreated to the bench and buried his face in a white towel, surrendering to the inevitable. His college basketball career was over. Photographers swarmed the sideline. Grim-faced coaches and trainers milled around, waiting to accept the runner-up trophy. A few steps away, Earvin "Magic" Johnson draped an arm around Michigan State's Judd Heathcoate, his rumpled and diminutive coach, and told a national television audience that reports of his departure for the NBA were nothing more than "rumors."

Bird didn't move, until a teammate stood over him. "C'mon, man, let's get that trophy," said forward Brad Miley. "Thirty-three and one. A hell of a year."

Michigan State beat Indiana State for the NCAA championship on March 26, 1979, and it was clear already that these two young men—Bird and Magic—had outgrown college basketball. This game was a transformative moment, every bit as important for American sports as the 1960 Kennedy-Nixon debates were for politics. The Bird-Magic rivalry would alter basketball at every level, from high schools to the Olympics. It transformed sports broadcasting, turned college hoops into a billion-dollar entertainment juggernaut, and resuscitated the NBA. That night, nearly a quarter of all television sets in America were tuned in to NBC's coverage from Salt Lake City, still the highest rating for any basketball game, college or pro, in history.

American sports fans clearly wanted more basketball. The following season, they would get it. On September 7, 1979, as Magic Johnson and Larry Bird prepared for their rookie seasons in the NBA, a cable-TV start-up in Connecticut broadcast its first episode of *SportsCenter*. In the early days, the Entertainment and Sports Programming Network relied on slo-pitch softball and Australian Rules football to fill the airtime. But that December, ESPN broadcast its first college basketball game—a DePaul victory over Wisconsin—with a verbose ex-coach named Dick Vitale providing commentary. The network carried twenty-three games during the 1980 NCAA tournament, and suddenly college basketball fans could count on more than a single Game of the Week to satisfy their cravings. In the coming years, the NCAA would expand its tournament from forty teams to sixty-four. The broadcast rights to televise those games would grow from $5.2 million in 1979 to $48 million three years later and $96 million in '85. Basketball would soon succeed baseball as the national pastime, changing the economics of college sports and giving small schools like the University of Evansville unprecedented opportunity. UE could play on national television. UE could play in the NCAA tournament. UE could restore Evansville's proud reputation as ground zero for small-college basketball.

Dick Walters had a choice seat that night in Salt Lake City, directly across from the Indiana State bench. It had been a month since Evansville's season ended, and Walters had cause for optimism. UE was no longer a mom-and-pop program, isolated in the southwest corner of Indiana. In its first full season in the top tier of college basketball, the Aces boasted a respectable record of 13–16 and a schedule loaded with the best teams in the country. Two schools in the Final Four—Indiana State and DePaul—had played the Aces at Roberts Stadium in the span of three days early in the season. While the DePaul game was an utter disaster, Walters saw his team's potential in the loss to Indiana State.

In December, Evansville fans had packed the stadium for their final look at Larry Bird in a powder-blue Indiana State uniform. The Sycamores led by a point with twenty-nine seconds remaining when Bird snatched a game-saving rebound on a missed free throw. He finished with forty points, leading Indiana State to a 74–70 victory. Although Walters complained bitterly that Bird had climbed over a UE player's back to grab the rebound, he was proud of his young team.

"Much as I hate to lose," Walters said afterward, "I've never been prouder of a team. I think we made thirteen thousand friends, the way we played tonight."

After the 1978 season, Evansville's move to Division I seemed prescient, just in time to reap the benefits of college basketball's explosive expansion. The move had paid off handsomely. Attendance at Roberts Stadium for the 1978–79 season was nearly 112,000, surpassing 100,000 for the first time in seven years. Ticket sales grew in each of the following four seasons.

Skeptics remained in Evansville. But soon Walters and his team would prove them wrong.

When Walters summoned Steve Sherwood to his office after the Thanksgiving break in 1979, Sherwood feared the worst. He'd fractured an ankle during the holiday break, playing with a buddy at their high school gym. He limped into Walters's office at Carson Center, assuming the coach was angry that he'd injured himself.

Sherwood already felt discouraged. As freshmen classmates Leaf, Bullock, and Harris cracked the starting lineup, Sherwood barely played his freshman year. His two free throws at the end of a blowout win over Tennessee Tech were a rare bright spot. And because he was a walk-on, he and his parents had to shell out $4,800 a year for tuition and housing. Steve chipped in with money he'd saved as a kid, cleaning carpets, mowing lawns, and washing dishes. But he was running out of cash. And at home, in northern Illinois, money was tight. Sherwood grew up the fourth of five kids in rural Crystal Lake, northwest of Chicago. His mother, Anita, earned a modest living in an elected position in local government. Archie Sherwood, his dad, did carpentry for a small local construction company. When construction work slowed, the family income suffered.

As a high school senior, Steve averaged twenty points and fifteen rebounds a game. He also made excellent grades. A couple of small colleges recruited him. But he didn't like their engineering programs. He turned down an appointment to West Point because he didn't want to join the military. He asked the coaches at Valparaiso University, in northwestern Indiana, whether he could play there as a walk-on. But they told him it was doubtful. Then a family friend put Sherwood in touch with a UE grad in Crystal Lake who called Walters on Sherwood's behalf. The coach invited him for a visit, and Sherwood flew down with his mom the next day, on their own dime. He handed the coaches film from his high school games and toured the campus with the dean of the engineering school. When Sherwood returned to Walters's office, the coach told him he saw raw potential and offered him a spot on the team with no scholarship and no guarantee he'd ever get one.

Sherwood moved to Evansville in June and took a job with a roofing company for $6.60 an hour. He and Theren Bullock rose for work at 3:30 a.m. and spent their days hauling five-gallon buckets of tar heated to 450 degrees that would be used to seal new roofs, where the temperature soared as high as 130. The roofing job ended that summer. But Sherwood enrolled for seventeen hours of classes in the fall term, leaving him little time for anything other than basketball and sleep. Making the transition from high school to college had been more difficult than he imagined.

Now he was nearly halfway through his sophomore year, hobbling around on a broken ankle and worried about money. Sherwood got a $1,200 annual grant through the engineering school. But it wasn't enough to cover his expenses. He considered borrowing money or playing for Indiana State University–Evansville, which fielded a Division II team. But Sherwood loved UE and its engineering school. He had also embraced an unlikely and high-profile role at the end of the Aces bench, as an animated, fist-pumping reserve, the first to greet his teammates on the sidelines during a time-out. Fans roared their approval on the rare occasions when he entered a game. The newspapers wrote feature stories and ran photo essays about him. Sherwood had found a home at the University of Evansville, and he didn't want to leave.

In the coach's office, Sherwood took a seat facing Walters, bracing himself for the coach's wrath. But, to his surprise, Walters wasn't angry about his ankle. In fact, he told Sherwood how much the coaches appreciated his hard work and admired the improvement he'd made since coming to Evansville.

Then Walters gave the walk-on a scholarship, erasing all doubts about Sherwood's future with the Purple Aces.

———

Late in the second overtime of a mid-December game against the University of North Carolina–Charlotte, Theren Bullock raced from beneath the basket in three giant strides, stopped at the free-throw line, and called for a pass. Eric Harris put up a shot instead, and Bullock drifted backward toward the baseline, watching the play unfold in front of him, following the ball with his eyes, moving into position. He gathered himself, leaped high with his right arm extended, and tapped the errant shot off the backboard. As it slipped through the net, a defender bumped him from behind and Bullock headed to the free-throw line. He calmly sank the shot, giving Evansville a four-point lead. As the

buzzer sounded a few moments later, the Aces walked off the floor
with a 79–75 victory in the University of Louisville's annual holiday
tournament. North Carolina–Charlotte had been to the Final Four in
1977. Louisville would win the national championship just four months
later. Before a crowd of fifteen thousand, Evansville's victory felt like an
NCAA tournament game.

"This is where we belong," Walters said afterward, expressing his
fondest hope as indisputable truth. In reality, Louisville had invited
three weaker teams to serve as cannon fodder, guaranteeing two sell-
outs and two easy wins. Schools from across the country, including the
University of Evansville, operated their holiday tournaments the same
way. But if Walters believed UE belonged among the greatest teams in
the land, why quibble over the details? Even the skeptics agreed that
the Aces were on the rise.

The victory over UNC–Charlotte marked the Aces' fifth win in
six games to start the 1979–80 season. Two weeks later, at the end of
December, Evansville's record stood at 9–2. Local TV stations had signed
on to carry eight to ten games that season. And in January, UE began
play in the Midwestern City Conference, a new league that included
Butler, Xavier, Loyola of Chicago, Oral Roberts, and Oklahoma City.
Playing in the MCC provided UE with new opportunities for money,
media attention, and postseason play. The MCC included three big-city
markets—Chicago, Indianapolis, and Cincinnati—and the potential
for regional and national television deals. The first conference tournament was scheduled for Roberts Stadium at the end of the 1979–80 season, a financial boon for UE, which still relied on basketball to fund the
entire athletic department. Perhaps most important, the MCC champion would eventually receive an automatic bid each year to the NCAA
tournament. Walters, as ambitious and media savvy as any coach, had
pushed hard for the creation of the conference.

But he always wanted more. More TV coverage. A nicer locker
room. Better housing for the basketball players. His ambitions reflected

his philosophy that style and substance need not conflict. Excellence need not be limited to the playing floor. His basketball program would be every bit as impressive as his suits. Building a top-tier program required amenities that UE lacked.

Walters lobbied for every upgrade imaginable. He commissioned redecorated locker rooms at Roberts Stadium, with plush purple carpeting, a new stereo system, and full-length mirrors surrounded by lights. Players relaxed on new recliners and drank Pepsi provided by the local distributor. UE purchased a purple van to ferry recruits to and from the airport. An advertising firm donated eight billboards that said "Welcome to Evansville, Where Basketball Is King." Five championship banners were hoisted to the rafters at Roberts Stadium. UE played in Florida and Hawaii, trips meant to entice recruits and boosters alike. The Aces stayed at nicer hotels on the road.

But in Evansville, the Aces lived at Franklin House, a ratty old three-story brick building owned by the university and located across the street from campus. Three players shared each of the five two-bedroom apartments, which included a bathroom, a living room, and a kitchen. With peeling paint and fading carpets, it looked like typical student housing. Walters wanted to replace it with something more . . . *comfortable*. He envisioned a new house near campus with a whirlpool, a steam room, a film room, and study space, all swathed in plush purple carpet. The front lawn would feature an Ace Purple statue spouting water. He also called for a new court at Roberts Stadium, because the old one had too many dead spots. "Get rid of the wooden bleachers," he suggested, "and add more padded seats." Kentucky's Rupp Arena, he pointed out, had twice as many seats as Roberts Stadium.

"Sometimes I'm impatient," he said one day, outlining his plans for conquering college basketball. "We've come a long way in the rebuilding process. But to me it seems like we're moving at a snail's pace. I want to run with this thing."

One luxury that Walters couldn't provide his players was chartered air travel, which made for longer road trips. The Aces now flew commercial, which meant they left Evansville the night before the game and returned the day after. It wasn't convenient, but it was nonnegotiable.

Still, Walters wanted to rebuild Evansville's program every bit as much as the most rabid Aces booster. He wanted to give UE fans what they so desperately wanted: a basketball team to restore their civic pride. So Walters asked the university for everything and then some. He certainly held up his end of the bargain. The Aces finished 18–10 in 1980. With Evansville's weak schedule, its respectable record wasn't nearly enough to qualify for the NCAA tournament, or even the National Invitation Tournament. But UE's momentum was palpable and Walters had begun competing with Top 20 schools for top recruits. He was obsessed with Kenny Perry, a long, lean southern Indiana boy with a smooth jumper. He battled Missouri's Norm Stewart—just like Bobby Watson!—for the services of Richie Johnson, a point guard in a power forward's body. He also snagged a slender, multilingual 7'1" center from Istanbul named Emir Turam.

But in stark contrast to Arad McCutchan, Walters's ambition wasn't limited to the University of Evansville. Mac had waved off other schools that came to him with more money and a bigger recruiting budget. He wasn't going anywhere. Aces fans appreciated his hometown loyalty and rewarded him with utter devotion. Mac was one of us. Even Bobby Watson, the outsider, expressed his devotion to Evansville. In his very first press conference, Watson promised that he'd stay at UE "as long as you'll have me." That evening, the *Evansville Press* splashed Watson's quote across six columns at the top of its sports page. Evansville wanted a coach who was absolutely, unquestionably committed to the city and its basketball team. In the eyes of the Aces faithful, UE was not a stepping-stone. It was a destination.

Walters, however, liked to keep a fresh résumé on hand at the end of the season, when big schools snapped up promising young coaches from their smaller rivals. But instead of networking quietly behind the scenes, he negotiated in public, happily sharing the latest opportunity with any reporter who cared to listen. He couldn't keep his ambition to himself. This did little to endear him to UE fans.

In April 1979, not long after he'd finished his first season at UE, Walters told Evansville sportswriters that Oklahoma State University had pursued him aggressively. Oklahoma State flew Walters and his wife down for the weekend, wined and dined them, and then offered a contract worth $38,000, with $12,000 from television appearances, about double what he made in Evansville. If it had been a mere $7,000 or $8,000 more, Walters said, he wouldn't even have considered it. But double his salary? Well, he felt he owed it to his family to at least listen to such a generous offer. Sometimes, Walters said, he heard about coaches making $15,000 more than he did, and it made him wonder about his own value on the open market. But, he added quickly, money isn't everything. So he turned down the offer from Oklahoma State to stay at UE.

"Evansville is just going to have to put up with me for a few more years," he said, "and yell and scream whenever I make substitutions or run a four-corners offense."

A year later, he assured UE fans that he wouldn't apply for the vacant job at Purdue.

"I'm very happy here," he said. "I'm not looking to leave Evansville."

———

Walters's style—brash and bratty—rankled some of UE's old-school fans. From early on, they pegged him as a big-city coach who drove expensive cars and wore flashy clothes, an outsider who was the hero of every story he told, eager to exploit Evansville for his own gain.

"Just because I wear three-piece pin-striped suits, everybody thinks I'm a big-city person," Walters complained a few weeks before his first game at Roberts Stadium. "And because I coached in suburban Chicago, they associate me with that area . . . I doubt there's anybody in Evansville more country than I am."

In fact, Chatsworth, Illinois, was a farm town of thirteen hundred about ninety miles southwest of Chicago. Chatsworth was a slice of small-town Americana on the Illinois prairie. In Chatsworth, Barry Goldwater beat LBJ, and young men raised families on a single income from the clay tile factory or the screen door manufacturer. When Walters was a boy, Main Street was a busy shopping district and the railroad cut through the center of town. There was a movie theater but no public pool. There was a lovers' lane southeast of town. But when it rained, the road got too muddy and nobody parked. The kids didn't smoke marijuana, and the boys who drank beer kept it to themselves. For fun, Dick and his friends rode their scooters on old country roads all summer long. Many of Walters's classmates lived on nearby farms. But Dick was from Chatsworth proper, the son of Gladys and Albert Walters.

Gladys and Albert had grown up in the Depression and, as Walters tells it, endured their share of hard times before he was born. At one point, to make ends meet, they washed eighteen-wheel semitrucks for a quarter each in the middle of bitter Illinois winters. Albert fumbled around as a young man, starting a TV repair shop and then an auto repair shop next door. His family's fortunes rose in the mid-1950s when Albert bought a local car dealership. By Chatsworth standards, the Walters family was well-off, and Dick's parents indulged their son well into his adulthood. Their daughter, Pat, Dick's only sibling, moved out when he was a boy, and Dick grew up basking in his parents' attention like an only child. Albert put up a basketball goal above the garage on the side of their house and installed four three-hundred-watt lights so Dick could play at night. He spent hours and hours under those lights, even in the winter, wearing warm gloves on frigid evenings.

Dick ran track and played football at Chatsworth High School. But basketball was his obsession. He played for four years and earned letters as a junior and senior. In the 1964–65 season, Dick played guard and wore number 40. He handled the ball well and scored consistently from fifteen feet. He wasn't the fastest Bluebird. He was smart, though, and played solid defense because he anticipated each pass and shot like a grand-master chess player. Even as a teen, he showed flashes of the intensity that would carry him to Evansville, politely challenging the referees on questionable calls.

In the senior class prophecy in the back of the 1965 Chatsworth yearbook, Walters's classmates predicted that Howard Diller would be the mayor, Darla Dehm would be an attorney, and Warren Shafer would fly airplanes. For Dick Walters, the class prophecy wasn't too far off the mark: his school friends pegged him as the coach of a fictional basketball team called the Arabian Nights.

———

Kenny Perry was a southern Indiana kid, nearly seven feet tall and painfully shy. It seemed on some days that every coach in the country wanted a piece of him, and they wore out the roads leading to Rockport, making their pitch, hoping for the best. UCLA was especially aggressive. With John Wooden retired, the program was no longer the dominant force in college basketball. Still, the Bruins were one of the top teams in the country and UCLA coach Larry Brown wanted Kenny Perry. So he invited Perry for an official visit to the UCLA campus in October 1979, and the kid from Rockport returned with starstruck tales of his encounters—real or imagined—with Kareem Abdul-Jabbar, Wilt Chamberlain, and one of Charlie's Angels.

Dick Walters couldn't muster the same star power. But he wanted Kenny Perry more than Larry Brown.

He wanted Perry more than any kid he'd ever recruited. Walters believed Perry would transform his basketball program, attracting a long line of blue-chip recruits. So he adopted a strategy that coaches from far-flung schools couldn't match. He lavished Perry with personal attention, making the thirty-five-minute drive to South Spencer High School dozens of times. He presented Perry with a petition signed by UE students, urging him to play for the Aces. Busloads of Tip-Off Club members crowded the bleachers for South Spencer games. Walters invited Perry to his home, where they shared a bowl of popcorn and talked about the future.

"I didn't put any pressure on him," Walters said afterward. "I just want to become such a close friend of his that it will be impossible for him to look me in the eye and say no."

At 6'10", with a lithe frame and a feathery touch from twenty feet, Perry was overwhelmed by all of the attention. Hundreds of colleges sent letters and brochures, filling nearly five laundry baskets. Bob Knight drove down from Bloomington to charm Perry's parents. Missouri's Norm Stewart, who lost out on Mike Duff three years before, made a hard sell. Larry Brown and his assistants visited Rockport over and over. Coaches from Kentucky, Louisville, Georgia, Michigan State, and Tennessee scouted games and practices. South Spencer coach Mitch Haskins, who'd been a college recruiter before coming to Rockport, sat down with his star player and sorted through all of the mail. Perry narrowed the list to twelve schools, and Haskins sent a letter to coaches, laying down the rules: All contacts start with the South Spencer coaching staff. Recruiters could visit practice only with permission. No personal contact was allowed in the fifteen minutes following a game. Postgame visits were limited to ten minutes. Eventually, Haskins had to send a second letter, notifying coaches that personal contact was forbidden and practices were closed. That didn't stop a few enterprising recruiters from calling Perry's house, claiming that Haskins had given them permission.

Walters relished the competition. He loved recruiting every bit as much as he enjoyed practices and games. Ultimately, every recruiting trip was a sales job. And Walters was a master salesman. He couldn't compete with the Charlie's Angels and Wilt Chamberlain. But Perry was a southern Indiana boy, and Walters didn't intend to lose him to Larry Brown or anyone else.

At 5:00 p.m. on February 28, 1980, five weeks before recruits could sign a National Letter of Intent, TV crews, newspaper photographers, and sportswriters gathered in the South Spencer gym. After Haskins introduced Curran and Joyce Perry, Kenny's parents, he summoned the young man from a side entrance to deliver a brief, carefully prepared statement. Kenny, with prematurely thinning hair and a wispy mustache, strode onto the court in a three-piece suit. He hated public speaking. But Haskins had refused to read the statement for him.

"After many months of careful consideration," Kenny said, "I feel it is my best interest and the interests of those very close to me that I attend the University of Evansville and play for Coach Dick Walters next season. Any questions you might have will be answered by Coach Haskins or my parents. Thank you."

Walters watched the press conference on TV, exulting in his victory. He called it "one of the brightest days in UE history."

Hyperbole aside, Perry's commitment was a shot over the bow, an unmistakable warning to opposing coaches: Walters would bring the best local players to Evansville. In the fall, Perry would return to UCLA wearing a University of Evansville jersey.

FOURTEEN

Where Basketball Is King

BRAD LEAF AND THEREN Bullock were best friends and polar
opposites, with games as different as their personalities. Despite
their contrasting styles, though, they shared a single-minded drive to
make UE basketball matter again. Walters named them cocaptains in
September 1980, at the start of their junior year, and the team quickly
coalesced around them. There were clear signs of a resurgence at UE.
But the Aces remained a small-college curiosity in national basketball
circles. That didn't faze Leaf and Bullock. They were true believers, dead
set on leading UE into the Top 20 and the NCAA tournament. After
that, who knows? The Final Four? Bullock, in particular, harbored no
doubts and his attitude rubbed off on Leaf and their teammates.

The cocaptains approached their leadership roles from opposite
directions. Leaf left the pep talks to others, preferring to let his maniacal work habits speak for him instead. Bullock, on the other hand, was
UE's den mother, its spiritual leader. He counseled underclassmen worried about playing time and called team meetings when the Aces played
poorly. After games, he greeted little kids waiting for autographs like
long-lost friends. Occasionally, his intensity got the best of him. Walters

kicked him out of practice once when he faced off against Kenny Perry
after an errant elbow.

"I'll knock your head off," he shouted at Perry.

But Bullock's intensity didn't sour his relationships. He was also
the Aces social director, hosting marathon beer-fueled backgammon
tournaments and poker games. His teammates trusted him, following
his lead, no questions asked.

"If we're playing lackadaisically," Leaf said, "he gets us off our butts.
If he says something is wrong, it must be wrong or he wouldn't say it."

When Bullock got excited, he spoke in superlatives, every sentence
ending in a line of exclamation points. He was often chosen to meet
with out-of-town reporters writing about the revival of the basketball program. He told them he liked to stop at the memorial as he
walked through campus and always considered Mike Duff, John Ed
Washington, and all of the rest as his teammates.

"Sometimes," he said, "I talk to them because they know what's
happening and this is for them, too."

But he also wanted to change the perception of UE's basketball program. Bullock had grown weary of playing for a small-town underdog.

"Whenever I tell someone I play for Evansville, the first thing that
comes into their mind is the plane crash," he said. "I want to change
that so they say, 'Evansville? Weren't they 24–4 and in the NCAAs last
year?'"

On a humid afternoon in September 1980, Emir Turam landed at Dress
Regional Airport following two days of travel from Zagreb, Yugoslavia,
with stops in London, Boston, and Chicago. Turam was UE's first
international recruit, a 7'1" nineteen-year-old from Turkey who spoke
flawless English. His arrival was big news in Evansville. When Turam
stepped off the plane, accompanied by Dick Walters, he found two

assistant coaches, two television crews, two sportswriters, and a new teammate waiting to greet him on the tarmac. He did his first interviews before he'd even made it inside to the terminal.

"Is this all for me?" Turam asked, wide-eyed, astonished to find himself a celebrity in a town he'd never visited and a country he'd never seen.

Gary Marriott, a UE assistant and one of Walters's first hires, accompanied Turam from Boston and introduced him to sophomore point guard Murray Lendy.

"You must be nice to Murray," Marriott told him. "He's the one who passes you the ball."

Turam didn't miss a beat. "He must be nice to me," he replied, "or I won't remember him with the rebound."

Turam was quick and agile, a prolific shot blocker who played for Turkey's top amateur team, averaging nearly twenty-four points in an international tournament that summer. He'd caused barely a ripple among American recruiters. But Turam had made a name for himself on the youth basketball circuit in Europe. Along with Kenny Perry, he gave UE two bona fide Division I big men. He also gave Walters's program a certain cachet in an era before international players made their mark on American basketball. In fact, the UE coaching staff had never seen Turam play before he came to Evansville and he'd never been to the United States. UE recruited him through the mail, with the help of Evansville's miniscule Turkish population.

Marriott first heard about Turam when he was an assistant coach at Wyoming. A Turkish student came to visit the coaches' office one day to talk about his friend Emir, the basketball player. The language barrier posed a problem, and Marriott showed little interest until the young man told him that his friend was over seven feet tall. Thus began a three-year recruiting effort that continued once Marriott came to Evansville in 1978. He wrote to Emir on a regular basis, and Turam responded by sending along clippings about his play from Turkish newspapers, which

UE students translated for the coaching staff. An American friend who played with Turam told Marriott he was a smart kid and a good shot blocker with a soft touch around the basket. Emir was also a good student who spoke German and French, in addition to English. His father was a German-born attorney for a major bank, and his mother was a British-born English teacher.

Ali Akin, a gastroenterologist from Istanbul who lived in Evansville, visited Turam on behalf of the UE coaching staff. Akin and his wife had dinner with Turam and his family, reporting later that UE's newest recruit needed to gain weight if he hoped to hold his own against American big men. Kentucky had also expressed interest in Turam. But when Wildcats basketball came up during dinner, Akin changed the subject.

"I told him about the Aces and their five national championships," Akin said when he returned to Evansville. "I didn't explain they were all in Division II. But then, he didn't ask me."

A few weeks after he'd retired in 1977, Arad McCutchan took a seat next to his old friend John Wooden, the only college basketball coach who'd won more national championships. The "Wizard of Westwood" had retired two years before but remained one of the most recognizable faces in the game, with a thatch of graying hair parted precisely on the left and eyeglasses perched on his prominent beak. McCutchan, on the other hand, looked like everyman: unfashionable black glasses, only a few wisps of dark hair atop his head, and a face that formed a V at the tip of his chin. Two old coaches, friends for three decades, passing the time with a pleasant chat. The only distraction was the line of fans and autograph seekers waiting for a brief audience with Wooden, bypassing the amiable and anonymous fellow sitting next to him.

"But finally," McCutchan recalled with delight several years later, "one youngster approached us and held out his program for me to sign, not John. That was one of my greatest moments."

The basketball programs the two men left behind would never recapture the national dominance they'd enjoyed when Wooden and McCutchan were at their peaks. But by late 1980, when the Aces traveled to Los Angeles in mid-December to face UCLA, the Bruins remained among the elite. UCLA was undefeated and ranked third, nine months after losing to Louisville in the previous season's NCAA championship game. For UCLA, UE was little more than an early-season speed bump, a final chore before leaving for Tokyo to play a team of Japanese all-stars. The Bruins were favored to beat the Aces by twenty-one.

For UE, however, the glamour of a trip to UCLA was intoxicating. A luxurious hotel. An afternoon at the beach. And then on to the hallowed ground of Pauley Pavilion, ancestral home of Walton and Kareem, the pinnacle of college basketball. In their dispatches back home, Evansville sportswriters marveled at the weather. Kenny Perry recalled his star-studded recruiting visit. Several Aces out for a walk stumbled upon a TV crew shooting an episode of *Solid Gold* and performed an impromptu dance routine to a Donna Summer song as the cameras rolled. The crowd on the sidewalk gave them a round of applause. This sort of thing didn't happen when UE played in Terre Haute and Peoria.

UCLA players were pampered in ways the Aces could only imagine, with luxuries that left Brad Leaf in awe.

"We saw them come into the hotel," Leaf recalls. "They're all driving these really nice cars, these college kids. This was a whole other world."

The Aces kept it close, but lost 69–62. Perry called it a moral victory. But the score wasn't the point. The game reflected Walters's aspirations for the program. It was a powerful recruiting tool, certain to impress small-town kids from Indiana and Illinois. It made the boosters happy, providing a select few with a forty-eight-hour respite from the December chill of southern Indiana. It was also a measure of how far the UE program had come in less than three years. Playing a midwinter game against DePaul in Chicago was one thing. Traveling to Los Angeles to face UCLA was something else entirely. In fact, Walters was so eager to get on UCLA's schedule that he agreed to play the Bruins in LA despite UCLA's refusal to reciprocate by coming to Roberts Stadium the following season. Walters had previously declined to play Kentucky in Lexington because the Wildcats didn't want to play in Evansville in return. But he'd always been drawn to Southern California, and he admired Wooden. While he was at the College of DuPage, Walters once flew out to visit Wooden on his own dime. He joined the coach for lunch at Wooden's favorite neighborhood lunch counter, savoring every moment.

Walters revered older coaches and enjoyed a warm relationship with Arad McCutchan. Mac vowed at his retirement that he'd keep a polite distance from the program so Bobby Watson could create a team in his own likeness. But in Evansville, Arad and the Aces were like a single entity that couldn't be separated. He continued to teach for several years after Walters arrived and later did commentary on UE television broadcasts. On the road, Walters invited him to practice the night before the game and they'd sit in the bleachers together, two coaches from two generations talking basketball. Walters absorbed criticism from every corner of the community, but always appreciated McCutchan's support.

"He was wonderful," Walters recalls, "a perfect gentleman."

———

When Jimmy Carter sat at his Oval Office desk on a Sunday night in July 1979 and told a national television audience that the United States suffered from a "crisis of confidence," it sounded as if he was speaking directly to the people of Evansville. At the turn of the decade, the city was a microcosm of the nation's limping economy.

In the midst of a faltering presidency, Carter had initially planned to speak to the country that night about the energy crisis. As he prepared to face the nation, Carter spent ten days talking with business leaders, labor chiefs, teachers, private citizens, mayors, and governors. He came away from those meetings believing the country needed more than a point-by-point plan for energy independence. He realized that the problems the United States faced were far deeper than the country's dependence on foreign oil.

"I want to talk to you right now about a fundamental threat to American democracy," Carter said during his somber thirty-three-minute address. "The threat is nearly invisible in ordinary ways. It is a crisis of confidence. It is a crisis that strikes at the very heart and soul and spirit of our national will."

In Evansville, the response to Carter's address was tepid. Dairy farmer Lee Riggs wasn't impressed with the president's speech or the fuel efficiency proposals that followed.

"The best thing the government can do for me," Riggs declared, "is to leave me alone."

Carter had never been especially popular with Evansville voters. Despite long-standing union support for Democrats, the political climate in the city had moved toward the center in the 1970s. Mayor Russell Lloyd was a moderate Republican, and in Vanderburgh County, Gerald Ford beat Carter by four points in 1976. When Senator Edward Kennedy campaigned for president at the Whirlpool Local 808 headquarters four years later, he told the union workers that Carter didn't care about the working class. That November, Carter lost Vanderburgh County to Ronald Reagan by nine points.

Evansville reflected the nation's mood. That summer, service stations closed on the weekends as their fuel supplies ran low. Striking truckers protested rising diesel fuel costs. And in February 1980, nearly forty-two hundred members of Local 808 again filed into Roberts Stadium to vote on a Whirlpool contract that union leaders told them wasn't enough. Many who raised their hands in favor of the deal recalled the fear and uncertainty of the strikes in 1971 and '74 and decided to cut their losses and accept a raise of thirty-five cents an hour. After peaking at nearly ten thousand in 1973, the hourly workforce at Whirlpool now totaled half of that.

Elmer Hall ignored his misgivings and voted "yea" that day, the first time he had ever supported a contract offer from Whirlpool. He felt like he had no choice.

"You can't beat them," he said afterward.

The new contract wasn't enough to slow the spiral at Whirlpool. Two months later, amid high interest rates and sagging new home construction, the company cut production of refrigerators, freezers, and dehumidifiers at the plant near the airport. Union employment that year fell to forty-one hundred and continued to decline, one year after the next.

Elmer Hall was right. You can't beat them.

FIFTEEN

A Coach Reborn

IN EARLY 1980, BARELY two years after his son had perished near Dress Regional Airport, Ed Siegel rode the school bus with his Marion County Championship Pike High School basketball team as an escort of fire trucks and police cruisers led them back home. When they reached the Pike parking lot, Ed hustled his boys through the winter chill and into the packed gym, where they were met by the pep band, cheerleaders, and an electric wall of noise. The players filled a row of chairs at midcourt as Siegel grabbed the microphone. He was forty-eight years old, portly, and graying, savoring this moment and beaming at the boys who had restored his passion for coaching. He introduced each kid, from the starters to the youngsters at the end of the bench, detailing their individual contributions to Pike's success. David Gadis was a senior, and he'd never seen his coach so happy.

When David was a freshman, in the final weeks of the 1977 season, Ed called him up to practice with the varsity. It was a singular honor for an Indiana kid, like a rookie being summoned to a big-league base-ball club in September for a brief chance to prove his worth. David guarded Mark Siegel every day, challenging him even as he tried to emulate his game. Mark told his dad that David was the quickest kid he'd played all season. After Mark graduated, David took over at point guard, leading Ed's team with the same natural poise and confidence Mark had always shown. Ed rode his ass in practice. But David never flinched. He understood. The coach and his point guard had come a long way together.

During that awful Christmas break after the crash, David and four of his teammates paid Ed a visit. When Carmen Siegel opened the door and led them into the den, they found her husband sitting in a rocking chair, shrunken and diminished beneath a blanket, one of the only times in their lives they had seen him quiet. Pike had postponed two games after the crash, and Ed hadn't returned to practice, leading his players to fear he would quit. They sat with him for an hour that day, told him about what he'd missed, and asked him to come back: "We need you." Ed thanked them for stopping by, for coming to the funeral, and said he'd think about it. But he wasn't sure. He'd spent so much time with Mark in the Pike gym, so many evenings in the car after practice, talking basketball as they headed home, passing the strip malls on the west side of Indianapolis. How could he face those painful memories, day after day? Ed visited his pastor and prayed for guidance. He decided, after a few weeks, that Mark would want him to keep coaching. When Ed returned to the bench in early January 1978, Pike High School retired Mark's jersey—number 14—in a pregame tribute.

For Ed, the two years that followed Mark's death were steeped in anger and despair. It started in the first days after the crash, when he couldn't get a straight answer about whether the university would pay for Mark's funeral. The Siegels joined other families who hired an attorney to press for answers about UE's burgeoning memorial fund. Ed sobbed during his testimony before the Indiana legislature, arguing that a state law limiting compensation in wrongful death suits was archaic and unfair. He recounted the anguish of cleaning out his son's dorm room and finding Christmas presents Mark had bought for Ed and Carmen.

"My son at nineteen years old, with the tremendous potential that was ahead of him—you're trying to tell me my son was only worth $4,500? Is that all his life was worth—$4,500? That's hard for a father to swallow."

In the months after the crash, Ed needed to know every detail of that night. He wanted to know what it looked like in that muddy field, what the rescuers discovered when they reached the smoldering remnants of the plane. Early in 1978, as the weather grew warmer and the days longer, Ed drove his family down to Evansville so he could get a good look at the crash site. He visited with Dr. Stephen Troyer and his wife, Lois, who had treated passengers at the scene soon after the plane went down. From the Troyers' backyard, Ed and his younger son David climbed down to the edge of the airport property. Walking the soft soil and taking in the view of the ravine where the plane broke apart and burst into flames filled the gaps in Ed's imagination and provided him a fleeting sense of peace.

But basketball is what saved him. It gave him such joy to see David Gadis and his teammates grow and improve. Ed had changed, too. Rather than let his assistants take care of the hands-on coaching, as he had done for years, Ed spent more time demonstrating what he wanted from his players, the proper stance on defense, a fluid release on a free throw. He didn't scream at them as much and accepted mistakes more readily. After more than three decades as an educator, Ed Siegel returned to Pike High School as a better teacher. That season, David Gadis was a sophomore point guard, leading a green team with more potential than talent. Pike struggled. But Ed knew David could play Division I basketball and convinced him that by the time he was a senior, Pike would be one of the best teams in Indianapolis. Ed also knew that the obstacles David and his teammates would face went well beyond turnovers and missed free throws.

One day he warned his players that their upcoming game in Franklin, a small town south of Indianapolis, was likely to get ugly. Three-quarters of his players, including David and his younger brother Mack, were African American, and Ed told them to expect a hostile crowd shouting racial epithets.

"They will call you every name but the one your mama gave you."

Ed instructed his kids to maintain their composure and represent their families and Pike High School with dignity and respect. Also: kick Franklin's ass and point to the scoreboard on the way to the bus. Ed's predictions were prescient. Fans brought signs and jeered at David and Mack and their teammates, screaming racial slurs.

"Go back to the ghetto!"

David heard it, but paid no heed. He led Pike with twenty-four points and hit two free throws with a minute left to seal the game. He and his teammates played just as Ed had instructed, ignoring the taunts, focusing on basketball, escaping Franklin with their pride intact and another notch in the win column.

By David's senior year, Pike was a deep and experienced team. Three starters had returned, the top three reserves were veterans, and Mack was already making a name for himself as a sophomore. David was one of the top guards in the state, pursued by recruiters from Louisville, Oklahoma, Southern Methodist, and other big schools. David led the Red Devils that season, making the perfect pass, scoring the crucial basket. In the semifinal game of the Marion County tournament, as the first-half clock ticked toward zero, David heaved a shot from midcourt to give the Red Devils a lead they never relinquished. The following night, after Pike won the championship, David and his teammates celebrated on the bus during the half-hour ride home, dancing and singing in the aisles. When the bus stopped near the Pike campus, the players crowded into the front for an unobstructed view of the fire trucks and police cars that would escort them the rest of the way to the Pike gym, where their classmates and families waited.

The rally that night was Ed's gift to his players, a grand gesture for fulfilling the promise he saw in them three years before when David Gadis was just a freshman, matched up in practice against the cherished point guard he would soon replace.

SIXTEEN

Rivals

WHEN LOYOLA UNIVERSITY TRAVELED from Chicago to Evansville to play the Aces in early 1982, eleven thousand UE fans booed Darius Clemons each time the public address announcer uttered his name and then cheered for each of the three fouls he committed. The boos didn't rattle Clemons or his teammates. Brimming with confidence, Loyola boasted a lineup studded with elite talent. Clemons was a fearless, whippet-quick point guard who grew up on Chicago's south side and forever played in the shadow of Mark Aguirre and Isiah Thomas, two of the greatest players in the city's history. He'd made a name for himself in Evansville two years before when he stepped to the line late in a close game, encouraged booing Aces fans by waving his arms—*Bring it on!*—and then sank two free throws to seal the victory. Although he scored less as a senior, Clemons led the nation with ten assists per game. Wayne Sappleton, a 6'9" senior center, led the nation in rebounding with fifteen a game, to go along with twenty-one points. Alfredrick "the Great" Hughes was a well-regarded freshman. All three were considered NBA prospects. The Ramblers played a simple, free-flowing offense. The first guy with an open shot usually took it.

The Ramblers considered themselves tough city kids, raised on Chicago's playgrounds. They considered Evansville a hick town. The Evansville newspapers played up the rivalry, dubbing Loyola a "glamour team" and labeling Clemons as Public Enemy No. 1. One reporter wrote about how much the sports information director from Loyola admired Clemons for overcoming the poverty of his childhood.

"For him to get where he has is a credit," the SID said. "He's a ghetto kid who didn't get caught in the jungle by crime or drugs."

Beneath the racially coded story lines, the rivalry was more complex than any in college basketball. The animosity between the Ramblers and the Aces was real, and it flared up on several occasions in 1982. But Clemons and his teammates also knew that when they came to Evansville, the Aces played with the weight of the city on their backs, with an intensity that Loyola didn't see in other teams, an urgency absent from other arenas.

"Their mission was beyond basketball," Alfredrick Hughes says. "We definitely knew they were playing for something bigger."

Evansville had finished the 1981 season 19–9, having drawn 127,000 fans to Roberts Stadium, more than any team since 1966, the apex of the McCutchan years. Walters was deeply disappointed that they didn't receive a bid to the National Invitation Tournament.

But UE entered the 1981–82 season awash in optimism, for good reason. Brad Leaf and Theren Bullock were seniors and cocaptains, poised for their best season yet. Richie Johnson, a 6'9" sophomore transfer from Missouri, seemed as if he could play any position on the floor. Rick McKinstry was a long and lean transfer from Clemson expected to contribute off the bench. And this year, for the first time, the winner of the Midwestern City Conference tournament would receive an automatic bid to the NCAA tournament.

But to get there, UE would have to beat the Ramblers three times in three gyms in six weeks, relying on the kid the old sportswriters called the Towering Turk.

The summer of 1981 had been long and lonely for Emir Turam, with late nights alone at Carson Center, shooting over and over, working out his frustrations on the rim. It was a steady routine, 350 shots each night, every night. He dunked, worked on his footwork in the paint, and practiced midrange jumpers. Emir had a key to the gym and let himself in at all hours. Walters stopped by his office once at 10:30 on a Sunday night and found Turam shooting, consistent as a metronome. When Emir wasn't shooting, he was running. When he wasn't running, he was eating. He lived that summer a block or so from campus with Dale Campbell, a railroad engineer and old friend of Arad McCutchan's who'd rented rooms to players over the years and fattened them up with pork chops, burgers, fried chicken, and banana milkshakes thickened with protein powder. If anyone needed fattening up, it was Emir. At 7'1" and 215 pounds, he was built like a Popsicle stick. His goals that summer were gaining weight and building muscle. On Mondays, Wednesdays, and Fridays, he headed downtown to lift weights at the Pit, a haven for muscleheads who began their workouts with primal screams and ended them by vomiting. Turam didn't exactly fit in among the Pit's typical clientele. But he didn't miss a workout because he couldn't bear to endure another season like the one that had ended in March.

Turam realized, a few weeks after his arrival in Evansville, that he'd have to adapt to the American style of play. It was nothing like what he'd grown up with in Turkey. In pickup games at Carson Center, Emir got knocked around under the basket. His new teammates were faster and more physical than players he'd faced in Europe. He couldn't simply rely on his height to dominate other players.

Once the 1980–81 season started and he tried to play more aggressively, he found himself in foul trouble. The officiating frustrated him. He'd get confused in practice and question coaches when they gave him instructions: "Why?" Walters thought at first that Turam was a smart-ass, but realized after a while that Emir wasn't joking around. He was an inquisitive kid, trying to learn the game from a new perspective. Once, on the day after Christmas, Walters lost his patience with Turam during a listless practice and kicked him out of the gym. Emir said later that Walters had misunderstood. He didn't have a bad attitude. He'd been sick. Once he'd recovered, Turam returned to practice with renewed vigor and played his best games of the season in the UE holiday tournament, with fifteen points and five rebounds against Akron. Turam walked off the court to a standing ovation that night. But the celebration was brief. Kenny Perry usually started at center, and Emir played less and less as the season wore on. Gary Marriott recalls a sensitive kid, easily discouraged by his coach's criticism. When Walters yelled at him—"You're 7'1" and you're jumping like you're 5'1"!"—Emir would shut down, giving minimal effort, which angered Walters even more. The upbeat, confident teen who found the media waiting for him on his first day in town was gone, replaced by an uncertain kid who couldn't understand what had happened to his game.

"I'm playing nowhere like I'm capable of playing," he said one day after practice. "I'm three of thirteen from the free-throw line. Why should that be? There's no difference in the baskets."

Marriott tried to help. He knew Turam responded to praise and worked with him one-on-one during practice. Turam was a lefty, so Marriott helped him develop his right-hand moves: layups, jump hooks, baby hooks. Nearly every day, just the two of them. He boosted Emir's confidence, praising his progress and encouraging good work habits. He told him that if he wanted to get a big contract in Europe or the NBA, he'd have to work harder. Marriott also invited Turam to his house, out by the airport, for dinner with his family. As Gary fired up the grill, his kids and their friends from the neighborhood crowded around their enormous guest, asking Emir about Turkey and his accent. Turam also made friends with a half dozen Turkish students at UE and with Ali Akin, the Turkish physician who had visited him in Istanbul before he arrived at Evansville. Emir desperately missed his parents and siblings. The cost of international travel was prohibitive and a three-minute phone call was ten dollars. So Turam cut out articles from the Evansville newspapers and mailed them home. His family sent him huge packets of Turkish newspapers. They were usually a few weeks old by the time they arrived. But Turam read every one of them, front to back. Academically, his transition to the US was a breeze. He'd grown up in a family that prized education, and he loaded his schedule with economics, math, algebra, and physics classes. It took him fifteen minutes to do his homework most days. So when he showed up at the team's mandatory study table at night, he read books and wrote letters home.

At the end of his freshman season, after averaging three points a game, Turam met with Walters to talk about his future. He was heading back to Turkey in April and wanted to know whether he should return to UE or give up on his college career. Walters was blunt. "I told him that if he went to Turkey and didn't come back for the summer," he said, "he should just stay there."

Turam came back to Evansville in June 1981, giving up a summer on the beach at home and giving Evansville basketball one more chance.

———

Eric Harris had also given Evansville basketball one more chance. And now, as his senior season approached, he had little idea what role he'd play for Dick Walters. Would he start? Would he be the sixth man? Or would he spend the year watching from the bench, wondering how his college basketball career had skidded off the rails? Of the four freshmen that Walters brought to UE for his first season—Harris, Leaf, Bullock, and Sherwood—Harris had gotten off to the fastest start and endured the most painful fall from grace, a confusing stumble from starter to sub.

Harris started at point guard for most of his freshman season, leading a team of strangers built on the fly with the quiet self-assurance of
a veteran. He averaged eight points and passed out 103 assists, a single-
season record at UE. Once Leaf and Bullock became starters midway
through the season, it seemed as if Walters could pencil all three of
them into the lineup for the next three years. As sophomores, Leaf and
Bullock made giant strides, but Harris regressed. Surgery to remove
calcium deposits from an ankle slowed him during his second year in
Evansville, as did an elbow injury late in the season. He was no longer
a full-time starter as a sophomore and averaged less than five points.
There were three games when he never left the bench. As his playing
time diminished, his relationship with Walters suffered. Complicating
matters was the fact that he'd become discouraged about academics.
Harris majored in biology and hoped to enroll in medical school after
graduating from UE. But because the Aces traveled so much, he found
it difficult to keep up with his studies. Harris had begun to doubt the
cornerstones of his college experience: basketball and academics. He
didn't talk to any of his teammates or coaches about his ambivalence.
That wasn't his style. But he talked to his parents, who encouraged him
to make his own decision about his future and promised they would
support him no matter what he chose. So, after his sophomore season,
Harris decided to transfer to Georgia and play with his high school
teammate, a high-scoring forward named Dominique Wilkins.

"I thought a change would help me," he said. "I was constantly
battling with myself. It was hard to come to a decision."

But announcing his decision to leave Evansville didn't ease his mind.
He had friends at UE. He'd been one of Walters's original recruits. He
felt obligations to his teammates and the UE fans who'd been so supportive after he lost the starting job. The pressure he'd felt in the days
after the season ended began to fade, giving him the clarity he'd lacked.
Three weeks after declaring his intention to transfer, Harris met with
Walters to say he'd changed his mind.

Walters welcomed him back but warned Harris to temper his expectations. UE had already recruited a junior college point guard to be the top backup, so Harris would be a third-stringer. Eric accepted the demotion with characteristically quiet disappointment. And then he endured an absolutely dreadful season. The low point, perhaps, had been the UCLA game at Pauley Pavilion. Harris entered late in the first half and heaved up an off-balance jumper from seventeen feet that clanged off of the front of the rim. On another possession, he was stripped of the ball, a steal that led to an easy UCLA layup. Walters pulled him out immediately and left him on the bench for the rest of the game. For the season, he played in only eighteen of UE's twenty-eight games and scored fourteen points, less than one per game. The quiet but confident kid who had directed traffic so nimbly as a freshman seemed a distant memory. He tried to use his time on the bench wisely, studying the game from a new perspective, figuring out how he would play opposing guards. He also changed his major to computer science and accounting. It wasn't exactly easy. But at least he could keep up with the homework more easily when the Aces were on the road.

Despite the heartache of the previous two seasons, Harris approached his senior year intent on preparing himself for whatever the future held. During the day that summer, he worked as a full-time intern at a window manufacturer, learning about computers and programming. At night, he lifted weights and played one-on-one with a former teammate. He also jumped rope, worked on offensive and defensive drills, and took up martial arts to improve his balance. He had not given up on his college basketball career. When practice started in October, Eric played with a sense of freedom that he hadn't felt since he was a freshman. He was on the second team during the preseason, but poured in twenty-three points during a scrimmage. That performance, combined with his understanding of the Aces' offense, convinced Walters to put him in the starting lineup for the season opener against Baltimore. It was his first starting assignment in thirty-nine

games and he didn't waste it, hitting all four of his shots and both of his
free throws, for ten points. He added four assists and three steals in an
Aces blowout. He scored sixteen the following week against Southern
Illinois and held the Valparaiso point guard scoreless on December 14,
blocking three of his shots. By early February 1982, Harris was averaging
eleven points a game and leading UE in assists. He ran the offense like
a maestro, scanning the floor, seeing plays as they developed, watching
his teammates as they moved into position, and getting them the ball
where they wanted it, where they could do the most damage.

Eric was still a serious kid, more likely to be studying than drinking
beer with his teammates. But after all of the uncertainty, after spending
game upon game on the bench, he had returned to the starting lineup,
wiser and more mature, as crucial as any player on the roster.

———

The first half of that first Loyola game at Roberts Stadium—January
23, 1982—was as ugly as expected, punctuated by trash talk and stray
elbows. But then it got worse, setting the tone for the two games that
followed.

Early on, Kenny Perry and Loyola forward Brian Liston jawed at
each other, until referees had to separate them midway through the
first half. But that was just the beginning. Referees later ejected Liston
for throwing a punch at Perry, eliciting protests from Loyola coach
Gene Sullivan, who claimed Perry started the whole thing by spitting at
Liston. No matter the details, the lingering tension seemed to embolden
the Aces. Bullock and Leaf played as if they had been preparing for the
entire season to seize this very moment. Over and over, Leaf sneaked
into the lane and drove to the rim past Sappleton's outstretched arms,
drawing fouls and draining free throws. He scored a career-high thirty-
one points, despite feeling ill late in the game. Bullock dropped in

twenty. When the buzzer sounded, the Aces left the floor with an 84–80 victory and a 13–3 record.

It wasn't a win-or-go-home game, and it did nothing to ease the antipathy between the two teams. But the victory gave the Aces a shot of adrenaline heading into the final six weeks of the season.

Afterward, Perry shrugged off the confrontation with Liston. He admitted that, yes, perhaps he had elbowed the Loyola forward. But it wasn't intentional. And he wasn't about to apologize, not in the midst of this burgeoning rivalry.

"Hey man," he said, "it was either us or them."

The next morning, the Aces traveled to Dress Regional Airport to catch a flight to Detroit for a game the following night. Walking to their gate, they encountered several familiar faces. It just so happened that Loyola was waiting for its flight home. Brian Liston headed straight for Kenny Perry, sharing a few thoughts about their encounter the night before. Perry didn't respond, and instead slipped into the middle of the UE entourage. Crisis averted.

Loyola is a Jesuit school, with a Latin motto that translates as "For the greater glory of God." Its fans, however, did not exemplify the university's idealism. Loyola would host the Aces in four weeks, and the Ramblers didn't intend to turn the other cheek.

———

For all of Evansville's success since Walters's arrival—the steady ascent, year after year, the blue-chip recruits, the national media attention—there was one glaring gap on the Aces' résumé: after four years in Division I, UE had still not beaten a big-name team or made it into the Top 20.

Earning a spot in one of the weekly Top 20 polls would be another impressive milestone in Walters's rebuilding project. But in practical terms, a Top 20 ranking had little bearing on whether UE would make the NCAA tournament. Beating a big-name school, however, would be a great leap forward for the Aces. A victory over an elite team would catapult UE into the national conversation on college basketball and bolster the Aces' case for a spot in the NCAA tournament. It would also give UE a certain legitimacy, helping Walters and his program move past the crash and its aftermath.

On February 10, UE traveled to Chicago to play DePaul. At 20–1, DePaul was ranked third in the country. The Blue Demons had won fifteen straight games and sixty-seven of sixty-eight at home. It was a dream matchup for Walters, played on his home turf and broadcast to seventeen million homes across the country on cable television's WGN.

The Aces led for most of the first half and trailed 59–58 with five seconds left and one final possession. A basket would give Evansville its most impressive win since the 1971 Division II championship game and a burst of momentum through the final weeks of the regular season. For the last shot, Walters called time-out and devised a strategy that surprised no one. On the inbounds pass, Eric Harris would look for Leaf and then Bullock, leaving the Aces' fate in the hands of its seniors. It was only fitting. But it didn't turn out the way Walters had drawn it up. On the inbounds play, Bullock slashed through the lane toward Harris but couldn't shake his man. Leaf sprinted toward Harris from the top of the key, but was smothered by DePaul guard Skip Dillard. This left Eric with only one option. After he'd looked off Bullock and Leaf, Harris spotted Kenny Perry moving out past the free-throw line with his hands in the air. He whipped a high pass that Perry caught above his head. Moving to his left, Perry took one dribble and two steps before launching an off-balance fadeaway jumper with three seconds left. It was an ugly desperation shot and it caromed off the front of the rim as the buzzer sounded, leaving Evansville with another near miss and a 17–4 record. The loss gnawed at Walters for days.

"I haven't quit thinking about it yet," he told one writer. "I can't get to sleep at night from thinking about it."

It was too late for moral victories. But the loss served as a building block, preparing the Aces for the most important games to come.

———

Alumni Gym was a relic, built in 1923 on the northwest side of the Loyola campus, not far from Lake Michigan. It was an unpleasant stop for visiting teams. Opposing players were forced to dress in the basement and climb two flights of stairs to the court. The gym was no more hospitable, with seating that nearly spilled onto the court. Sometimes players inbounding the ball had to step out of the way to let fans pass by. The stands, which included seating on a second-level track that encircled the court, held about twenty-five hundred fans whose screaming bounced off the walls in a deafening echo. Other than the court, the rest of the gym was dimly lit, contributing to an unsettling atmosphere that left visitors intimidated long before the opening tip. Loyola enjoyed an unmistakable home-court advantage at Alumni Gym. Over a period of eight days in early 1978, the Ramblers pulled off an improbable hat trick on their home floor, beating Marquette, Indiana State, and Georgetown. All three schools were ranked in the Top 15. Alumni Gym humbled even the greatest teams.

When the Aces visited on February 20, Jerry Sloan showed up to cheer on his alma mater, just days after he'd been fired as head coach of the Bulls. Sloan was one of the few friendly faces among the three thousand fans who had wedged themselves into the stands, straddling the line between fervent and hysterical. During a time-out, the Evansville bench was splashed with beer by a fan seated on the balcony above. Ramblers fans hounded Kenny Perry, waving a spittoon and peppering him with obscenities. They also doused him with a cup of water. One loyal soul, in the name of Brian Liston and all that was righteous, spat at Perry as he headed to the locker room at halftime.

Perry waited until late in the game to respond. Walters waved
him onto the floor with 1:45 left. Perry had endured a disappointing
sophomore season at UE. He'd started at center as a freshman, but
Walters envisioned him at power forward, where he could loft feathery
jumpers over smaller rivals. Perry started the first two games as a sophomore before Walters sent him to the bench in favor of the electrifying
Richie Johnson, who started at power forward the rest of the season.
But against Loyola, Perry provided a timely reminder of the skills that
had made his arrival at UE such a coup. He played that night as if he
had stumbled upon a pickup game at the South Spencer High School
gym. With the Aces clinging to a 73–71 lead, he blocked a Loyola shot,
drew a foul, and sank two free throws. He blocked another shot on
Loyola's next possession. Ramblers sub Gerry Mundt answered with
a jumper from twenty-three feet to make it 75–73 with fifty seconds
remaining. It felt for a moment like the thunderous Loyola crowd
would bring Alumni Gym crumbling to the ground. But the noise and
the pressure, the roar of the Rambler fans, the profanity, the projectiles,
the pure hostility raining down on him throughout the game, none
of it seemed to distract Kenny Perry. As the seconds ticked away on
the scoreboard clock, he maintained his cool. With fourteen seconds
left and the Aces up by four, he calmly sank two more free throws and
then grabbed a rebound on Loyola's final shot. The Aces sprinted off
the court with a victory and a 20–4 record, eliciting high praise from
their most famous fan.

"This," Jerry Sloan said, "is as good a team as Evansville's ever had."

—————

It was only practice and it was almost over. But the pressure weighed on
Emir Turam as he stood alone at the free-throw line, his teammates eye-
ing him hopefully. They'd run five lung-searing sprints, and each time
a teammate missed a free throw, they lined up for another. Now they

waited on Turam, a 58 percent free-throw shooter. When he missed, and the grumbling began, Walters interrupted to offer them a deal.

"You guys willing to gamble on Big E? I'll give Emir another chance. If he hits, just the five laps you've already got. If he misses, ten. How about it?"

Ten? It was hard to fathom ten. No one wanted to run ten. They wanted to shower. They wanted to go home. Studying seemed a better option than running ten more sprints. But the Aces were a team, tight as a fist. Theren Bullock spoke for all of them: "C'mon, Big E," he muttered wearily. "Put it in."

Turam flicked his wrist, the ball floated toward the rim and then splashed through the net. His teammates converged on him at the free-throw line, celebrating, as Turam beamed in the middle of it all, enjoying the moment.

It was not the first time Walters gave Turam a second chance, and it wasn't the first time Emir nailed it. Turam's solitary summer at Carson Center had paid off. He didn't miss a single weight-lifting session at the Pit and reported to practice in October weighing 233 pounds, about fifteen more than in his freshman season. He came in with a new attitude, as well, playing with an aggression that had been absent the previous season. He'd grown accustomed to the more physical style of American players. He'd also added some variety to his offensive game, practicing ball fakes and short jumpers, setting picks and rolling to the basket, looking for a pass. Turam had played well during preseason scrimmages and scored ten points with ten rebounds in an exhibition game. Walters had made him a starter for the opener against Baltimore on November 30. By December, Turam had proved his worth to skeptical Aces fans and before the month was out had scored in double figures four times. His rebounding had improved and his size helped make the Aces' zone defense one of the best in the country. His mere presence prompted rival coaches to change their offenses and forced shooters to alter their shots. His added muscle was evident against DePaul late in the season, when rugged all-American Terry Cummings tried to overpower him at the rim. Turam fouled him, but turned back Cummings's dunk attempt, an achievement that would have been unfathomable twelve months before.

He still struggled on some nights, hacking and bumping opposing centers who were quicker and stronger. During one stretch in January, he committed twenty-two fouls in five games, and scored a total of just seventeen points. As a result, Emir sometimes spent more time on the bench than in the game. Or he played with such timidity that rival big men battered him around the basket, scoring and rebounding at will. Wayne Sappleton, Loyola's bruising center, humiliated Turam with thirty-four points when the Ramblers visited Roberts Stadium in January. Emir fouled out after missing his only two shots. For all of his improvement, he remained a work in progress.

But when Emir felt good, after he'd hit a couple of jump hooks or short jumpers, he got confident, and when he got confident, he was hard to stop. At halftime of the Aces' third game against Loyola, he told the coaches he wanted the ball. He knew he could beat Sappleton and he wanted to prove it.

After three months, twenty-seven games, and twenty-two victories, the entire Evansville season came down once again to Loyola. The Aces and the Ramblers faced off one last time in the championship game of the Midwestern City Conference tournament in Tulsa. The winner earned a bid to the NCAA tournament. The loser hoped and prayed for an invitation to the NIT. To the rest of the world, this game was little more than a blip, two small schools from the Midwest battling for the championship of an obscure new conference stacked with a bunch of other small schools from the Midwest. But for Evansville and Loyola, this game was Ali versus Frazier III, the Thrilla in Manila, the fitting culmination of a nasty rivalry laced with genuine hatred.

For Loyola, a win would salvage a season that had nearly spun out of control. The Ramblers entered the game rejuvenated. At 17–11, Loyola had won four straight after losing to the Aces in February. Darius Clemons had rebounded. After playing poorly in the first two games against Evansville, looking to pass more than shoot and scoring just nine points combined, Clemons dropped twenty-two on Xavier to lead Loyola into the championship game. For Evansville, a victory would be another milestone in the program's unlikely revival. The Aces had improved steadily each season, from thirteen wins to eighteen and then nineteen. This year Evansville was 22–5, its best season in a decade. The Aces finished 12–1 at Roberts Stadium and filled the arena for nearly every game. This is precisely what UE fans had wanted since the first day Walters showed up in 1978, wearing that handsome pin-striped three-piece suit.

Nothing from the first two games suggested the third matchup against Loyola would be an easy one for the Aces. UE had won twice by a total of ten points, and the third meeting would be just as close.

The Aces led by three at halftime, a lead Loyola erased in the first minutes of the second period. Then Emir Turam went to work, backing Sappleton down in the paint, taking the ball to the rim, using all of those lessons he'd learned working one-on-one with Gary Marriott at Carson Center. Loyola couldn't stop him. Turam scored eight points in a four-minute stretch early in the second half, giving UE a 50–41 lead. He also blocked two of Sappleton's shots and finished with fourteen points and twelve rebounds, his best game since stepping off the plane and into the humid Evansville summer eighteen months before. The Aces danced to the locker room with an 81–72 victory. The University of Evansville—and Emir Turam—had finally fulfilled their promise. After four years of playing the plucky underdog, pushing that boulder up the hill, inch by inch, shouldering the expectations of the entire city, the Aces were headed to the NCAA tournament, college basketball's marquee event. It seemed almost like a fever dream, as if it had happened before our very eyes but was not, in fact, tangible and real. We had wanted it so desperately, and yet who among us really believed it could happen?

Dick Walters believed. Absolutely and without reservation. All of the preposterous promises he'd made—the lofty predictions, demands for better hotels, upgrades to Roberts Stadium, new recliners in the locker room, the purple van, the billboards ("Welcome to Evansville, Where Basketball Is King")—all of it led to this magnificent moment in this delirious locker room in Tulsa, Oklahoma. It could have been his moment alone, the culmination of his unceasing ambition, fuel for his insatiable ego. Instead, as his players and coaches celebrated, Walters paused to consider the meaning of the victory and all that the city had endured.

"The Purple Aces didn't win tonight," he said. "Evansville did. This one's for them."

———

The plane, an Eastern Air Lines jet, silver and blue, had begun its descent over Dress Regional Airport when the stewardess's voice echoed through the cabin. "There are two thousand people at the terminal, awaiting the arrival of the Purple Aces," she said.

And sure enough, as Steve Sherwood emerged from the plane in his letterman's jacket and peered out onto the tarmac, he saw thousands of rabid Aces fans lit by klieg lights from the TV cameras. The crowd numbered closer to five thousand, and many of the fans had been waiting for two hours—since 5:30 p.m.—in temperatures that dipped to twenty-seven degrees. Fans in the first row pressed against a waist-high fence, fathers holding toddlers aloft, decked out in purple; grade-school kids and college kids waving signs and gigantic foam fingers declaring the

Aces No. 1. Someone had handed out white caps with "Aces" splashed in purple across the front. The tarmac was so crowded that those who couldn't get outside formed a line that ran through the terminal and out the other side, to the front of the airport. Sherwood, carrying a purple travel bag, waved as he climbed down the steps, and the crowd erupted. Then came Eric Harris, Richie Johnson, Kenny Perry, Brad Leaf, and Theren Bullock, each greeted with cheers and high fives. Turam was welcomed with a chant of "E-meer! E-meer!" The players gathered around a podium, and the crowd hushed when Walters, flanked by Leaf and Bullock, stepped up to the microphones.

"This is the most heartwarming thing that's ever happened to us," Walters said. "We're very, very proud to represent you."

This brought another roar, and soon the Aces waded through the joyous crowd, signing autographs, as they hurried to vans that would take them to Carson Center.

Then, the thousands who'd come to welcome their arrival—the students, their parents, the kids in junior high, the TV guys, the newspaper reporters, and their photographers—all made their way back through the terminal and out to the parking lot, climbing into their cars and their pickups, heading home on a Sunday night. Just like that, the celebration ended in the very same place where we'd lost Bobby Watson, Mike Duff, John Ed Washington, and everyone else on Air Indiana Flight 216. We'd grieved their loss and welcomed their spectral presence at the campus memorial, at Roberts Stadium, and every year on December 13. But we put those thoughts aside that night for a few moments so we could celebrate these Aces and all the new memories they'd made for us.

SEVENTEEN

Dying Young

KEVIN KINGSTON'S BEDROOM, AT the top of the stairs in the big house on the outskirts of Eldorado, looked much the same as it did before the crash, filled with souvenirs and trinkets that only Kevin would keep. A *Gone with the Wind* poster tacked to the wall over his trundle bed. A framed *Bonanza* poster, with the faces of his friends covering the faces of Ben Cartwright and his boys: Hoss, Little Joe, and Adam. A photo featuring Kevin and a cherubic preschool boy wearing a replica Eldorado Eagles uniform, ticket stubs from Barry Manilow, Bob Seger, and Doobie Brothers concerts, eight-track tapes he'd altered by placing his own face on the cover, a black-and-white photo of Kevin in his track uniform from junior high, after he'd won the state title in the 880-yard run, his pen-and-ink drawing of Yosemite Sam, a brochure advertising the Bobby Watson Purple Aces Basketball Camp, a ticket to a speech by President Ford, elementary school yearbooks featuring photos of Kevin as the sixth-grade class president. Don and Wanda Kingston couldn't part with the mementoes that Kevin had collected, and so most of it remained where he'd left it the last time he'd been home. Leaving Kevin's room untouched gave his family a measure of

peace and comfort. Sometimes, Valery Kingston slept in her brother's
bed, holding his memory close while she could.

But after a year, those keepsakes seemed more and more like rel-
ics. Without Kevin, the room was lifeless. Valery's friends felt sorry for
her every time they walked past. So, Don and Wanda commenced a
renovation of the upstairs that they had planned before the crash. They
knocked down a wall to expand the master bedroom. They added two
small leather couches to create a sitting room, where Don and Wanda
could watch TV. They put shelves on the wall for hundreds of Don's
books. They kept Kevin's trophies and photos. But they cleaned out
his closet, giving clothes to his friends. One boy, several years younger
than Kevin, was given a warm-up suit. When the remodel was completed, the Kingstons felt as if they'd made a fresh start. Don was named
head coach of the Eldorado football team, after taking several seasons
off to watch Kevin play. He also took on the role of athletic director.
Wanda bought antiques at rummage sales and auctions, refinished them
with Don, and then sold them at flea markets. They were resolute in
remembering Kevin's sense of humor and charisma. They didn't miss
any of Valery's track meets, and when UE awarded Kevin a posthumous
degree, the Kingstons asked their daughter to accept it on their behalf.
Kevin's parents vowed that his death would not define their family. Nor
did they try to push it aside. Don and Wanda accepted that their loss
was the community's loss as well.

They grew closer to Kay Barrow, sharing a grief that friends and
neighbors couldn't fathom. Kay and Don met to review applications
for an annual scholarship given to an Eldorado High School student
in memory of Kevin and Mike. They appeared together on the night
the Eldorado gym was renamed the Duff-Kingston Memorial Gym.
Mike and Kevin would be forever linked in Eldorado, and so would the
Barrow and Kingston families.

Valery could tell when her mother struggled. Wanda didn't like
to talk about the crash and couldn't bear to imagine the terror that

Kevin felt as the plane dropped from the foggy night sky. Don was different. He was something of a Renaissance man. He'd always been intellectually curious, his shelves crammed with books on the French Revolution, English history, twentieth-century philosophy, the lives of Van Gogh, Churchill, and Hemingway. He collected dictionaries and language guides to learn French, Spanish, German, and Italian. He liked crossword puzzles, Louis L'Amour Westerns, and American literature. He was also a gifted writer, the author of *Sugar and Salt*, a slim collection of verse and essays. Many of the poems were short and whimsical, about dogs, indignant pigs, and a rabbit skipping away into the woods. The essays were folksy odes to his childhood, his family, and growing up poor during the Depression. He encouraged readers to embrace "the sweetness of life with a grain of salt."

Don confronted Kevin's death with existential questions that he turned over and over in his mind. What would Kevin be doing if he were still alive? What would he have been like as the years passed? Don wasn't a churchgoer. Valery and Kevin, on the other hand, had attended Eldorado First Baptist Church every week with family friends. When she was in sixth grade and Kevin was a high school senior, they accepted Christ as their savior and were baptized on the same day. After Kevin's death, Don started watching Billy Graham crusades on television. He sat down with Valery to talk about her faith. What, he asked her, was it like to be baptized? But most of the questions he wrestled with after Kevin died were questions that his family and friends could not answer. These mysteries led Don down the same spiritual path his children had traveled. Like Valery and Kevin, he believed that Jesus would forgive him his sins. Don came to understand Kevin's death with a new clarity. He knew now that he would someday join his charming, sweet-natured son in the world to come, and it gave him a peace that he'd never known before.

Kevin was buried in the Wolf Creek Primitive Baptist Church Cemetery, on the gently rolling hills west of Eldorado. His grave is

marked by a handsome granite stone with a small photo of Kevin at
the top and the dates of his birth and death—May 8, 1956–December
13, 1977—at the bottom. Don's love of poetry and Kevin's hometown
legacy are reflected in the four lines carved just beneath Kevin's name,
the first stanza of A. E. Housman's "To an Athlete Dying Young":

> THE TIME YOU WON YOUR TOWN THE RACE
> WE CHAIRED YOU THROUGH THE MARKET-PLACE;
> MAN AND BOY STOOD CHEERING BY,
> AND HOME WE BROUGHT YOU SHOULDER-HIGH.

EIGHTEEN

The Winning Edge

IT WAS WINTER BUT the days were warm and full of promise. So warm that Paul Ford had got to thinking about fishing. But when his conversation with a reporter turned to basketball, he paused to consider Evansville's chances in the NCAA tournament. UE was headed back to Tulsa, where the Aces would play Marquette University on March 11. Ford was a retired steelworker who lived near Roberts Stadium, and for twenty-five years he'd walked to Aces games along narrow side streets dotted with the modest homes of his neighbors. At first, he doubted the school's move to Division I, figuring UE was too small to stand up to Indiana, Kentucky, and Louisville. But the Aces had proved him wrong, and Ford had come to believe in this team.

"I told my wife she'd better make no damn plans for Thursday night," he said. "I'm going to be right there, watching the Aces. I think they'll win that game."

It was an optimism born of hope and history, and it swept over the entire city in the days before the game. The collective longing was apparent on US 41, the highway that split the town in half. The sign at the gas station said, "Go Aces Go." The Ramada Inn declared, "Aces Are No. 1." The sheriff's station near the airport: "Purple Aces Beat

Marquette." Mayor Michael Vandeveer opened his State of the City address before the Downtown Kiwanis Club by saying he wished he could be in Tulsa instead. Sheriff Jim DeGroote, who had spent hours traipsing through the muck by the airport on the night of the crash, marveled at how far the basketball program and the city had come. "I wondered if we'd ever get back to the glory days of Division II," he said. "And now, in just four years . . ."

Outside the Great Hall on the UE campus, two days before the game, an impatient crowd lined up an hour early for a rally to wish the team good luck. Fans were so overcome with school spirit that they began chanting even before they got inside. "We want [clap-clap] Marquette. We want [clap-clap] Marquette."

When the doors opened, a crowd of one thousand poured in, filling the hall beyond capacity and leaving those who arrived late trying to squeeze in at the doorway in the back. As an NBC crew shot a feature for the nightly news, the band, the pep squad, and Ace Purple led cheers near the stage. UE students stood next to white-haired alums, who stood beside parents holding toddlers waving purple foam fingers and pom-poms. Theren Bullock emerged from the wings and led the Aces onto the stage, to a roar. Microphone in hand, he acknowledged the optimism of his teammates and assured the crowd that it wasn't an underdog's naivete. The Aces would fight and scratch for every advantage, he promised. It would be a fitting finale for the four seniors.

"There is no tomorrow for myself, Brad, Eric, and Steve Sherwood," Bullock said. "There's no next year for us."

Walters took center stage to chants of "Dick, Dick, Dick." Decked out in a crimson sweater recalling the days of Arad McCutchan's Redshirt Army, he remembered the night in December 1978 when the Aces returned to campus after beating Murray State University for UE's first victory since the crash. The bus driver told him there was "some kind of riot" in front of Carson Center. But it wasn't a riot, Walters said. It was a crowd of UE fans, waiting to welcome the Aces home.

When Aces assistant coach Greg Meiser traveled to Milwaukee on March 9 to scout the Marquette-Wisconsin game, it seemed like everyone on press row asked the same question: Is Dick Walters going to take the Wisconsin job?

As Evansville fans celebrated UE's march into the postseason, Walters's relentless ambition provided an unwelcome distraction during an otherwise-giddy week of anticipation. Newspapers in Chicago and Evansville reported Walters was already "signed, sealed, and delivered" as the next coach at Wisconsin. Badgers coach Bill Cofield had resigned the previous week in the midst of a 6–21 season, and the consensus suggested that Walters would soon replace him. In an unfortunate accident of timing, Marquette hosted Wisconsin just forty-eight hours before facing the Aces. Walters wanted to scout the Warriors himself, but opted to skip the inevitable media circus and sent Meiser instead.

Walters was indeed a hot prospect. At just thirty-four years old, he had resurrected a venerable program, winning seventy-three games in four seasons. The media had just voted him Midwestern City Conference Coach of the Year. As network television crews chronicled the Aces' rise, Walters had cultivated a national profile. He was handsome and telegenic, a rising star at the dawn of the TV sports boom, perfect for big schools in rebuilding mode. Arizona, for example, had contacted UE for permission to speak with him. Walters wasn't interested. He also batted down a rumor that he would coach at Stanford.

But the Wisconsin job would be different. The Big Ten was bigtime. Walters could remain in the Midwest, where he maintained a Rolodex full of contacts, and he could recruit heavily in Chicago, his old stomping grounds. With a handful of junior college kids and freshman recruits overlooked by the likes of Indiana, Kentucky, and Notre Dame, he could transform the program in a year or two. Taking the Wisconsin job would be a big step up.

"The Big Ten can give Walters what he wants most in life: publicity," Dave Johnson wrote in the *Evansville Press*. "Publicity—with money a close second—is what turns Dick Walters on."

Walters acknowledged that he had interviewed for the position seven years before, when Cofield was hired. And he admitted that he was a good friend of Elroy Hirsch's, Wisconsin's athletic director. But he adamantly denied that he was interested in coaching the Badgers.

"I swear to God," he said. "I don't even know how much the Wisconsin job pays. I've never even been to the campus."

It was a dubious claim. The Wisconsin rumor lingered for weeks, and there was more to it than Walters would admit. But the chatter about another big school pursuing Walters merely reinforced what Aces fans had learned about him in the past four years: he was an excellent young coach with a very bright future, and there was no guarantee that he would stay at UE. Now, after coming so far, Evansville didn't want to lose its coach, no matter his ego or eccentricities. Walters's swaggering arrogance and big-city ambition were not impediments to UE's resurgence. They were its foundation. The very qualities that turned off so many fans were what enabled Walters to resurrect a broken basketball program. And in raising up that broken basketball program, Walters had lifted the rest of the city, too.

Aces fans lobbied on his behalf.

"I think Dick Walters deserves a raise and if that is what it takes to keep him in Evansville, then fine," wrote Mr. Robert E. Zoss in a letter to the *Evansville Courier*. "Either pay him what he's worth or lose him!"

On the afternoon before his team faced Marquette, Walters took a seat in the hotel restaurant for a late lunch of iced tea and cream of broccoli soup. He seemed . . . relaxed, draping an arm across the back of the red booth, as if awaiting an exhibition game against the Polish national team and not the most important game of his career.

"I really feel no pressure at all," he said. "I'm as loose as can be."

His players felt the same way, he added. Confident, prepared, eager. The Warriors did not intimidate them.

Marquette was a fitting matchup for UE, a small, private school with church ties in a faltering rust belt town. Like Evansville, Milwaukee had been battered by a shrinking manufacturing base and haunted by the loss of industries that once defined the city. And, like UE, Marquette had its own championship history. As Bobby Watson zipped through the Midwest to restock the Aces roster, the Warriors won the NCAA title in 1977 under the leadership of charismatic coach Al McGuire, a feisty, wisecracking New Yorker well known to Aces fans. In 1959, McGuire led tiny Belmont Abbey into Roberts Stadium and promised UE fans that if Arad McCutchan's boys beat his team the following year, he would buy ice-cream cones for everyone. Belmont Abbey did indeed lose on its return trip to Evansville, leaving McGuire with nothing to offer the crowd of twelve thousand. A local dairy owner saved the day by passing out thousands of ice-cream bars on McGuire's behalf.

McGuire retired from coaching after Marquette won the championship, replaced by longtime Warriors assistant Hank Raymonds. But McGuire's legend lingered, and Marquette fans still considered their team a national power. In 1982, heading into the NCAA tournament, Marquette had won twenty-one and lost eight with a schedule far more difficult than Evansville's, including games against Iowa, Minnesota, Stanford, Arizona State, and Notre Dame. Marquette was led by a big and speedy guard combo that more than compensated for the Warriors' lumbering and erratic front line. Senior Michael Wilson and sophomore Glenn "Doc" Rivers were both 6'4" and led Marquette in scoring, blocked shots, steals, and assists. Wilson was a pure shooter, and Rivers was a dominant defender and leaper who could drive the lane and score, destined for a long career in the NBA, as a player and a coach. Dean

Marquardt, a 6'9" center and Marquette's leading rebounder, anchored the front line.

Overall, the Warriors were bigger than the Aces, and their guards were more athletic than Eric Harris and Brad Leaf. But the Aces boasted one of the stingiest defenses in the country, relying mostly on a 1-3-1 zone that featured Harris up front, at the top of the key, harassing opposing guards. Richie Johnson joined Turam and Leaf playing in the middle, and Bullock patrolled the baseline beneath the basket. The 1-3-1 limited the mobility of rival guards who preferred to drive the lane or pass to big men looking for easy shots inside. It forced teams like Loyola and Marquette, with slashing guards, to shoot from long range. It worked especially well for UE because Johnson and Turam were so big and agile that it was difficult to pass over them. It helped that Bullock was long and relentless on the baseline, moving from one corner to the other with a suffocating intensity. Because man-to-man defense was more prevalent around the country, other teams struggled against UE's zone, shooting less than 50 percent against the Aces. Raymonds believed that Evansville's zone was the best in the country.

Walters saw no reason to change the Aces' game plan as he prepared for the Warriors. His team was 23–5 and ranked twentieth in the country by *Sports Illustrated*. Better to stick with what got them this far. His primary goals were controlling the tempo and preventing Rivers from waltzing through the lane as he pleased.

No one gave much thought to stopping Dean Marquardt.

———————

Brad Leaf woke up on game day dead set on fulfilling two lofty ambitions against Marquette. He'd come to Tulsa to prove himself to the rest of the world, to show NBA scouts he belonged among the best in the country. Perhaps more important, he wanted to leave Evansville fans with a lasting memory to assuage the wounds that lingered from December 13, 1977.

Leaf had enjoyed a good run in Evansville. Since that bitterly cold night in Milwaukee during his freshman year, when he regained his confidence and set aside thoughts of transferring, Leaf had carved a reputation as one of the better shooting guards in the country. As a senior, he averaged more than seventeen points and four rebounds. At 6′5″, he was still a step or two slow. But he was big and strong enough to muscle his way to the rim and shot consistently from eighteen feet. He was also money from the free-throw line. The day before the Marquette game, Leaf was named honorable mention all-American by the Associated Press.

But those accomplishments were achieved over a period of weeks and months and years, a slow accretion of free throws and jumpers and layups. They spoke to his tenacity, the hours he spent in the gym, the effort he invested in fine-tuning his shot, perfecting his form. Brad regarded the Marquette matchup as a predraft tryout for the NBA, a chance to showcase his skills in a high-profile, high-stakes environment. Never had he enjoyed such visibility, playing on network television on the first night of the NCAA tournament. An explosive performance would give him a nice bump as pro teams considered their options among college shooting guards.

Brad also felt a powerful obligation to Evansville. He knew little about the city or the university before he committed to play for Walters. He wasn't familiar with Arad McCutchan's legacy, and the crash at first seemed an abstraction to him, something that happened in another place, at another time. All Brad wanted when he arrived on campus was directions to the gym. But once he earned playing time and returned for his sophomore year, the depth of Evansville's loss slowly dawned on him, as if blinders had been removed and he could clearly see what the city had endured. He felt a palpable sense of sadness on campus. He heard fans comparing his team to Bobby Watson's Aces and began to understand the impact of the crash from the people who'd lived through it. His girlfriend, Karen Leach, was an intramural jock, a member of the Chi Omega sorority, and a UE cheerleader who'd grown up in Evansville fully immersed in Aces basketball. Her parents, Jerry and Roma Leach, had met when they were both students at Evansville College. Jerry later served on the alumni board at UE, Roma taught nursing there, and each year they bought season tickets for basketball. The Leaches had a pool at their house on Evansville's north side and often invited Brad and his teammates over for a swim or a cookout. The closer Brad grew to Karen and her family, the better he understood what Aces basketball meant to the city.

Now, after nearly four years, as Brad's college career neared its end, he had one last chance to fulfill an unspoken commitment to his adopted hometown.

Tip-off was set for 7:00 p.m. at the Mabee Center at Oral Roberts University. It was the first night of the tournament and a turning point for college basketball. For the first time, the tournament would be televised by CBS, which had snatched rights for the event away from NBC the year before with a staggering $48 million bid for three seasons. At $16 million a year, it was 60 percent more than NBC had paid for the rights in 1981. NBC had carried the tournament for twelve years, providing the foundation for college basketball's rapid growth in the 1980s. But it was CBS, with its deep pockets and marketing muscle, that made the tournament a major event on the sports calendar.

The University of Evansville was one of forty-eight teams to play that weekend at eight sites, from Uniondale, New York, to Pullman, Washington. Each of the four regionals included schools that had long dominated college basketball. North Carolina, led by a skinny freshman named Michael Jordan, was the top seed in the East Regional. Kentucky was sixth in the Mideast, right behind Indiana, which had won the championship the year before. In the Midwest, Ray Meyer's DePaul Blue Demons had captured the top seed. UE was seeded tenth in the Midwest, and Marquette was seventh. The winner of their matchup would play Missouri, which had received a bye. Norm Stewart's Tigers finished the season 26–3. But his best player, center Steve Stipanovich, injured his right ankle before the tournament, and his status for the second round was uncertain. So, in a perfect world, the Aces would beat Marquette and then face Missouri without its best player. What a delicious possibility: five years after Bobby Watson beat Stewart in the Mike Duff sweepstakes, UE could beat him again. Only this time, the stakes were much higher.

The UE-Marquette game would be carried in Evansville on two radio stations and the local CBS affiliate. Aces fans all over the city gathered in bars and living rooms and basements, waiting, hoping.

Arad McCutchan and his wife watched at a friend's house, not far from the UE campus. McCutchan taught a math class that evening, but changed the start time from six o'clock to five so he and his students had plenty of time to get in front of a TV before tip-off. Mayor Vandeveer watched with his wife and two daughters, "a family affair," Mrs. Vandeveer said. The elderly residents tuned in at Buckner Towers, a high-rise apartment building for seniors, and the regulars lined up at the bar at Ensor's First and Last Chance Saloon, in nearby Boonville.

At the University of Evansville, hundreds of students crammed into the Harper Dining Center. Harper, with its tall ceilings and wide windows, sat facing Walnut Street and the Carson Center gym, and it wasn't usually so rowdy. The students crowded around televisions at the front of the room, one a behemoth provided by the local CBS station and the other smaller, with its antenna pointed toward the ceiling for the best reception. Students had come two hours before tip-off, prepared to celebrate. Some snuck beers in under their coats, fully prepared for a victory toast. The entire room crackled with electricity.

Chris Weaver threw a party at the Executive Inn, the nicest hotel in Evansville, splurging on a sixty-dollar suite for a dozen friends. It had been five years since he'd met with Bobby Watson, back when Weaver was vice president of the UE student association and Watson was a young coach drumming up support for his new team. As a senior in the spring of 1978, Weaver had gotten to know Dick Walters during meetings with student leadership. Walters was intense, Weaver thought, and not as personable as Watson. But he was perceptive, and Weaver admired how Walters acknowledged the tragic circumstances that brought him to Evansville and the raw emotions that lingered, while simultaneously looking toward the next season and the season after that. Weaver didn't begrudge the new coach's big-city persona or his naked ambition. Walters's arrogance was a necessity, given the Herculean task he faced. And if he got a better job after building a winner at UE, good for Walters and good for the university. After Walters's success, the top job at the University of Evansville would be coveted by coaches all over the country.

Weaver graduated in 1978 and stayed in Evansville, working first for the reelection campaign of US representative David Cornwell, a southern Indiana Democrat. After Cornwell lost, Weaver took a job as the executive assistant to Mayor Vandeveer. The crowd in the suite for the Marquette game included coworkers from City Hall, UE alumni, and friends—men and women, middle-aged and recently graduated. Drinks in hand, they gathered in front of the television, nearly overwhelmed by the anticipation.

"At tip-off," Weaver recalls, "people were either yelling and screaming in pure joy, or crying like babies."

———

I harbored great expectations that night, sitting on the floor in our living room, just two blocks from Harper Dining Center.

I was fifteen, a freshman in high school, and no longer interested in accompanying my dad to Roberts Stadium. But to me this game was a once-in-a-lifetime event, like Halley's Comet, when everyone gathers to take in the spectacle and then spends the next day talking about it. It was important to me that the Aces were playing on a national network, that maybe people who knew nothing about my hometown would be rooting for our basketball team that night.

And this team, unquestionably, was ours. We'd seen Brad Leaf and Theren Bullock emerge as if from a cocoon, watching them grow from gangly freshmen to veteran cocaptains. We'd seen Steve Sherwood evolve from a cheerleading benchwarmer to a rugged lunch-bucket sub. We'd witnessed the roller coaster of Eric Harris's career, from starter to invisible sub, and back to starter again. These were our boys, and I felt a special affinity for them. We were practically neighbors. They lived just a few blocks away. I occasionally saw them in the summer at Carson Center. Once, when I was in elementary school and shooting around in the nearly empty practice gym, Brad Leaf made a half-hearted attempt to block my shot as he walked off the court. The thrill lingered for days.

Perhaps more than anything that night, I wanted to see the underdogs—*our* underdogs—prove the doubters wrong.

My dad watched the game with me, relaxed as always in the orange recliner as I sprawled on the deep-pile carpeting only a few feet from our enormous faux-wood television console. Dad still maintained that a small school like UE couldn't compete with national powerhouses, that truly elite players like Isiah Thomas and Michael Jordan would never choose Evansville over Indiana or North Carolina.

"I'm not a pessimist," he'd say. "I'm a realist."

I had no evidence to dispute his theory. But I was a rebellious teenage smart-ass, learning to smoke ditch weed and choke down warm beer with my friends, and an Aces victory would allow me to remind him that he was wrong. That prospect appealed to me a great deal.

But looking back now, nearly forty years later, I realize that claiming victory over my father was only one of the reasons I hoped for an Aces win. Despite the mushrooming drama of my teen years, I held on to the same unrealistic hope I'd felt four years before, as an eleven-year-old boy grateful to spend a Saturday night with my dad at Roberts Stadium.

NINETEEN

First Dance

TONIGHT, IN THE LATE-WINTER twilight, the Mabee Center resembles a spaceship from an old Martian movie, saucer-shaped, having landed on a sea of blacktop here on the edge of the Oral Roberts campus. Encircled by narrow white columns that stretch from roof to ground, it appears from a distance that a gust of wind could lift the whole building up and send it spinning away over the oil fields that dot the Tulsa landscape.

Inside, a couple hundred Aces fans have positioned themselves in a single cluster, a vocal minority in a half-empty arena. This is the first game of a doubleheader, and the NCAA parceled only 313 tickets to the University of Evansville. And anyway, the main attraction is the second game, which will include Houston, with Clyde Drexler, Hakeem Olajuwon, and the rest of their Phi Slama Jama teammates. No matter how compelling its story, Evansville remains an understudy. No one is mistaking Brad Leaf for Clyde Drexler. And yet, the beauty of the NCAA tournament is that underdogs always have their day. The previous year, a single day produced some of the most memorable upsets in the tournament's forty-two-year history. On March 14, 1981, tiny St. Joseph's beat top-seeded DePaul on a layup with two seconds left.

Arkansas beat defending champion Louisville on a forty-nine-foot heave at the buzzer. And Kansas State beat second-ranked Oregon State on a jumper with two seconds left. That was the day that March Madness was born.

At the Mabee Center, as the pregame scoreboard clock ticks down to zero, UE assistant Gary Marriott assesses the Aces from the sidelines. He doesn't like what he sees. Missed layups. Clanking jumpers. The Aces do not look confident, prepared, and eager, as Walters had promised the day before. They look intimidated. They look as if the pressure of the past four years, the enormity of the moment, and the weight of the city's expectations have worn them down.

Even Rick McKinstry is feeling it. Which is odd, because McKinstry played in some big games as a freshman at Clemson in 1980. That season, the Tigers made a run in the NCAA tournament that ended just shy of the Final Four, when they lost to UCLA in the West Regional Finals. McKinstry transferred from Clemson after that season because he felt limited in a college town that offered him little more than practices and games. He's a quiet kid, majoring in business, and a member of the Midwestern City Conference all-academic team.

"I'm not just a basketball player," he said before the season began. "I'm a student and a social being."

He had to sit out a year in Evansville, but played in every game this season. At 6'6", Rick is a gifted athlete. Sometimes, though, he has to remind himself to play with Theren Bullock's intensity because it doesn't come naturally to him. In high school, McKinstry had forged a reputation as a great scorer, and Walters had hoped he would provide instant offense off the bench. But it hasn't worked out that way. Rick averages less than three points a game, and he is absolutely dreadful from the free-throw line.

At Ensor's First and Last Chance Saloon, the walls are lined with pennants, fifty-seven to be precise. Major League Baseball. The National Football League. Colleges and universities. All donated by regulars.

"You had to be at the game to get one," says Junior Fisher.

Ensor's sits along the Southern Railway tracks smack in the middle of Boonville, northeast of Evansville. It's a workingman's bar, always has been, dating back to the horse-and-wagon era, when men had bloody gunfights out front. Legend has it that the saloon got its name from its proximity to the railroad tracks: it was the first and the last place a fella could get a drink, whether he'd just arrived in town or he was on his way out. These days Ensor's is populated by coal miners, railroad workers, carpenters, and electricians. On some days, you'll find the local gravedigger sitting at the bar. They play cards and watch sports and bullshit each other, from the middle of the day through to the end of the night. Ensor's is owned and operated by a woman named Pinky, who serves up burgers, grilled cheese sandwiches, and her own home-made potato salad. Ensor's is only fifteen miles from the UE campus, but a world away from its close-cropped lawns, budding trees, and kids sneaking beers into Harper Dining Center. Tonight, though, the regulars at Ensor's nurse their drinks and dine on chicken wings and french fries, awaiting the opening tip with a cautious optimism. Pinky's son Stan is tending bar. He's taking the Aces by a point.

"I'd take Marquette," says one of the regulars, "but I can't bet against my heart."

They meet at center court, Dean Marquardt and Emir Turam. Could they be more different? One kid, an oversize linebacker from a Wisconsin factory town. The other, skinny as a garden snake, from a multilingual family in Istanbul. One, thick and muscular, averages less than three points a game. The other, after working his ass off the previous summer, lifting weights, shooting for hours a day, is enjoying his best season in college. Tonight, only one of them will play the greatest game of his career.

Turam stands four inches taller. But they weigh about the same, and Marquardt has spent the entire season banging around in the paint against bigger and more talented centers than Turam faced in the Midwestern City Conference. So it's no surprise when Marquardt controls the tip, and no surprise when Michael Wilson dumps a pass down low to Marquette forward Brian Nyenhuis for an easy basket in the lane.

Thirty seconds in, Marquette by two.

Larry Calton sits at the broadcast table, calling the action for Evansville fans in his sing-song baritone. Calton is always bullish on the home team, unabashed in his zeal for the Aces. But tonight, as the game progresses, his delivery swings from utter despair to hopeful hysteria, from disgust at the referees to love for Brad Leaf. He's already expressed his irritation that tournament officials invited the Marquette pep band but didn't make room for UE's. He's also prepared Aces fans for the potential that their team might play a little tight early in the game.

But barely a minute has passed and now every sentence out of Calton's mouth is an exclamation. It's the first hint of things to come, the first subtle shift in momentum. Maybe the Aces aren't nervous. Maybe Gary Marriott was wrong about UE's warm-ups. Maybe everyone is feeling like Brad Leaf, confident and eager to show the whole country that this season was no fluke, that the University of Evansville is no sob story.

It begins with Richie Johnson, whom the sportswriters have dubbed "Magic," because his game resembles Earvin Johnson's. Richie is 6'9" and a masterful passer on the break. He also possesses a decent midrange shot, and both of those skills are on display soon after the Nyenhuis basket. First, he slips into the corner along the baseline, takes a pass, and launches a fifteen-foot jumper. Good! Then he dishes to Bullock in traffic. Theren scores, draws a foul, and drains his free throw. Suddenly the Aces are in control. Now it's the Warriors who appear tight. They try a full-court press, but it doesn't slow UE. Each time the Aces get the ball, they run. Leaf streaks toward the basket on the left side of the floor and, as a defender closes in from the opposite side, Brad drives to the rim, twisting, and lays the ball in with his left hand.

Marquette's brutish front line is throwing elbows and forearms, treating Turam like a stuffed animal. But they have no answer for the balletic ferocity of Theren Bullock, all arms and legs and yet playing with purpose and precision.

"Bullock gets it in to Leaf on the left side," Calton says, his voice rising in anticipation. "Brad heads for the bucket, puts it up, no good. Bullock rebounds. He scores! Bullock scores, and the Evansville Purple Aces lead it 13–7! Thirteen minutes to go!"

———

Pandemonium erupts at Harper Dining Center. UE students have been standing since before tip-off, their arms raised, screaming at the television. But now the clamor drowns out the play-by-play on TV. When Wallace Graves appears on the giant screen, cheering from his seat at the arena, the students are chanting.

"We are . . . UE! We are . . . UE!"

They are kids, eighteen, nineteen, twenty years old, full of unreasonable expectations, most born and raised within an hour or two of campus. They've been sheltered. They're too young for cynicism. They've never been laid off or divorced. They don't yet understand the disappointments of middle age, and that's a blessing for them, because they can lose themselves in this night, they can stand and bellow at the screen until the final buzzer sounds and their throats are red and raw.

Their synchronized shouting ends once Theren Bullock's inspired play gives way to a stretch of Aces basketball so incomprehensible and alien that it sucks all the energy out of Harper Dining Center. This shift happens so slowly, like the steady erosion of a dusty farm field, that the damage is clear only when it's over.

Evansville's 1-3-1 defense works against Doc Rivers every bit as well as it did against Darius Clemons. The Aces have sealed off the lane, leaving Rivers no path to the basket. But with four UE defenders focusing on the Warriors' two guards, Marquardt and Nyenhuis run Bullock ragged along the baseline. Hank Raymonds has found the soft spot in the 1-3-1: big men who can shoot from the corner, before Bullock chases them down. Marquardt is hitting free throws and Nyenhuis, a 6'10" bruiser in a bowl cut who averages four points a game, is playing like Moses Malone. After Eric Harris overthrows a pass to Leaf, Nyenhuis responds with a basket, a steal, and a dunk. Marquette leads 17–15 with less than nine minutes to play in the first half.

Now, clearly, Brad Leaf's moment has arrived. He knows it. His teammates know it. Just get the ball in his hands and the rest will take care of itself, as it always does.

And yet, when the Aces look to Leaf in the first half tonight, believing in him with the faith of apostles, his gift inexplicably vanishes at the moment UE needs it most. His open jumper from the right wing clangs off the rim. Seconds later, he lofts an air ball from the same spot. Since that twisting layup that gave the Aces an early lead, Leaf has missed seven straight, shots he makes every day in practice and twice a week in games.

After the air ball, UE guard Murray Lendy misses a jumper, Johnson travels, and Leaf loses the ball on his way to the basket. A few seconds later, he loses it again. Marquette responds to this sudden spasm of ineptitude with twelve points in a row, including two free throws from Dean Marquardt. Evansville trails 27–15. The Aces are playing as if they're underwater, the crowd noise muffled, their legs heavy and slow. Larry Calton is glum. "I don't think I've ever seen any basketball team go as cold as the Aces have here in the first half."

Evansville endures nine minutes and fourteen possessions in a row without a basket. There will be great debate about how this happened, whether it was a self-inflicted wound or a canny scouting report. Either way, Marquette leads 29–20 at halftime and Leaf trudges off the floor after hitting just one of his twelve shots.

———

At Ensor's, Junior Fisher is pissed.

"They got to get the lid off the basket," he says. "Walters, get your shit together."

But Junior is more hopeful than Lloyd Titzer. Lloyd is ready to give up. Why hold out hope for the second half? Unlike the students at Harper, the men at Ensor's have endured their share of failure and regret. Better to throw in the towel early than be disappointed at the end.

"If Leaf's off," Titzer says, speaking to no one and everyone at the same time, "it's all over."

———

The most astonishing story for Marquette tonight is not Dean Marquardt's scoring. Marquardt is big enough to force his way to the rim, and he'd always had a nice jumper. But that isn't the miracle of the evening. The miracle is the fact that Marquardt is even in uniform, that he is even alive.

Marquardt was a high school senior in 1978, a big kid from Milwaukee and one of the top recruits in Wisconsin. His long list of college suitors included Kentucky, Minnesota, and Cincinnati. But in the end, it came down to Marquette and Wisconsin. Marquardt had cheered Al McGuire's national championship team in 1977 and worked on his game at McGuire's summer basketball camps. When he chose to play for the Warriors, Hank Raymonds called it "a beautiful day for Marquette University."

Marquardt played well enough as a reserve in his freshman year to start at center as a sophomore. He spent the summer of '79 shoveling gravel on an asphalt crew and playing basketball every night. He'd gained thirty pounds and felt stronger and more confident as the summer ended. But early on a Sunday morning that August, less than two months before the start of practice, his car collided with a pickup at a Milwaukee intersection. A couple who happened upon the crash tried to provide first aid, but couldn't get into the car. Firefighters on a nearby call had to pry one of the doors open to pull Marquardt out. The crash killed a passenger in Marquardt's car and left him with fifteen broken ribs, a broken collarbone, and a collapsed lung. His left arm was shattered, and he lost twenty to twenty-five pounds after three weeks in the hospital. Back at his parents' house, he couldn't tie his shoes or shower by himself. A walk down the driveway and back to the house left him exhausted. Doctors told him it would take a year, at least, to fully recover. But he couldn't give up on basketball. In the months after the crash, he needed it more than ever. He started physical therapy that fall. He was playing again by the end of the year, slow and sluggish, with heavy braces on his chest and arm. His averages of 1.4 points and 1.6 rebounds that season were cause for celebration.

Marquardt was an excellent passer and a consistent shooter from fifteen feet. But he was planted in the post for most of every game. Raymonds didn't run plays for his big guys. With Wilson and Rivers at guard, he didn't need to. So Marquardt rebounded, set picks, played defense, and scored when he happened to find himself with the ball beneath the basket. He'd never scored more than seventeen points at Marquette.

But at halftime at the Mabee Center, Raymonds gives Marquardt a new role. After he noticed that the Aces' 1-3-1 gave Marquette room along the baseline, where Theren Bullock has to run from one corner to the other, Raymonds tells Marquardt to drift out from beneath the basket and fire away. It's a novel strategy, counterintuitive, sending your center out to shoot from long range. With Nyenhuis in control beneath the basket, however, Marquette can afford to leave Marquardt in the corner, all by himself.

―――――――

Steve Sherwood sits at the end of the bench tonight with an ankle so swollen that he couldn't fit it into a normal shoe without removing the laces. He won't play at all.

But at Harper Dining Center, Sherwood's fan club fills the first row and their hero's injury doesn't dampen their spirit. Geek's Guerillas was hatched in a double dorm room they called the Jungle, which is decorated with a plastic palm tree, piles of dirty laundry, and a drink machine that dispenses pure grain alcohol. Sherwood doesn't even live there. But the guys are engineering and business majors who adopted him as one of their own and borrowed his nickname to create T-shirts with "Geek's Guerillas" on the front and his number—54—on the back. A dozen or so guys came to home games that season and whipped the small student section into a frenzy. They had plenty to cheer about. Sherwood had advanced in four seasons from a little-used walk-on to a solid sub and campus cult hero. Geek's Guerillas could count on their man to score a bucket or two and grab a couple of rebounds each game, giving Emir Turam and Kenny Perry a breather and providing Walters with a brawny center who relished his all-grit-no-glory role.

Sherwood's ankle injury is a bummer, and not just for Sherwood and his buddies. Turam and Perry might as well be in street clothes tonight, given the way Marquardt and Nyenhuis are playing. Sherwood could, at the very least, rough up Nyenhuis for a few minutes, maybe draw a couple of fouls and change the tenor of the game.

Anything would help. Trailing by nine after twenty minutes, the Aces desperately need a jolt of energy.

———

Brad Leaf jogs from the locker room, unbowed. He cannot explain the first half. The open jumper from the right wing? The air ball? This has never happened before. He's at a loss. Could it be that he's stuck in a moment that is simply too big for him, that he's overwhelmed by the pressure to audition for the scouts and the bottomless obligation he feels to Evansville?

Hank Raymonds would dismiss such questions as existential gibberish. He can easily explain Brad's lousy first half. In preparing for the Aces, Marquette's coaches noticed that Leaf needed an extra second or two before he set himself to shoot. He did more than merely flick his wrist. Leaf's form was deliberate, and Raymonds believed Marquette could disrupt his rhythm by going at him belly to belly. So he ordered Wilson to get in Leaf's face at every opportunity. Cut him off, don't give him the time or space to get set.

It looked like a brilliant strategy for those first twenty minutes. But shooters shoot. It's the only way to break a slump. And Leaf is one of the purest shooters in the country.

It takes him a few minutes to get warmed up in the second half. But he's not panicked. He doesn't fling the ball to the rim every time he touches it. Instead, he waits, looking for a seam in the defense, empty space he can claim as his own if only for a split second. With nearly five minutes elapsed, Leaf moves in a broad arc from the top of the key to the baseline, taking a pass from Eric Harris.

"Eric from long range," Calton says, "into the right corner to Leaf. Brad maneuvers in, puts it up. And it is good! Maybe that will get Brad started."

Indeed, it's as if a dam has broken and now the shots fall from all angles: drives in the lane, jumpers from the corner, free throws. It is a relief, yes, finally. This is what Brad expected all along, what his teammates had seen the entire season, at Carson Center, Roberts Stadium, and all the other gyms they'd passed through during this remarkable four-month run, twenty-eight games, twenty-three victories, barely hanging on for number twenty-four. This is what Jerry Leaf had prepared him for, all those summer nights in the driveway, charting his shots: fifty free throws, fifty from the corner, fifty from the top of the key. Brad was built for moments like this.

But nearly every time he scores, Marquardt answers. No one expected a shootout between Brad Leaf and Dean Marquardt. And yet, they trade baskets seven times in the second half. No one expected much from Brian Nyenhuis either. And yet, he's making sport of Evansville's big men. Marquette leads 47–34 midway through the second half, and Hank Raymonds looks like a genius.

Evansville's run starts with seven minutes to play, Marquette up by ten. Harris drops two jumpers from twenty feet. Leaf sinks two free throws. He has fourteen points. The Marquette lead is now four, and Larry Calton is shouting into the mic, which is not unusual for him.

On some nights, his booming voice misses the mark and overwhelms the action. Pedestrian plays gets swallowed up and exaggerated. But tonight his delivery is spot-on, pitch-perfect for this moment, and exactly what his listeners back in Evansville want to hear. Because they're shouting, too.

"Bullock on the left side, comes to the top of the key, gives it to Leaf. Brad goes to the right. Still dribbling. Now down the middle, Leaf stops. Puts it up in traffic . . . It's good! Oh what a shot! Sensational shot by Brad Leaf! And it's 51–49!"

———

In Boonville, the guys are chanting and, for a few seconds at least, the small crowd at Ensor's First and Last Chance doesn't sound much different from all the kids at Harper Dining Center: "Aces! Aces!"

———

The load he's taken on in the second half has left Leaf exhausted, dragging. He's spent so much energy bringing the Aces back, running past screens, enduring elbows and hip checks in the lane, that when Walters pulls him for a breather, he slumps into his seat on the bench, head hung low. He's scored sixteen. Bullock has seventeen. Harris has come around, too. The seniors, carrying the Aces again.

But they've received little help. Turam, who'd come so far this season, who had transformed himself into a true Division I center, fouled out early after missing all three of his shots. Kenny Perry, his replacement, who turned down UCLA and the good life in Southern California, hasn't scored either. Two years ago, Walters envisioned twin towers with complementary skills, Perry's smooth jumper a potent contrast to Turam's dominant inside game. Tonight, though, UE's vaunted big men have been humiliated by two guys who barely showed up on Evansville's scouting report.

———

Marquette, 55–49, less than four minutes to go. Walters has no choice, no time to waste. He summons his leading scorer from the bench.

Soon after reentering, Leaf is fouled and steps to the free-throw line. This is a boon for Evansville. The clock is stopped. The Aces get a moment's rest, and their best free-throw shooter is at the stripe. The first goes down easily. The second is long, but falls.

Doc Rivers responds, slicing down the middle, shoveling a pass to Marquardt, who waits patiently on the right side and sinks yet another. He now has twenty-one, a career high. Leaf, like a punch-drunk fighter staggering forward, flailing away, blood in his eyes, knocks down a jumper from the left side, his sixth basket in seven attempts since halftime, giving him twenty.

Marquette by four.

The final minute passes slowly, the Aces again pushing the boulder up the hill, step by agonizing step. Walters chooses a particularly ugly strategy to buy time, hacking Nyenhuis to stop the clock, hoping he'll buckle at the free-throw line. The fluid give-and-take between Leaf and Marquardt is replaced by a stop-motion series of fouls and free throws. It's not a novel approach, but it works. When McKinstry fouls Nyenhuis, the big man blows the free throw.

"Bullock on the backboard. With fifty-four seconds to go. It isn't over yet. Harris to Richie Johnson. Johnson down the middle. Puts it up and in!"

Marquette, 61–59.

Forty seconds remain and the arena is nearly full now, more than eight thousand people suddenly caught up in the back-and-forth, roaring for the upstarts from southern Indiana, happy to forget about the Houston game for the moment, hopeful for a Cinderella moment, even if it comes during the undercard, even if it's ugly.

"Nyenhuis fouled by Leaf. Nyenhuis going to the free-throw line again . . . If he misses, the Aces have the ball, thirty seconds to go, they'd be down by two. Big, big free throw for Nyenhuis. Twelve points in the game. Hitting only 55 percent.

"Free throw"—and here Larry Calton's voice drops an octave, dripping with disappointment verging on suicidal despair—"good . . . Second one coming . . . Nyenhuis back to the free-throw line . . . the second free throw is in the air and it is . . . off the rim . . . good. He hit them both."

Marquette, 63–59, thirty seconds left.

Aces' ball. No need to panic. Not yet. Plenty of time. But the options grow more limited as each second slips away. There's no three-point line in college ball. So the Aces need two baskets and a stop to force overtime. Or UE can hack Nyenhuis again to kill the clock and hope for the best. Either way, Evansville needs at least two possessions and maybe a lucky break.

"Here comes Leaf into the front court. Left corner to McKinstry. Rick fakes, and it's going to be a foul on Marquette! A foul on Marquette! And McKinstry . . . will go to the free-throw line."

Raymonds calls time-out. McKinstry heads to the bench, holding the season in his unsteady hands. He shoots 32 percent from the line.

"Well, we have twenty-four seconds remaining, twenty-four seconds to go, Evansville trailing, 63–59. Obviously, McKinstry must hit the free throws . . . The last time he went to the line, the first free throw went off the backboard and down. The second one he missed."

―――――

Rick McKinstry will look back many decades later and marvel at this time in his life, at this team, this group of guys. He's a middle-aged man now, a family man, working for IBM in Texas, and the fond feelings he has for Brad Leaf and Theren Bullock—all of them, really—have not faded. It's almost too much to put into words. These Aces had a rare bond. They were a true team, greater than the sum of their parts, like family, like brothers, all of the clichés, held tight by their captains. Brad, so open and genuine and guileless. And Theren, charismatic and exacting. Everyone following his lead. Their time together was fleeting, only seven months from the start of classes till this final game. They left school and scattered all over the world. Most of them lost touch. But this season left them with powerful memories, even as their hair turned gray and their children grew up, long after the sting of their losses had faded.

―――――

The time-out ends and McKinstry walks solemnly from the bench. The referee hands him the ball. Marquette by four, twenty-four seconds to play.

"Here at the free-throw line, it's McKinstry . . . It's no good. The rebound goes to Marquette."

―――――

Now just fifteen seconds remain. The Aces need two baskets while holding Marquette scoreless.

"It's not impossible. But it's going to be very, very difficult."

Michael Wilson inbounds the ball and Richie Johnson fouls Marquardt before any time comes off the clock. It's a brilliant move, perfectly timed, and it sends Marquardt to the free-throw line. As amazing as he's been tonight, emerging from near anonymity in the paint to sink jumpers from the corners, Dean Marquardt is no sure thing from the line.

When he misses and Bullock grabs the rebound, Evansville briefly finds itself with one final miraculous opportunity. A quick score. A steal on the inbounds play and another basket and suddenly: overtime.

But Theren can't hold on to the ball and as he loses it, he overcompensates for his mistake and commits his fifth foul. The lanky kid from Blue Island, Illinois, the beating heart of this team, is finished. Bullock walks slowly to the bench and takes a seat, his head down, no doubt now about how it all plays out. Marquette will play Missouri. The Aces will go home.

The scoreboard says Marquette 67, Evansville 62.

———

The Evansville locker room is funereal, crowded with young men unaccustomed to failure, tears welling in their eyes. Walters takes a long look around, feeling protective, and closes the doors, barring the media. Nothing he can say will ease their disappointment. They had come so close, scratching and grasping, playing for far more than a trip to the second round.

"I feel like tomorrow should be practice as usual," Eric Harris says as he dresses at his locker. "I never wanted it to end."

———

The regulars at Ensor's First and Last Chance Saloon offer a clear-eyed postmortem, as if they knew all along that it would never happen, that the Aces were just lucky to be in the same gym as Doc Rivers, Brian Nyenhuis, and Dean Marquardt.

"Five minutes of the first half is what killed them," one fellow says, though the first-half drought lasted nearly twice that.

Now, however, is not the time to quibble. It's over. Maybe one more beer and head home. Work tomorrow morning.

Behind the bar, Stan Ensor takes the long view, summing up the past six months, speaking for all of southern Indiana. "Hell," he says, "they had a super season."

———

At Harper Dining Center, it takes a moment to sink in. Is it really over? UE was supposed to win this one and then prepare for the next round. And then, who knows, right? Right?

Now a guy stands up in the front row and turns around, rousing the crowd from its stupor, summoning one last burst of school spirit.

"Come on, you deadbeats. Fire it up."

And they all join in, because there are no cynics in this crowd.

"Aces! Aces! [clap-clap] Aces! Aces! [clap-clap]"

This is not the celebration they'd expected. They smuggled bottles in beneath their coats to cut loose, because kids at other schools around the country do this every year, knock back a few beers, toast the victors, and run outside screaming for joy in the cool, dark evening, jumping into fountains and on top of cars, defacing statues, kissing strangers. There will be no toasts for UE fans tonight. No storybook ending.

But it feels as if something has changed, as if the ground has shifted. Evansville is no longer the underdog, no longer the small city with the little college, recovering from the unspeakable. Maybe that, all by itself, is worth celebrating.

EPILOGUE

IN EARLY APRIL 1982, three weeks after he led his team off the court in Tulsa, Dick Walters stood before a group of Aces boosters at a downtown social club for a postseason banquet. During a question-and-answer session, someone in the crowd piped up. "We'd like to keep you here," he shouted, and the room broke into applause.

"It would be very difficult for me to leave here," Walters said, motioning to his players seated nearby. "I'm so committed to these guys."

The uncertainty of Walters's future lingered long after the loss to Marquette. Wisconsin's interest was no longer a rumor, and Walters no longer denied his plans to visit Madison for an interview. The narrative had already been set: it was Walters's job if he wanted it—at a salary substantially higher than the $36,000 he made at UE. Walters was typically coy, saying the invitation to interview in Madison "came out of the clear blue sky" only after the NCAA championship game a few days before. No one believed him.

Once he returned from Madison, published reports suggested the Badgers had indeed offered Walters the job. Based on his annual flirtation with other schools, it seemed a foregone conclusion that he'd soon be packing his bags and selling his house.

But on April 4, back in Evansville, Walters met with Wallace Graves for forty-five minutes in the morning and spoke with him again that afternoon. Then the Tip-Off Club got involved. A booster had already given Walters a new Corvette as a courtesy car. Now a group of well-heeled Aces supporters agreed to supplement Walters's salary as part of a new five-year contract. With three kids in school and the momentum of the '82 season at his back, Walters seemed finally ready to settle down.

But there was little time to savor UE's success. Walters had to reload immediately. Bullock, Leaf, and Harris were gone. Kenny Perry and Emir Turam eventually left, unhappy with their playing time. A fifteen-point upset of eleventh-ranked Purdue at Roberts Stadium in December 1983 suggested better times ahead. It was the signature win that had eluded Walters for five seasons. But the Aces couldn't maintain that momentum. By spring 1985, the afterglow of the '82 season had faded. Walters couldn't restock the roster or recapture the enthusiasm that had carried Evansville to the postseason. Home attendance plummeted by almost 40 percent.

One night, Wallace Graves invited Walters to dinner at an upscale steak house and posed an uncomfortable question.

"He said, 'Which one of us is more important to the university?'" Walters recalls. "I laughed and he said, 'No, I'm not kidding.'"

Walters told Graves he understood his place at UE, that the basketball team was just one part of the larger campus community. The president ran the university, and the basketball coach worked at the discretion of the president.

"But I knew then he felt I had gotten too big for my britches."

Graves fired Walters in 1985 and he never coached again. He believes other schools assumed he'd violated NCAA rules at UE. Why fire a coach who'd resurrected your program?

Ultimately, Dick and Jan divorced and Dick moved to California, where he dabbled in television commentary and worked for a company that manages college bookstores. Now retired, Walters says he regrets turning down the Wisconsin job. It was everything he'd always wanted: a big school in a major conference. The Badgers were the Big Ten's doormat. But Walters knew how to rebuild a basketball program.

Walters left UE with a record of 114–87 in seven seasons. The coach and the city had never been a perfect fit. Evansville was an insular town and Walters was an outsider. He stepped on toes and said the wrong things. There was the annual question of whether he'd stay or go. But the city and the coach needed each other. Evansville rescued Walters from the anonymity of the junior college circuit and offered a challenge that no coach—before or after—had ever faced.

In return, Walters performed a modern miracle.

———

Evansville welcomed its new basketball coach in March 2018, soon after the end of another uninspiring season. But Walter McCarty needed no introduction. He's an Evansville native with an NBA pedigree, and many of the hundreds who turned out to greet him on his first day were family and friends. On his way to the podium, McCarty stopped to wave, shake a few hands, and offer an elderly woman a peck on the cheek. It was a fresh start for the Aces with echoes of all the fresh starts before, from Sloan to Watson to Walters and beyond.

For Evansville fans, McCarty represents the latest, greatest hope to return Aces basketball to some semblance of its old self. After UE fired Walters, the Aces returned to the NCAA tournament four times, winning just once, and haven't been back since 1999. The Aces play in a new arena downtown, and on a good night, the crowd is half of what it was back in the day. But, honestly, it's not a fair comparison. So much has changed since the crash, now four decades ago. So many of the institutions that knit the city together are gone.

In 2010, Whirlpool moved production of its refrigerators to Mexico and closed the plant out by the airport, where FDR once toured to buoy the spirits of workers making fighter jets.

Whirlpool's move left most of its remaining eleven hundred Evansville workers unemployed with limited prospects for jobs that paid such generous wages. The company had whittled the local payroll year after year, one round of layoffs after another. The end was inevitable. Still, closing the Whirlpool plant was an especially painful moment for the city. Once the Refrigerator Capital of the World, Evansville no longer churned out refrigerators.

Roberts Stadium was demolished after UE played its last game there in 2011. The stadium had been remodeled over the years, but couldn't match the grandeur or the revenue potential of the new college arenas, with their plush suites and big corporate sponsors. Roberts Stadium's successor, the Ford Center, seats eleven thousand. Next door, the Indiana University School of Medicine has opened a branch campus expected to bring five hundred new students, high-paying jobs, and millions of dollars in urban development.

Like the arena and the medical school, Walter McCarty faces outsize expectations. Aces basketball, even in its diminished state, remains central to Evansville's identity. White-haired boosters from the McCutchan era still buy tickets and fetch their purple sweaters from the back of the closet each winter. They returned to campus for the rally to welcome McCarty home and made their way downtown to witness his inaugural season. McCarty's credentials are impeccable. He played on Kentucky's 1996 NCAA championship team and then bounced around the NBA for a decade. After retiring, McCarty took a series of assistant coaching jobs, first with the University of Louisville and most recently with the Boston Celtics. His mentors include Celtics coach Brad Stevens and former Louisville coach Rick Pitino. But almost as important as his résumé, McCarty grew up in Evansville. He's one of us, a hometown kid, and that still means a lot in Evansville: all three finalists for the Aces job were Evansville natives.

The university and its new coach have done their best to reignite enthusiasm for the program. Before the start of his first season, McCarty made all of the requisite speeches around the region. After he threw out the first pitch at a Minor League Baseball game, he mingled with young families and posed for selfies. One day students found him strolling around campus, passing out donuts. Like Walters, he's added amenities for his players. Only, instead of a Pepsi machine, he put an Xbox in the locker room. Like Watson, he's installed a wide-open, fast-paced offense. But donuts and selfies are not rebounds or free throws. The Aces finished McCarty's first season at 11–21.

Evansville is no longer an insular factory town, and its basketball program may never again be a national marvel. And yet, on some days, it seems as if nothing has changed. This winter, when McCarty leads his team onto the Ford Center court, Evansville will once again turn its attention from snowfall predictions and presidential politics. McCarty has inspired new hope for the basketball program that Arad McCutchan built sixty years ago from a cramped office on the edge of campus. Frank Deford's assessment from 1978 still rings true.

"It's a basketball town," he wrote, "in the basketball season."

—April 2019

ACKNOWLEDGMENTS

I CONDUCTED NEARLY 250 interviews for this book. Those who were especially helpful include: Kay Barrow, Dick Walters, Stafford Stephenson, Craig Bohnert, Steve Sherwood, Valery Helton, Mike Blake, Lois Watson Ford, Cheri Partain, Charlie Butler, and Chris Weaver.

This book would not have been possible without the following:

Dan Conaway

Barry Harbaugh

Erin Calligan Mooney

Debra Gwartney

Tom Bissell

Michael McGregor

Paul Collins

Mike Blake

Mark Tomasik

Joe Atkinson, for providing advice, insight, and hours of raw video. His documentary, *From the Ashes: The University of Evansville Purple Aces*, is a moving tribute to the legacy of Evansville basketball.

Kyle Keiderling, whose book *Trophies and Tears: The Story of Evansville and the Aces* is a compelling and encyclopedic history of Purple Aces basketball.

Shane White and the staff at University Libraries

Evansville Vanderburgh Public Library
Eldorado Memorial Library
Chatsworth Township Library
Evansville African American Museum
Amanda Ford Beitler
Ian Pestrak
Lloyd Baker
Delaney Broderick
Alecia Giombolini
Peter Ames Carlin
Peter Zuckerman
Jack Hart
Steve Mayes
Carol Gray
Bob Boxell
Dave Coverly
Mike Moon
Larry Bingham
Keith Beaven
Nancy Beaven Korff
Linda Ford
Martha Beaven Hancock
Mom and Dad, for everything

A NOTE ON SOURCES

I RELIED HEAVILY ON the archives of the *Evansville Press*, the *Evansville Courier*, the *Sunday Courier & Press*, *Chicago Tribune*, the *Eldorado Daily Journal*, the *Indianapolis Star*, *Evansville Living* magazine, UE's *Crescent Magazine*, the *LinC*, the *Courier-Journal*, *Sports Illustrated*, the *Washington Post*, the *New York Times*, the Athletic, and the *Pittsburgh Post-Gazette*. I also made extensive use of the video archives of WFIE-TV channel 14 and WEHT-TV channel 25. The authors of *Evansville, at the Bend in the River: An Illustrated History* provided crucial detail about the city's first 150 years. The writings of Evansville historian Darrel E. Bigham were critical to my understanding of the history of race in Evansville and the city's development during World War II. George Klinger's research was especially helpful to understand the earliest days of the university and its relationship with the rest of the city. The work of writer Seth Davis provided detailed accounts of John Wooden's life and career, as well as the Indiana State–Michigan State championship game. Evansville was fortunate to have three newspapers stocked with editors and reporters who cared deeply about Aces basketball. I am indebted to the work of Mark Tomasik, Dave Johnson, Tom Tuley, Anne Harter, Bill Fluty, Tom Collins, Pete Swanson, Rich Davis, Don White, and Pat Moynahan.

Books

An Evansville Album: Perspectives on a River City, 1812–1988, by Darrel E. Bigham

City of the Four Freedoms: A History of Evansville, Indiana, by Robert Patry

Drive: The Story of My Life, by Bob Ryan and Larry Bird

Evansville, at the Bend in the River: An Illustrated History, by Kenneth P. McCutchan, William E. Bartelt, and Thomas R. Lonnberg

Evansville: The World War II Years, by Darrel E. Bigham

Indiana Blacks in the Twentieth Century, by Emma Lou Thornbrough

The Road to Madness: How the 1973–1974 Season Transformed Basketball, by J. Samuel Walker and Randy Roberts

Trophies and Tears: The Story of Evansville and the Aces, by Kyle Keiderling

We Ask Only a Fair Trial: A History of the Black Community of Evansville, Indiana, by Darrel E. Bigham

We Face the Future Unafraid: A Narrative History of the University of Evansville, by George Klinger

When March Went Mad: The Game That Transformed Basketball, by Seth Davis

Wooden: A Coach's Life, by Seth Davis

INDEX

ABOUT THE AUTHOR

Steve Beaven is an Evansville native and a former staff writer at the *Oregonian*. His work has appeared in the *New York Times* and the *Chicago Tribune*. He lives in Portland, Oregon, with his wife and two sons.